# Screening Shakespeare
## from *Richard II* to *Henry V*

# Screening Shakespeare from *Richard II* to *Henry V*

Ace G. Pilkington

**DELAWARE**

Newark: University of Delaware Press
London and Toronto: Associated University Presses

Associated University Presses
440 Forsgate Drive
Cranbury, NJ 08512

Associated University Presses
25 Sicilian Avenue
London WC1A 2QH, England

Associated University Presses
P.O. Box 39, Clarkson Pstl. Stn.
Mississauga, Ontario,
L5J 3X9 Canada


The paper used in this publication meets the requirements
of the American National Standard for Permanence of Paper
for Printed Library Materials Z39.48-1984.


**Library of Congress Cataloging-in-Publication Data**

Pilkington, Ace G.
    Screening Shakespeare from Richard II to Henry V / Ace G.
Pilkington.
        p.    cm.
    Includes bibliographical references and index.
    ISBN 0-87413-412-9 (alk. paper)
    1. Shakespeare, William, 1564–1616—Film and video adaptations.
2. Historical drama, English—Film and video adaptations.   3. Great
Britain—History—1066–1687—Historiography.   4. Shakespeare,
William, 1564–1616—Histories.   5. BBC TV Shakespeare (Television
program)   6. Kings and rulers in motion pictures.   7. Great Britain
in motion pictures.   I. Title.
PR3093.P55   1991
822.3'3—dc20                                               90-50310
                                                              CIP


PRINTED IN THE UNITED STATES OF AMERICA

# Contents

# Acknowledgments

I wish to express my gratitude to Rank Film Distributors for giving me permission to photocopy the shooting scripts of Olivier's *Henry V;* to the British Film Institute and the City of Birmingham Public Library for providing copies of those scripts; to R. Russell Maylone, curator, Special Collections Department, Northwestern University Library, for a photocopy of Welles's shooting script of *Chimes at Midnight;* and to the Shakespeare Institute, University of Birmingham, for a copy of the dialogue script of *Chimes at Midnight.*

I have collected a large number of scholarly debts in the writing of the Oxford D.Phil. thesis, on which this book is based, and in the writing of the book itself. Dr. Susan L. Brock of the Shakespeare Institute, University of Birmingham, and Audrey Shumway and Carole Williams of the Dixie College Library were specially helpful in providing information and materials. I am indebted for encouragement and suggestions to Dr. Tim Bywater, Stephanie Chidester, Dr. Jerry L. Crawford, Dr. Dennis Kay, Professor Peter Levi, Dr. D. F. McKenzie, Elaine P. Pilkington, Melanie M. Starnes, Dr. Stanley Wells, Dr. John Wilders, and Phil Williams.

# Screening Shakespeare
# from *Richard II* to *Henry V*

# 1

# Introduction

## Shakespeare on Screen

Writing in 1971, Garrett, Hardison, and Gelfman stated as the basic contention of their anthology, *Film Scripts One,* "that film is not *an* art form of the twentieth century, it is *the* art form of the twentieth century."[1] They complained, nevertheless, that "to examine a film with the same care and thoroughness as a novel or a poem is difficult."[2] They point out, of course, that a large part of that difficulty comes when one tries to consult the filmtexts. The problem might best be solved using extensive archives and moviolas, thus making it possible to view and review entire films and even to examine individual frames, building detailed interpretations from frequent watchings in the same way that literary critics work from readings. However, they go on to lament, "this solution, though ideal, is at present impracticable. No archive can accommodate the large numbers of individuals interested in film, and . . . the constant use of films quickly destroys them."[3]

This is a clear statement of the problems faced by film critics before the arrival of the videocassette. Even the chance to watch a film has sometimes been hard to come by. Jack Jorgens describes Orson Welles's *Othello* as "infrequently seen,"[4] and Charles Eckert says "perhaps it has gained stature through its inaccessibility."[5]

Those considerations, together with the limitations of time and space, have also restricted most film criticism to the middling mode of impressionistic—even if often perceptive—journalism, retarding a more developed textual scholarship of film and many significant filmed readings of Shakespeare. That situation has now been completely transformed by the omnipresent, viewer-controlled videocassette. It is infinitely flexible—easily started, stopped, scanned, and compared, having the advantages of the moviola without its drawbacks. Three complete films of the same play, for example, can be contained in a space no larger than a paperback book; comparisons and contrasts, the poising of dif-

ferent scenes against each other, or the balancing of three incarnations of the same scene can be accomplished as easily as turning
pages.

The advantages are obvious. As many actors and scholars have
maintained,[6] in the case of a play, "the real, full text is any given
production, just as the text of the film is the film itself, and not the
scriptwriter's dialogue."[7] But it is difficult to freeze such an
ephemeral thing, what Philip Gaskell calls "the performance
text,"[8] unless it is also a film. Then it becomes, in a sense, a text
that can be "read," infinitely repeatable and susceptible to scholarly investigation. Such a text can be studied in the same way as
different editions of a play, novel, or poem (or their printed
interpretations) may be studied.

However, because a film is a "performance text," it has dimensions and possibilities a printed script does not offer. The structure of a play may be clarified in production, since drama is made
from movement, from stress and counterstress. Character can be
revealed by the same process, when static forms acquire motion
and flesh. Even the smallest of details can be examined, the flicker
of symbol and gesture caught and fitted into the visual and verbal
world of the performance. Such interpretations may serve as
confirmation or contradiction of other kinds of criticism, a crucible of practice in which theory may be tested. They form a significant body of criticism, hitherto imperfectly accessible to scholarly
inquiry and serious critical debate.

Any such study must, however, confront several prejudices.
The most obvious is also in some ways the most naive: namely,
filmed versions of Shakespeare are not Shakespeare, whether in
their displacement of the stage as his proper medium or in their
freer handling of his verbal text. These objections assume the
impropriety, in effect, of "adaptation." Shakespeare wrote for the
stage, not for the screen (so the argument goes), and moving the
plays onto film (or for that matter the films onto videotape) is a
translation that alters their essential meaning.

There are multiple answers to such objections,[9] including Walter Hodges's comment that the destruction of the Elizabethan
playhouses meant the extinction of authentic Shakespearean performance, "since when it may almost be said that no play of
Shakespeare's has been acted, except in adaptation."[10] As Peter
Hall puts it, "In a sense any production or even any criticism of a
play is an adaptation of the original."[11]

Dudley Andrew sets out the theoretical ramifications of such a
position, arguing that adaptation is much like interpretation the-

ory, since both involve the taking of meaning from another text. The hermeneutic circle in interpretation theory maintains "that an explication of a text occurs only after a prior understanding of it, yet that prior understanding is justified by the careful explication it allows." This "global conception" of a text's meaning makes analysis and discussion possible. Andrew sees adaptation as "similarly both a leap and a process. It can put into play the intricate mechanism of its signifiers only in response to a general understanding of the signified it aspires to have constructed at the end of its process."[12]

It is possible to take this a step further, as Bernice W. Kliman and Kenneth S. Rothwell do, and point out that "the attitude toward films as texts coincides with new critical movements that have made suspect the idea of *one* Shakespeare text; many now believe that *all* texts . . . are re-creations of Shakespeare."[13]

Many objections to the process of adaptation also ignore the flexibility of film. In Susan Sontag's words, "cinema . . . can encapsulate any of the performing arts and render it in a film transcription," becoming, as Jack Jorgens says, "a transparent medium." Donald S. Skoller would call this a first-category adaptation: "little more than a filmed recording of a stage play."[14]

Even when film is not simply "recording" theater, it is not an easy matter to dismiss it as a mechanism for revealing Shakespeare. Referring specifically to the work of Laurence Olivier, Jan Kott says, "The living Shakespeare of our time has been presented, first and foremost, in film. Film has discovered the Renaissance Shakespeare."[15] As Donald Skoller writes, "the sixteenth century stage was virtually without scenic dressing and yet it suggests a fluidity more in the spirit of cinema than of contemporary theatre."[16]

Those who would object on principle to filmed Shakespeare would regard any shift from film to television as merely accentuating the problem. One further answer to their argument is Susan Sontag's statement that "there, movies themselves become another performing art to be transcribed,"[17] and by Christian Metz's contention that "the student who studies a film on a moviola . . . or even on a TV playback system is nevertheless studying the full semiotic system of that film."[18]

As John Wilders points out in "Shakespeare on the Small Screen," "Television can restore to Shakespeare's plays the unbroken flow and continuity they almost certainly achieved in the Renaissance theatre." Discussing an acting style that does not need the slow elaborations necessary for projection on the modern stage, he goes on to say, "Not only does this speed of performance give to the plays a tighter unity, but it probably restores to them the pace and rhythm they achieved when they were first produced."[19] In a lecture that expands on this article, he goes even further, saying, "I do feel that if he [Shakespeare] were alive now, he would be a television script writer. I very seriously believe that he was actually a film script writer four hundred years before films first appeared."[20]

In an interview concerning his production of A *Midsummer Night's Dream,* a film released first on American television and then in theaters, Peter Hall also commented on the closeness between filmed and televised Shakespeare, the interconnectedness of the mediums, and the excitement that interaction can generate: "films will become more flexible, more varied because of it, let alone the possibilities that lie ahead in the cassette film."[21]

With more filmed Shakespeare available than ever before and with the mechanism of the videocassette making possible more complete and careful studies than were previously imaginable, it is time to reevaluate filmed and televised Shakespeare in terms of what they have accomplished and what they may yet be able to accomplish given sufficient funds and efficient imaginations. Such a reevaluation is particularly important now when technological innovations are blurring the differences between film and television, while pay cable and the videocassette market are changing the nature of audiences, of financing, and therefore of filmmaking.

## Difficulties of Shakespearean Film Criticism

Robert Jackson complained in his 1978 dissertation that "systematic and thorough examinations of filmed performances of Shakespeare's plays are rare, and a great deal of work remains to be done before we can say that filmed renditions of the plays are or are not artistically valid." The situation (except for the ease of examination of texts offered by the videocassette) has not greatly altered in the intervening years.

Part of the problem, as Jackson points out, is that "it is always possible to support generalizations, pro or con, with examples from somewhere in the films"[22] and overall surveys of Shakespearean films will find what the surveyor is seeking. The alternative, detailed examinations of individual films, requires ample time and space and calls into play a scholarly discipline largely absent from recent studies of novels and poems, that is, the description of the text itself. But any serious criticism should be able to assume certain common principles of textual authenticity and accurate citation, or at least clearly acknowledge any divergence from those principles.

An examination of a filmscript requires the accumulation and recounting of facts about what happens in the flickering medium of the film before any reliable conclusions can be drawn. In this sense the film critic is in the position of a literary scholar examining original manuscripts: he must transcribe his materials before he can analyze them, and he must verify the transcriptions of other film critics before he can trust their transcriptions. As Peter Davison says about his own comments on Olivier's *Hamlet*, "Film, especially transferred to video as *Hamlet* has been, can be seen again and again. That means that what is said here can be checked and there is evidence for disagreement."[23] There is also evidence to settle disagreements. Variant readings must be set against each other and checked with the text. That is a large part of what this book sets out to do.

As Garrett, Hardison, and Gelfman phrase it, "the study of film demands accurate recall not only of what happened but what was said, how it was said, and—film being visual as well as verbal—how it was conveyed in images."[24] Even a small detail such as a character's expression in a single close-up can provide the clue to the film's central interpretation.

This book, employing the videocassette and treating the films as texts, seeks to discover the evolution of the central interpretations in six films that use overlapping material from the second tetralogy: BBC television's version of the four individual plays, plus Laurence Olivier's *Henry V* and Orson Welles's *Chimes at Midnight*. The films offer a wide variety of approaches to the medium within the controlled space of four related plays.

Garrett, Hardison, and Gelfman point out the major difficulty in dealing with film is that it provides "more information than the human mind can retain. . . . Even the best observer has his limits and they are soon reached."[25] This means that mistakes will be more frequent and more serious than in similar examinations of novels and poems. Donald Skoller describes his own pre-videocassette research method, which involved viewing films from three to five times while making both written and tape-recorded notes. Also, during one watching "a dual track recording was made" containing the sound track and the researcher's "running description of the visualizations occurring on screen."[26]

He goes on to claim overoptimistically that "in combination with the several viewings of each film, the dual-track document prompted near-total recall of the film."[27] It is, of course, difficult to speak notes into a tape recorder and watch a film with attention at the same time. In addition, an accurate and detailed narration of a film's visual events would, of necessity, run much longer than the film. Unfortunately, the best his dual-track document (or any similar makeshift) can do is to prompt the viewer to recall some part of what he thought he saw. If he missed something (and he should certainly expect to miss many things), only the film itself could correct his false impressions. Skoller's account clarifies the difficulties of consulting a filmtext that has not been transferred to videotape and helps to explain the frequency of mistakes.

Clearly, before the use of the videocassette, mistakes could have been called almost unavoidable. I give here examples of various kinds of misreadings not to suggest that the scholars involved are anything less than careful researchers but to demonstrate the necessity for meticulous recountings of what happens in film, the frequency with which errors occur, and therefore the value of the new process of screening Shakespeare, which the videocassette makes possible. I have confined myself to misreadings of the filmtext of Orson Welles's *Chimes at Midnight;* similar misreadings may be found, of course, in studies of other films.

The transfer from playscript to filmtext may be one source of difficulties. David Bordwell, says, "Nym summarizes the complexity of the problem as Falstaff lies dying: 'The King is a good King. But it must be as it may.'" And Jack Jorgens, author of what is generally recognized as one of the best books about filmed Shakespeare, has either found the same mistake independently or followed Bordwell's lead (though he makes no mention of Bordwell as his source): "Nym comments sadly, 'The King is a good king, but it must be as it may'" This is given as scene 27 in Jack Jorgens's account of *Chimes at Midnight,* and the lines are spoken by the actor who is twice identified as Bardolph in what Jorgens (and the dialogue script) labels scene 21.[28]

Admittedly, this is an easy mistake to make; Bardolph and Nym take each other's speeches to such an extent in Welles's film that keeping them separate is difficult, and in Shakespeare's play (*H5* 2.1.128–29),[29] it *is* Nym who speaks the lines. Nevertheless, for anyone watching the film closely and repeatedly and still more for anyone who could easily go back to check a reference, the mistake would not be quite so likely.

Nor is there any confusion in Welles's scripts. The dialogue release script of *Chimes at Midnight* gives the scene as 28 and the line as Bardolph's.[30] The shooting script places the line in scene 29, but the line is still Bardolph's.[31] In fairness to Bordwell and Jorgens, I should point out that neither one of them was using any version of Welles's script, hence Jorgens's creation of his own, slightly different scene numbers.

If following another critic was Jorgens's problem in the previous example, Lorne M. Buchman has the opposite trouble. He denies the claims of other critics that Welles had used material from *The Merry Wives of Windsor* in *Chimes*, saying "In my study of the film I find no material from this later play and can only conclude that this assertion has become a common critical error."[32] Scene 21 of *Chimes* takes place in the tavern, and Falstaff says, "I must turn away some of my followers" (*Wiv.* 1.3.4–5).[33] In typical Welles fashion, threads of this scene are woven into the fabric with the Host's lines reassigned to the Hostess, before we get back to the main business of *2 Henry IV* 2.4.

Commenting on the set for this sequence, Charles Higham wrote, "When the set of the inn run by Doll Tearsheet . . ."[34] The inn (or tavern) in *Chimes at Midnight* is run by Hostess Quickly, as it is in Shakespeare's plays. Charles Higham may be suffering from a malady that afflicts some film critics—an unfamiliarity with Shakespeare's plays. His account of the Gad's Hill robbery might be taken as an indication of this: "Falstaff talks about his encounter with some assailants at Kendal Green, the story of his defeat of them becoming more exaggerated at every moment."[35]

The examples I have given so far are simple matters of fact and plot, and while they are certainly sufficient to demonstrate the difficulties involved in accurate film criticism, there is a more complex and equally serious kind of error to which Shakespearean critics (as opposed to film critics) of Shakespeare films are particularly prone. Barbara Hodgdon explains that a filmed adaptation of Shakespeare posits two auteurs, two kinds of textual authority, in the play and in the "so-called directorial signature." However, "another textual authority operating here—what I call the expectational text—contains my private notions about the play and about performed Shakespeare, notions that I may not even recognize until I find them denied."[36]

I would add that another part of the expectational text contains the critic's notions about film and/or television, and I would also point out that sometimes those notions are not clearly recognized or examined even after they have been denied.

In a medium that moves with light if not quite with its speed, it is all too easy to see what is not there. A single viewing (or even multiple viewings) coupled with a firm expectational text can result in misreading because the critic sees what he expects, not what is actually on the screen, or it can result in a misreading of another type when a critic, disappointed in his expectations, attacks the film he has seen not because it is a bad film or bad Shakespeare but because its critical stance differs markedly from his own.

The difference in interpretation such divergence in expectation can generate is remarkable. For instance, Jack Jorgens reports of what he calls scene 24 in *Chimes at Midnight* (scene 22 in the dialogue script) that one shot shows the new king turning to his subjects "distant as his father always was, undefined in the smoke and sunlight. Another shot shows the dead father behind the son—not only can Hal not escape duty and the past, he has in a sense been inhabited by the spirit of his father."[37]

Describing the same moment, Lorne Buchman says that with Henry IV's death and Hal's assumption of power the "light coming into the castle—that until this point had been a straight and narrow beam—disperses in a bright shower of the sun's rays. Through this visual metaphor, Welles makes clear the positive changes associated with the ascension of Henry V."[38]

It is simply a question of textual accuracy. If Shakespearean films are to be studied as texts, it must be possible not only to provide descriptions of them that get the facts and plot right but also, using those facts and those descriptions, to move beyond impressionistic reactions to a reliable account of the filmtext's central vision or interpretation. That is what this book sets out to do. With the videocassette, it is now possible for the first time.

## Central Interpretation

As Robert Jackson writes, "For many years the movies were scorned by the world of legitimate art, and that attitude, in spite of recent claims of legitimacy for film, is still around." It affects film and, to an even greater extent, television criticism. At least some of the mistakes I have just been discussing might well be attributable to such an attitude. Jackson goes on to say that in spite of a recent trend to "consider movies as the ultimate expression of modern art," they are simultaneously regarded as a form that "is practiced artfully by only a few great creative spirits around the world and is much more commonly contaminated by businessmen."[39]

In other words, while an auteur of the stature of Orson Welles is to be treated as an artist in control of his materials, most directors for film and television can safely be regarded as workers turning out a commercial product who must engage in a tug of war with actors and producers to achieve any sort of personal vision. Because films are extraordinarily expensive and are, of necessity, cooperative projects involving hundreds of people, there is, of course, some truth to this picture.

Describing the difficulties involved in shooting *Major Dundee*, Charlton Heston points out the divergent aims that hobbled the effort, "Columbia wanted a cowboy and Indian story, I wanted a film that dealt with the basic issue of the Civil War, and Sam, as it happened, wanted the film he later got to make."[40] Heston has described a three-way struggle among a studio, a director, and an actor whose stature (and contract) gave him some creative control. The result was a less-than-successful film. Some critics have maintained that many successful films are the result not of creative control, a realized intention, but of happy accidents.

Leslie Halliwell argues, for example, that *Casablanca* is such an accident.[41] He adduces in support of this view that the initial idea was to use Ann Sheridan and Ronald Reagan in the parts played by Ingrid Bergman and Humphrey Bogart and also that no one knew the ending until the first of two alternative versions was actually shot. I would claim that such an argument undervalues the qualities of the director, Michael Curtiz, and also ignores cowriter Howard Koch, who, as S. F. Bathrick puts it, composed "the brilliant script for *Casablanca*." She goes on to point out that *Sergeant York* (1941), *Casablanca* (1942), and *Mission to Moscow* (1943) all reflect his "genuine adherence to his stated principle that the screenwriter should play a socially conscious role in relation to the industry."[42]

However, there were noticeable disagreements during the filming. Ingrid Bergman tells of arguments between the producer and scriptwriters, between Mike Curtiz and Hal Wallis, and of the constant and confusing script changes that were the result: "No one knew where the picture was going and no one knew how it was going to end."[43]

Nevertheless, Bergman's account of how that ending was selected suggests that the process was not random. There were from the start of the shooting two possible endings under consideration, one where she would fly away with her husband and the other where she would stay behind with Humphrey Bogart. In the first ending to be shot, Bogart was left behind, walking off into the fog with Claude Rains and speaking the line, "Louis, I think this is the beginning of a beautiful friendship." As Bergman tells it, "Everybody said, 'Hold it! That's it! We don't have to shoot the other ending.' "[44] I would suggest that part of the problem here is, as Charlton Heston notes, "You have to work in film quite a while before you understand the subtle and shifting responsibility shared by actor, director, and editor."[45]

Even in a film that does not bear from the beginning the clear mark of an auteur, there may be a central interpretation that coalesces, an emergent form created as a result of a dialectic of discovery among producer, director, and actors. Thus, even a film like *Casablanca,* where disagreements were the rule, could reach a point at which the rightness of the first ending to be shot was instantly recognized and the second one was abandoned. Laurence Leamer, in his biography of Ingrid Bergman, calls it "an ending as perfect as a poem."[46] Such a clear demonstration suggests that films should be treated as other texts are treated, as serious works of art, and that the circumstances surrounding the making of the films, the variation from preliminary scripts to finished films, and the final filmtexts themselves should be carefully examined.

Umberto Eco, in a more sophisticated attack on *Casablanca* than the one mounted by Leslie Halliwell, assigns films to a category apart from printed texts. "A perfect movie, since it cannot be reread every time we want, from the point we choose, as happens with a book, remains in our memory as a whole, in the form of a central idea or emotion."[47] His classification would justify the subjective responses of many critics, making film a matter for memory and emotion and not for scholarly investigation. I suspect that one reason shooting scripts for Olivier's *Henry V* and Welles's *Chimes at Midnight* have hitherto remained unexamined[48] is that such attention to detail has seemed unnecessary to critics who regarded successful films as fortunate accidents and saw even perfect films as indivisible memories, beyond the reach of analysis.

But Eco's "principles" have already been overtaken by technology. This study sets out to demonstrate that films can be read and reread and that they are subject to the same kind of detailed and accurate examination which has traditionally been given to printed texts. Such serious textual examination of filmed Shakespeare will make it possible for Shakespeare film criticism to move beyond appreciations and reviews to full-scale analysis, including point-by-point comparisons of shooting scripts and release scripts and examinations of the expressed intentions of directors and actors. Finally, it should be possible in the case of the six film-scripts under consideration to trace the evolution of their central interpretations.

# 2

# The BBC Shakespeare Series

One of the most important factors in the creation of the BBC Shakespeare Series was the videocassette itself. John Wilders told me in a personal interview that the BBC had approximately two-thirds of the capital necessary to finance the project but needed outside support and sponsorship for the rest. The American corporations who joined the BBC venture did so because they believed "there would be a big videocassette market." He emphasized, "We couldn't have started it without the help of Time-Life, and Time-Life presumably would not have done it if they hadn't foreseen a big videocassette market."

In other words, "the biggest project ever undertaken by the BBC drama department"[1] can be directly attributed to the economic impact of the videocassette. In fact, the videocassette and the market the producers felt it represented became a matter of aesthetic style as well as economic substance. Wilders went on to say that the worldwide audience of millions of people affected the style which was adopted: "Time-Life themselves insisted that the productions must not be too . . . experimental. . . . They wouldn't have twentieth century versions of the plays."[2]

One way of describing this is to say that the BBC and its partners were attempting to create a product that would appeal to the markets they had identified. Another, equally valid (and for the purposes of this study, more important) description is that the BBC and its partners were attempting to make films that would conform to the expectational texts of as many of their prospective audience members as possible. The process was complicated because the films actually had two main markets to reach—the international television audience and, behind and beyond that, the audience that would eventually buy the videocassettes.

That trying to serve the two different audiences created tensions is clear from a variety of circumstances. For instance, earlier Shakespeare films had in general been much shorter than their BBC counterparts. Olivier had cut over half the lines in *Henry V*,[3]

22

and Orson Welles had compressed his version of the second tetralogy into 119 minutes in its longer version. But during the tenure of the first producer, Cedric Messina, and the initial pressure to do "definitive" and, therefore, complete productions, the BBC made relatively sparing cuts, resulting in productions that tended to be as long as or longer than their stage counterparts. *Richard II,* for example, ran two-and-a-half hours, "requiring very little editing for the television screen,"[4] while the last play overseen by Messina was "a virtually uncut, three-and-one-half hour *Hamlet* starring Derek Jacobi."[5] This makes excellent sense for videocassette viewers, who can start and stop the program at their own convenience, and it is important for educational institutions, which tend to favor complete texts.

At the same time, there was, as Stanley Wells reports, a contradictory tendency to view two-and-a-half hours as the outside limit for a television production, "and during the two years in which Messina was producing the series most plays were cut so as to fit within this limit."[6] Jonathan Miller, who was the second producer, "laughed at the notion that any production could be definitive,"[7] but while he was in charge, "even long plays such as *Troilus and Cressida* . . . [were] given with few cuts." Again, though, there were contradictions. *Othello* might retain almost all of its lines, while "*The Taming of the Shrew*—not a specially long play—was shorn of the entire Induction."[8]

The plan for the BBC Bardathon, Video Folio, Shakespearathon, or Canon in the Can, as it has been variously called, started at Glamis Castle with Cedric Messina's idea of filming *As You Like It* in the open air.[9] Officially, however, it emerged from his office in the form of a memo on 3 November 1975.[10] Shaun Sutton, who was then head of the BBC's television drama group and who eventually took over from Jonathan Miller as the third and final producer of the BBC Shakespeare, believed that Shakespeare's original audience "was neither very sophisticated nor literary," and he saw the mass television audience in similar terms, as a group to be educated but above all as a group for whom "the plays will be presented as they were first conceived—as entertainment."[11]

Cedric Messina's version of the same material also stresses the entertainment value of the project. Though he says that "for students, these productions will offer a wonderful opportunity to study the plays," he soon qualifies that with the statement that the BBC films "are not intended to be museum-like examples of past productions."[12]

These comments from Sutton and Messina demonstrate the struggle to appeal to the immediate television audience, which expected entertainment, and at the same time to create a lasting library of "educational" tapes for the new audience the BBC and its American partners had identified beyond the initial television viewers. Thus, Messina "spoke at the outset of doing *definitive* productions that for years to come would bring Shakespeare to the masses."[13] The Video Folio was to become a permanent library of tapes, instantly accessible and infinitely repeatable. And, of course, "Time-Life wanted to make a profit by selling videotapes to educational institutions."[14]

As a result of these mixed goals, the new BBC productions had to be conservative, instantly and widely acceptable as well as instantly accessible. The publicity handout that helped to launch the series said, "The settings are those the layman would *expect* to see when he hears the name of Julius Caesar or Richard II."[15] The productions were not "radically to depart from traditional interpretations. There was to be little pruning of texts, no modern dress. Messina even instructed the directors to 'let the plays speak for themselves.'"[16] Or as Graham Holderness puts it, "Conscious of this dependence on the market rather than on patronage and subsidy, the planners insisted that productions should aim for 'high quality' and 'durability.'"[17]

This conservative policy may well have appealed to the widest possible audience. Even a reviewer such as Richard Last, who is not completely in favor of the results, finds the policy logical. "Tradition and consolidation, rather than adventure or experiment, are to be the touchstones. In view of the BBC's proclaimed intention—to produce a 'definitive' compendium of all 37 plays—this was probably the only realistic option available."[18]

However, at the same time, the conservative policy distinctly limited the choices of the producers and directors. "Jonathan Miller is quoted as saying that his main problem in taking over the series was 'the original contract with the American co-producers—it had to be so-called traditional, in the costume of the period (whatever that meant).'"[19] Miller seems to have been faced with the problem from the very beginning. As Robin Stringer reported, "Jonathan Miller, brought in by the BBC to take over from Cedric Messina the . . . project to film all Shakespeare's plays, promised yesterday that he would not be putting them into modern dress or even into the 19th century."[20]

In Kenneth Rothwell's words, "Messina began with the premise that the series should please a hypothetical schoolmaster, a kind of

Jonsonian humour figure peevishly hostile to anything new or trendy in Shakespeare performance."[21] Given the monetary hopes of Time-Life and the restrictions imposed by the other coproducers, that schoolmaster was anything but hypothetical; he was a composite figure made up of all those professors who would (and, in the event, did) wring "the funds necessary to purchase the tapes from austere university budgets."[22] Since the films of Olivier and Zeffirelli were available on videocassette for well under $100 per play, while Time-Life was charging $225,[23] the BBC could not afford to antagonize this audience.

That the BBC's conservative policy could result in a restriction of options was demonstrated early in the history of the project. John Wilders, the literary advisor for all thirty-seven productions, asked some essential questions about the filming:

> Should we observe the conventions of the Elizabethan theatre and produce them in an empty studio? Should we . . . try to reconstruct the Globe Theatre? Should we . . . build sets which would create the impression of reality? Or should we carry realism still further and transport our company to an actual forest for *As You Like It* and scour the country for a suitable castle for *Hamlet?*[24]

Wilders "advised Cedric Messina to summon a meeting of television directors, a kind of seminar at which these questions could be discussed and solutions proposed."[25] Messina rejected the advice, arguing that "each play creates its own problems . . . and that we should not cramp our directors by imposing on them an inflexible 'house style.' "[26]

However, it seems clear that the actual reason for this rejection was the existence of a tacit (according to Jonathan Miller, it was explicit) "house style" almost from the beginning of the project. Russell Miller reported as early as 29 January 1978 that there was "general disenchantment" because the BBC was insisting "that the 'house style' of all the plays should be faithful to the Bard rather than the Box." The goal was "a thoroughly proper, perhaps scholarly version of the Compleat Works."[27]

To carry out John Wilders's proposal and open a wide range of issues to a seminar of television directors would have been to invite disagreement and possibly even innovation. In his article "The BBC Shakespeare and 'House Style,'" James C. Bulman argues that Messina favored directors with good television track records and little or no experience directing Shakespeare onstage because "directors who have done Shakespeare on the stage may be inclined to do dangerously unorthodox things with him."[28] How much more dangerous would it have been, then, to put together a group of directors, many of them with wide stage experience, and encourage them to make suggestions about the filming of the series?

In fact, many directors were excluded not only from the initial planning but from any participation in the project by the very house style Messina said he wanted to avoid. Stanley Wells reports Jonathan Miller saying "that the limitation to 'period' costume . . . represented an insuperable obstacle to the engagement of directors whom he would have wished to work for him."[29]

Messina's bias comes through clearly in his discussion of the first season's shooting: "We've not done anything too sensational. . . . There's no arty-crafty shooting at all. All of them are, for want of a better word, straightforward productions."[30]

Bulman sees a pattern with directors like John Gorrie, who directed *The Tempest* while he "admitted to having no particular approach to" it, and Rodney Bennett, who directed Derek Jacobi in *Hamlet* when Jacobi had just completed a two-year tour in the part, and Bennett "had never directed Shakespeare in his life." The result, Bulman says, was "traditional interpretations of the plays," many of them already tried out in performance by the actors who became, to some extent, auteurs as well.[31]

In Messina's words, "The directors are responsible for the interpretations we shall see, but as the series progresses it will be fascinating to see how many of the actors take these magnificent parts and make them their own."[32] Messina's view of the matter comes through even more clearly in a statement he made when announcing his plans for The Shakespeare Plays: "The productions will be taken over by the actors and there will be a lot of eye-to-eye confrontation. That's what television can give you—a front row in the stalls with two fine actors shouting at each other."[33]

However, not all the shouting came from the actors. Judging from the reactions to the first season of the BBC Shakespeare, both John Wilders's idea for a directors' seminar and Cedric Messina's confidence in the BBC, which, as he pointed out, was "not inexperienced in the presentation of Shakespeare's plays,"[34] should have been reconsidered. The initial film, a version of *Much Ado About Nothing*, was "completed at enormous expense, judged by the BBC planners to be a disaster, and then instantly thrown into the wastepaper basket."[35] The three productions that followed it, *Julius Caesar, As You Like It,* and *Romeo and Juliet,*[36] were judged by Jack Jorgens, among others, to have done "no service to

Shakespeare at all, being in the main poor TV and poor Shake-speare."[37] Indeed, *Romeo and Juliet* is by popular consent (or perhaps, more appropriately, dissent) the worst film in the entire series. I suspect that only the ignominy and expense of having to discard the first two productions saved *Romeo and Juliet* from sharing the fate of *Much Ado About Nothing;* there were certainly American critics who would have cheered heartily if it had been withdrawn and replaced.[38]

After the series had been completed, John Wilders summed things up: "I think that the worst fault of the television Shake-speares is that they tended to be cautious and rather too safe and unambitious and lacking in originality."[39] Even in the first season it was clear from the reactions of reviewers that while the BBC's conservative productions might meet many of the expectations of a mass audience, they often failed to produce the expected excite-ment.

Philip Purser, for instance, found "a curiously unsweaty, anti-septic smell to the proceedings" of the BBC's *Julius Caesar.* For Sylvia Clayton, "It was a cautious production . . . reverent in speech, conventional in movement." Sean Day-Lewis had a similar reaction to *As You Like It,* saying "it only intermittently engaged the emotions and never caught fire." Sylvia Clayton responded in the same way to *Romeo and Juliet,* pointing out it "offered helpful viewing for exam-crammers. And bell-clear enunciation, two hours of energetic feuding, no tricks or eccentricities." She went on to add, though, that the young lovers "aroused melancholy, not grief."[40]

The reference to "exam crammers" is one reminder that the BBC remained very much aware of the long-term financial pos-sibilities of the series. And, indeed, beyond the contrasting (and sometimes conflicting) expectations of the television and vid-eocassette audiences, there were other tensions, many of which, despite the additional funds obtained from the American corpo-rations, had to do with the budget.[41]

There is a feeling of constriction about many of the BBC productions that has very little to do with the size of the screen but is instead the result of the claustrophobic television distribution of time and its unfortunately interchangeable equivalent—money. Laurence Olivier spent £475,708 (about $2 million) and thirteen months shooting *Henry V;*[42] Orson Welles was occupied with *Chimes at Midnight* from the winter of 1964 to the spring of 1965.[43] By contrast, the announced budget for the entire BBC project was £7 million, or $13.6 million.[44] That works out to

£189,000, or $367,000, for each of the thirty-seven productions.[45] Shooting schedules were correspondingly restricted to a rigid six days per production.[46] As Stanley Wells says, "Miller has spoken of 'inadequate rehearsal facilities,' saying that 'you only have about a month to rehearse, and six days to tape. Most people who really take Shakespeare seriously feel that at least six weeks are necessary to rehearse, with 12 days of taping.'"[47] Some of what this means comes through in Anthony Quayle's discussion of the difficulties of playing Falstaff. He complains that while it is possible to fit the size of a stage performance to the size of a theater, for the small television screen it is easy to overact or underplay. "You've got to hit it like a moonshot, and I found it impossible to gauge. In a film you would do several tests. . . . With television you never can see yourself."[48]

By comparison, in wartime Britain, Olivier spent "just over a week . . . with tests of the artistes and make-up."[49] Anthony Quayle reports Giles saying, "'We'll do that scene again because it isn't quite as good as you can make it,'" adding "but time is very limited."[50] The reshooting of scenes would have been complicated because the material was taped in fairly large sections with a limited number of cameras. In Cedric Messina's words, "we've not shot them like films. We taped them, sometimes, for fifteen minutes without a break."[51]

Much of what is said about television Shakespeare uses the BBC project as a standard without taking these restrictions into account. One issue that is raised repeatedly is the difficulty for the actors in working without a live audience. But as Anthony Quayle's words make clear, the real problem was a lack of feedback of any kind, and the problem could have been easily if somewhat expensively remedied.

It was against these background tensions and expectations that the BBC version of the second tetralogy was constructed.

# 3

# The BBC *Richard II*

## Factors Shaping the Production

John Wilders told me in a June 1987 interview that two of the constraints on the BBC *Richard II* were (as might be expected from the general background of the series) time and money. He used the Mowbray-Bolingbroke confrontation as an example of a scene where "the camera tended simply to shift in a rather automatic way from one to another." And he went on to argue "that if more had been done with having many more cameras and many more camera angles and more interesting lighting and so on, it wouldn't have been quite such a routine, workaday production." He pointed out, however, that "we would not only have needed a bigger budget, a much bigger technical crew, but it would also simply have taken a very great deal more time in rehearsal and the actual recording it."

As John Wilders indicates, the production could have been improved with more time to rehearse and film. The coordination required among director, actors, and camera crew cannot be achieved without careful planning, no matter how capable the artists involved may be; the choreography required on a sound-stage must be almost balletic in its precision. Actors must, of course, hit marks to remain within the effective range of the camera. This is complicated when an actor crosses from one part of the set to another; it becomes still more complex when groups are involved. For instance, in a three shot, the actors must carefully restrict their movements and stay close together. They must also keep to the prearranged schedule, delaying or speeding up their dialogue and inserting pauses to allow the camera the time it needs for changes of movement and focus.[1] It is worth remembering in this context that the BBC productions were sometimes taped in blocks of as much as fifteen minutes.

There are, indeed, many signs in *Richard II* of the haste that lack of money creates. The framing is often sloppy, the actors

29

sometimes shuffle to get out of the way of the camera and each other, there is a worrisome sameness to the camera angles, and, especially in the early scenes, actors are often crammed into shots for no reason other than to add more costumes and bodies. Thus, through most of Bolingbroke's early speeches, he is in two and three shots with stony-faced actors who look blankly away from the action and even down at the floor in what seems much closer to actors' boredom than courtiers' embarrassment. Reaction shots in general tend to be slow (and with the notable exception of Jacobi's) not well thought out. There is perfunctory pointing of a camera at an actor as an illustration to go with a particular line instead of using the reaction shot as a means (like lines and often equally important) of advancing plot and characterization.

Here, for example, are some of the problems that occur in the first three scenes:

At 1.1.36, "And mark my greeting well," the back of a head bobs between Bolingbroke and the camera and then moves away again. At 1.2.9, "Finds brotherhood in thee no sharper spur?" there is an unsteady camera movement. At 1.2.58, "Yet one word more," Gaunt is partly out of the frame, the most common type of trouble.[2]

At 1.3.7, "Marshal, demand of yonder champion," Richard's face is too distant to be clearly visible in the shallow focus this production often employs. This too is a frequent difficulty, as the following examples show. At 1.3.78, "God in thy good cause make thee prosperous," Richard is visible in the background during Gaunt's speech, an excellent idea that comes to nothing because the king's features are so blurred as to be indistinguishable. At 1.3.116, "Attending but the signal to begin," Richard signals, but his face is again unclear.

At 1.3.141, "Till twice five summers have enriched our fields," there is a cut to Richard, but in the background Gaunt's shoulder and a fringe of hair rock in and out of the frame, partly, no doubt, as a result of the crowded acting conditions. At 1.3.166, "Within my mouth you have enjailed my tongue," Mowbray is in a two shot with a bored actor who looks down. This is a repeated difficulty; there are many useless faces. Shortly after this, for example, Bolingbroke is in a shot that should belong to him, but two less important actors are seen more prominently than he is. At 1.3.179, "Lay on our royal sword your banished hands," Gaunt is the cause of a similar problem; he is visible, shuffling from one foot to the other in a way unmotivated by anything but finding an unobtrusive place to stand.

At 1.3.268, "Will but remember me what a deal of world," there is a more complicated difficulty than sloppy framing. Bolingbroke turns upscreen to speak to Gaunt, and as a result, we lose most of his expression. This would be an excellent place to employ a reverse angle shot, perhaps giving the film a three-dimensional feeling by shooting the reverse angle over Gaunt's shoulder. The result of that strategy would have been to add visual variety plus give us more of Gaunt's expression than we had of Bolingbroke's and all of Bolingbroke's reaction as well.

The difficulties I have so far listed might most readily be ascribed to a too-short shooting schedule. However, there is an overall problem of attitude as well, which appears most clearly in 2.1. This scene should, in my opinion, have been reshot, but, as I'm about to argue, it should first have been rethought. It follows the most cleverly filmed of the early scenes, the king and his courtiers in the baths, and has in addition Shakespeare's excellent stage (and even better screen) transition from Richard's "Pray God we may make haste and come too late!" to Gaunt's "Will the King come" to start things off. One of Giles's better ideas was the juxtaposition of the informalities at the baths with the informalities we see in the dress and attitudes of the two brothers. It is a vital scene for the plot, containing important confrontations and strong performances, made more prominent still by the decision to use this scene (or at least the first two-thirds of it) as the end of part 1 in the three-part structure, which the BBC imposed on the play. But the filming is marred not only by absence of time but also by the presence of Messina's conception of television Shakespeare as a "front row in the stalls with two fine actors shouting at each other."[3]

For instance, at 2.1.11, "More are men's ends marked than their lives before," York crosses downscreen between Gaunt and the camera on Gaunt's line for no discernible reason, and then Gaunt looks back to where York had been to deliver his next line. Surely something odd must have happened to leave two veteran actors in such straits. At 2.1.72, "What comfort, man? How fares it with aged Gaunt?" there is a desperate camera movement to bring a sliver of Richard to the screen while he speaks his line. At 2.1.113, "Landlord of England art thou now," there is another example of confusion. Gaunt, who has been advancing on Richard during his speech, steps back at this point, which happens also to be the time when the camera switched to Richard for a reaction shot. Since Gaunt and the camera operator had not synchronized their movements and since only one camera appears to have been involved,

Gaunt was left very clumsily out of frame before an equally clumsy cut to Richard.

At 2.1.117, "Darest with thy frozen admonition," the camera is shooting over Gaunt's shoulder at Richard, who is upscreen, but instead of a shot that might have given us the two of them reacting to each other, all we get is the back of Gaunt's head. In fact, we do not see Gaunt's face from this point until the last half of 2.1.124. Far too often in this scene we are deprived of Gaunt's face, of Richard's, or of both. At 2.1.141, "I do beseech your Majesty, impute his words," there is a similar problem. York is shouting upscreen at Richard, who is facing the wall.

Much in this scene was not caught by the camera. At 2.1.148, "Nay, nothing, all is said," we fail to get Richard's first reaction to Gaunt's death because Richard is out of focus. At 2.1.151, "Be York the next that must be bankrout so!" we have only the back of York's head. At 2.1.155, "So much for that," Richard moves quickly offscreen and then back; the camera can't keep up. At 2.1.175, "Than was that young and princely gentleman," York moves completely out of frame. At 2.1.181, "Which his triumphant father's hand had won," we have the back of Richard's head, while York is turned upscreen with his hand blocking what little we might otherwise have seen of his profile. At 2.1.184, "O, Richard, York is too far gone with grief," York now turns downscreen and his face falls out of the frame. At 2.1.200, "Now afore God—" York follows Richard behind the other actors and neither is visible.

Many of the problems with what otherwise could have been a very strong scene come directly from giving the audience a seat in the stalls while two actors shout at each other. There is plenty of shouting, and the camera (there often appears to be only one) does seem to have been confined to the front seats of a hypothetical theater: it is capable of moving in for close-ups but not of shooting from the wings, from the back of the stage, or from anywhere overhead. As a result, we are burdened with the difficulties of the stage and television together. We have not the freedom of watching anything the director does not show us, and the sight lines are so clumsy and the camera's freedom of access so limited that much of the scene is not visible to anybody. Undoubtedly many of these problems could have been corrected with longer shooting time and more retakes, but many of the difficulties could also have been eliminated if the initial idea had been to film television rather than to record a stage production from the front rows.

In fairness to David Giles and his company, I should point out that the problems I have so far listed are at their worst in the early scenes of *Richard II*. There is a steady decline in the number of technical mistakes through the four BBC Shakespeares he directed and a corresponding increase in the flexibility of camera placement. In addition, the efficient handling of many specialized group shots in the difficult circumstances of *Richard II* demonstrates his expertise.

Several critics commented on Giles's skill. For Clive James, Giles "showed his firm hand immediately, framing the actors' faces as closely as possible while they got on with . . . speaking the text."[4] Jorgens similarly praises the "scene where Bolingbroke sentences Bushy and Green to death." He points to "the confident use of the camera, which includes and excludes characters with precision," providing "a striking contrast with the randomness of earlier productions."[5] I have indicated that it also provides a contrast (if not a striking one) with some other scenes in this production, but I do not mean to deny Giles's effectiveness. He should certainly be credited with the victories and finesses that emerged from a rough process.

In addition to the neat juxtaposition of informal scenes from Richard in the baths to Gaunt and York alone together, Giles has made other interesting connections. The last part of 2.1, from 224 to the end (the plot of the three conspirators), was cut away and set at the beginning of part 2, in Westminster, the Cloisters.[6] And this whole miniscene was cleverly handled. We begin with Northumberland in close-up, speaking, it would seem, to himself. Then Ross, on his first line, turns back into the screen to make it a two shot, and finally Willoughby neatly steps in for a three shot. There is movement provided soon after by Northumberland crossing correctly behind prior to the three of them walking off as a group. Once they are all onscreen, their three faces are adroitly crammed together, providing a visual illustration for Ross's "We three are but thyself, and speaking so / Thy words are but as thoughts" (2.1.275–76). This visual concentration also helps to make them seem more positive, more certain of the success of that coming man (in two of the word's senses), Bolingbroke. The elimination of the first ninety-nine lines of 2.2 gives Giles an all-but-perfect jump cut from the absolute plan for action of Northumberland, Ross, and Willoughby to York's plaintive "I know not what to do" (2.2.100).

That Giles is also capable of handling larger groupings is proved with the arrival of Bolingbroke in 2.3. The whole scene is nicely done, with especially crisp camera movement between Bolingbroke and York during their confrontation. At 2.3.122, "If that my cousin king be King in England," we get a three shot with Northumberland cannily watching Bolingbroke's persuasion from the background. When Ross and Willoughby are added, we have a neat five shot with Bolingbroke standing silent in front while other voices speak his arguments for him. It is a visual summary of the progress from the three conspirators' certainty to York's dithering, Bushy, Bagot, and Green's fear, and the arrival of Bolingbroke himself. The film has told us, even without the text, that one of the next moves will be against the favorites.

Michael Manheim points to the symbolic use of long shots and close-ups as the strength in the filming of 3.3: "That both Richard and Northumberland are seen at a distance establishes the highly political, patently insincere nature of their exchange." When "close-ups take over . . . Richard speaks his real feelings to his entourage."[7] A similar juxtaposing of private and public takes place in 4.1 when Bolingbroke, who has been using his private voice, switches at 4.1.199, "Are you contented to resign the crown?" to a public style of declamation, a contrast that the intimacy of television easily heightens. Giles has demonstrated his skill by achieving more than might be expected in such difficult circumstances.

In addition to time and money, there were other factors in the construction of the BBC's *Richard II*. The decisions made by the designers and directors in that first season reflected the concerns of the producer and his corporate sponsors, which were in turn dictated by the audience expectations they perceived and hoped to fulfill. Messina's initial idea for the series had involved an open-air production of *As You Like It*, which meant, according to set designer Tony Abbott, "that the studio productions must be able to go alongside the ultra-realism of the location productions."[8] Here again is the feeling of restriction I noted earlier. Despite William Walton's music for the opening, despite the reassuring presence of John Gielgud, there is a sense of smallness, of sameness, so that there will be fewer visual styles in a whole season of different plays than in Olivier's *Henry V.* The decision, however, was part of the producer's concern for the expectations of his audience. And according to at least one reviewer, Messina may not have been conservative (or consistent) enough. Philip Purser complained that if the BBC had decided to limit itself to "reliable texts in a straightforward studio setting—an acoustic cube as the modern equivalent of Shakespeare's wooden 'O,' " it should not then go "frolicking off on location in Scotland for 'As You Like It.' "[9]

Tony Abbott describes the style that finally emerged in *Richard II* as "stylised realism."[10] That there were distinct limitations both on the realism and the stylization is clear from the handling of the tournament scene (1.3). David Giles says the scene was "an absolute swine." He goes on to explain the impossibility of doing the scene realistically in a television studio but points out that they used real horses to avoid the alternate danger of too much stylization, because "if we had gone too stylised with the list scene we would have had to stylise the play all the way through." Giles is apparently aware that a mixture of styles in the same film (or the same season) was not one of his options.

He is also suspicious of too much stylization because "on television where what you see is a real head against a bit of stylised background you can only stylise if you design it shot by shot." Though later productions in the series, such as *The Winter's Tale* (and his own *Henry V*), tend to contradict Giles's initial assumption, it seems to me that his comments are another example of the pressure of truncated rehearsal and shooting schedules. He continues, "There certainly wasn't time for that here and I'm not sure I'd have wanted to do that anyway."[11] He is slightly defensive and almost apologetic about the only part of the filming that was noticeably unusual.

Perhaps David Giles has good reason to sound apologetic. It was, in fact, this sequence that prompted those remarks by Cedric Messina about "arty-crafty" shooting, which I have already quoted. After discussing what he saw as the healthy habit of shooting for fifteen minutes without a break, Messina mentioned that Richard's soliloquy had been cut into ten different shots; he then went on to defend this seeming deviation from his policy of plain shooting: "We've done nothing sensational in the shooting of it—there's no arty-crafty shooting at all."[12]

Again, such comments indicate Messina's attempts to fulfill the expectations of his mass audience. He says he hoped the productions would "stimulate people who . . . notice *Hamlet* advertised in their neighborhood theatre to say, 'I saw it on the box; I think it's a good play. Let's go in and see it.' "[13] Apparently, as Messina envisions the viewing experience, his audience must be introduced to art gradually, with no visual shocks to warn them that they have switched to something different from their ordinary fare.[14]

David Giles's decision about the costumes for *Richard II,* which brought him into conflict with the overall costume policy and with Robin Fraser-Paye, the costume designer for the production, tends to support my reading of Messina's remarks. Giles said he did not want the costumes to resemble *The Book of Hours* but

> to look as much like clothes as possible.[15] Robin . . . said to me, "But they're extraordinary clothes." I said, "Yes, I know . . . and I do know Richard spent £2000 on one suit . . . but I want them to look real—everyday clothes that the audience can accept."[16]

In this case the goal for the costumes in the histories "to be historically accurate to the period in which the play is set"[17] had to give way to what Giles (and Messina behind him) thought his "unsophisticated" audience could accept as real clothes.[18] Robin Fraser-Paye solved the problem by toning down the color palette and omitting the more extreme fashions.[19]

Many of the decisions that moved the production toward realism and away from "arty-crafty" shooting were also designed (as might be expected) to reduce the director's impact and importance. David Bevington, for example, calls Giles's direction (of *1H4* but the description applies equally well to *R2*) "low-key" and his "interpretation less insistent than that in the [stage] productions of Burrell, Seale, Hall, Hands, Nunn and others."[20] I see this reduction of the director's influence as designed because of Messina's obvious desire to avoid "arty" direction and let "the plays speak for themselves." Of course, plays do not speak, actors do, and this too is clearly one of Messina's designs—to let the actors speak to the audience with as little interference as possible. In the process David Giles has become much less important than some of his stage counterparts, while the actors have emerged as—to some extent—auteurs.

There is nothing particularly unusual about the actor as auteur; both Olivier and Welles might—by stretching a point—be so described. Indeed, Patrick McGilligan argues that a performer who "shifts meanings, influences the narrative and style of a film and altogether signifies something clear-cut to audiences despite the intent of writers and directors" is an auteur.[21]

Obviously, Orson Welles and Laurence Olivier do much more than this, while the actors in the BBC Shakespeares do less. But McGilligan discusses an intermediate situation, where the actor may also be an auteur. In the work of three Warner Brothers directors of the thirties and forties—William Keighley, Roy Del Ruth, and Lloyd Bacon—McGilligan identifies a straightforward, quick style of making movies, which "gave the actors . . . free rein to interpret their roles: indeed, there was little time for anything else."[22] Bacon, for example, shot *Picture Snatcher* in fifteen days,[23] a feat that is perhaps comparable to filming a Shakespeare play in six (allowing for the relative difficulty of the material and for the fact that Bacon had no time for separate rehearsal).

In short, given the preconceptions of the producer (including a bias toward realism that foregrounds the individual performance at the expense of any overall pattern), the extremely brief time allowed for shooting, the tendency to film the plays in large chunks when possible and to do retakes only when absolutely necessary, and keeping in mind that many of the actors had more experience with the material than the director did, it makes sense to look at the BBC *Richard II* (and the other plays of the second tetralogy) as the result of a combined effort. Of course, any film is a combined effort of many artists, but in the circumstances I have just described, the impact of any one of the chief players might be as great or greater than that of the director, and any analysis of the film must be arranged accordingly.

A clear example comes in Michael Manheim's review of *Richard II*. It is one of the most favorable reviews the production received, and it is undoubtedly strongly influenced by Manheim's admiration for the cast in general and Jacobi in particular. He ascribes the film's success to "the superb realization of the characters" and goes on to say, "Derek Jacobi is for me the best Richard witnessed in over thirty years."[24] Cedric Messina had to some extent anticipated this, calling the play "the tragedy of one man."[25]

What emerges from this description of the making of the BBC *Richard II* is the clear subordination of an individual production to an overall "house style." It might well be argued that such subordination is dangerous. As Messina himself had said, "Each play creates its own problems,"[26] and shaping *Richard II* perforce to fit the preconceptions of BBC television realism meant rejecting a number of other forms the production could have taken. It might have been more logical to look first at the text and only then to determine the film to be made from it.

In examining Shakespeare's aims in the play, Stanley Wells says, "Shakespeare made a decision of fundamental importance. He decided to write this play entirely in verse." He goes on to discuss the effects of this degree of "stylisation and artificiality in the language," maintaining that "a number of the characters are so lacking in individuality that they seem mainly or entirely choric in function."[27]

However, since pointing up such a choric function or fore-grounding the stylization of the language can be undertaken by actors only when directorial decisions have paved the way, certain elements in *Richard II* were, of necessity, played down or shut out. Messina no doubt viewed this as part of the process of meeting the expectations of his various audiences, "what the layman would expect to see when he hears the name of . . . Richard II." Hence, "in all the histories the aim is to be historically accurate to the period in which the play is set."[28] This principle (violated only when even stronger audience expectations got in the way) emerged in tragedies with historical settings as well, even when the tight budget might not have seemed able to support it. Russell Miller "was told by a disgruntled employee" that during the making of *Romeo and Juliet,* the only researcher was in the British Museum, "wading through Italian books to try and find out what a town square was like in Italy in the fifteenth century. And she can't even speak Italian."[29]

Costume designer Odette Barrow indicates the kind of detail that was expected in the "semidocumentary style" for *1 Henry IV:*

> I had a problem with Hotspur. Historically, when his mother died he incorporated her arms with his. But Shakespeare manages to have her appear in Part 2 *after* Hotspur's death; so we thought, well, we'll have to give him his arms as they were before she died. So far as history is concerned his arms at the battle of Shrewsbury are therefore inaccurate, but as far as Shakespeare is concerned, they're right.[30]

Clearly, David Giles was not meant to be an auteur, making Shakespeare's material his own after the fashion of Orson Welles. Many of the options that would have made a directorial imprint possible had been eliminated. There was not even the inspiration of continuity, of seeing *Richard II* as the beginning of a four-part sequence. Despite Cedric Messina's description of the histories as a "sort of Curse of the House of Atreus in English,"[31] there was initially no plan to produce the plays in the second tetralogy as a group. It is true that many of the actors do continue throughout the series, and Giles did direct all four; however, at the time he made *Richard II,* he "was not expecting to continue with the three Henrys."[32] Thus, it is not safe to regard decisions in *Richard II* as direct preparations for the later plays. The omission of Henry's reference to Hal, the inclusion of his mention of Glendower, and the change of actors in the part of Hotspur are therefore likely to be influenced by factors other than the connection between *Richard II* and *1 Henry IV.* For example, the choice of Tim Pigott-Smith for Hotspur was probably the result of his success as Angelo in the first season's production of *Measure for Measure.*

The central interpretation that grew from David Giles's *Richard II* was, as I have indicated, as much a matter of what could not be done (or what was not allowed) as of what could. It had to fit (or at least seem to fit) Messina's vision of audience expectations, and it had to take into account the naturalism of the production and the interpretive importance (and even control) of the actors, especially Derek Jacobi. It also had to fit in with the BBC's emphasis on the history of the period in which the play was set. In the circumstances, it is not surprising that the central interpretation which emerged was the result of cooperation between Giles and Jacobi (who had read history at university) and that it used the play's historical background as a starting point. In a way, Giles's creative use of history anticipated Jonathan Miller, who was able to work within the restrictions of BBC house style by focusing on the history of Shakespeare's period. Miller said, "It's the director's job, quite apart from working with actors . . . to act as the chairman of a history faculty and of an art-history faculty."[33]

## The Critics, Giles, and History

One logical means for charting the central interpretation of the BBC *Richard II* is to look at the critics' reactions. Often, the unfavorable responses are even more revealing than the favorable ones because they show where the critic's expectational text has been revised by Giles and company. Malcolm Page is right when he says, "Commentators gave moderate praise to the television *Richard,* grudgingly observing that it was rather better than others of the first six."[34] But as Manheim's judgment makes clear, Page is describing a consensus or average from which individual conclusions diverged widely.

The most sweeping condemnations were made (as might be anticipated) in those instances when Giles seemed to be deliberately revising the expectational text. Sheldon P. Zitner criticizes the whole of the BBC second tetralogy and *Richard II* in particular for "the effort to 'clarify' the text." However, the example he gives is surprising: "the camera cuts to Bolingbroke in exile, informing us that before he returns to England he knows about the death of his father and about Richard's proposal to confiscate his property. Not so in Shakespeare."[35] And not so in the BBC *Richard II* either. As happens disconcertingly often in Shakespeare film criticism, a check of the production in question fails to verify the description of events. Bolingbroke's first appearance after the death of Gaunt is in 2.3 with the scene's first line, "How far is it, my lord, to Berkeley now?" There simply is not an interpolated French scene, and, in any event, how would such a scene without lines indicate Bolingbroke's royal ambitions? But Zitner's hypersensitivity to the remote (and in this case nonexistent) possibility is revealing.

At least part of Zitner's objection is expressed more directly by Martin Banham: "When a television (or, to be fair, a film) director . . . shapes our image of the action, he is intruding his own interpretation of what is significant." Banham sees in this the danger that the director will "interfere with our imaginative liberties" and may even destroy "the sensitive integral framework of the play itself." He maintains that one result of this interference "has been to give these Shakespearean productions on television a linear feeling."[36]

This comment seems to me to come (on one level at any rate) from an uncritical idealization of the stage and an equally uncritical condemnation of television and film. Surely, as John Barton's 1973–74 production of *Richard II* for the Royal Shakespeare Company makes clear, a stage director may also interfere with the audience's "imaginative liberties."[37] In fact, as David Bevington's analysis indicates, David Giles's "low-key" direction results in an interpretation that is "less insistent" than that of many of his stage counterparts.

Nevertheless, several factors contribute to the feeling that Giles has more control than is actually the case. I have already pointed out that the shooting schedule and the conscious decisions of Messina and of Giles himself effectively reduced the impact of the director on the films of the second tetralogy. But the large number of close-ups, the small number of reverse-angle shots, and the use of "a very long lens on the camera, so what you see in focus is clear but everything else is blurred" for exterior shots,[38] all added up to what Samuel Crowl called a "claustrophobic *Richard II*."[39] While that adjective may be too strong, there is a closeness (and even, perhaps, a visual flatness) about the production that can give the misleading impression of a linear progression imposed on the viewer by the director.

I do not, of course, wish to suggest by this that David Giles did not make directorial decisions, some of which had strong impact. It is likely to be certain key decisions Giles made that are annoying Banham, even though he does not directly say so. Michael Manheim, who approves of those decisions, praises Giles for serving "as teacher as well as director." We are, he says, being taught history we may not have learned "when, following Bolingbroke's accusation that Norfolk has murdered the Duke of Gloucester, Giles has the camera switch not to Norfolk but to Richard, the real culprit in Gloucester's death."[40] Such a camera movement will not work, of course, unless the actor playing Richard is ready for it and shares the director's vision of the historical events that preceded the opening of the play. But Giles and Jacobi did have a shared vision that shaped the film.

It is in all probability this shape that Banham dislikes. He finds the "linear feeling" uncomfortable because the line moves away from his expectational text. One of the strongest objections to the production from another critic hits at this precise issue of the interpretation of the history behind the history play. Pointing to Cedric Messina's conventional description of the history plays and a television talk given by Paul Johnson as a curtain raiser for *Richard II*, Graham Holderness argues that "the second tetralogy emerges from this production as a constituent element in an inclusive and integrated dramatic totality, illustrating the violation of natural social 'order' by the deposition of a legitimate king."[41] Additionally, he maintains that the naturalistic conventions which Messina and Giles favor further endorse this ideology,[42] and he contrasts this with what he sees as the more open and radical version of history and history plays that emerged from Jane Howell's direction of the first tetralogy.[43] I find some of Holderness's assumptions concerning the BBC *Richard II* useful because, though I believe his reading to be incorrect, I think the part of the filmtext that makes him uneasy is the center of the interpretation which Giles and Jacobi created.

Certainly, a naturalistic style of production can be used to endorse Tillyard's thesis, but style does not guarantee the political nature of content. As Henry Fenwick points out, "television casting is able to open up hitherto neglected portions of the play," and one of the examples he gives is "the tiny part of the Duchess of Gloucester played by Mary Morris."[44] The naturalistic television scene (1.2) foregrounds the Duchess of Gloucester's grief, Richard's guilt, and John of Gaunt's expressed belief that God will avenge Richard's crime as emphatically as the same scene was foregrounded in John Barton's stylized and nonnaturalistic stage production.[45] A good Tillyardian or even a director who wanted to simplify characterizations might have been expected to cut the scene.

Despite Cedric Messina's remarks about an English Curse of the House of Atreus, there was no concerted effort to produce a version of the second tetralogy conforming to Tillyard's Elizabethan world picture. In fact, the emphasis on the history of the period resulted in the contradiction of many of Tillyard's points.

Paul Johnson did say (as Holderness indicates), "According to the orthodox Tudor view of history the deposition of the rightful and anointed King, Richard II, was a crime against God, which thereafter had to be expiated by the nation in a series of bloody struggles."[46] But shortly before that he had called Richard "an ideologue, a fanatic, an early supporter of the theory that kings ruled by divine right." He also accused Richard of "illegal exactions and confiscations" and of exploiting parliament "to commit judicial murder against the nobles and despoil their estates."[47] It would seem that the "orthodox Tudor view of history" was not shared by Paul Johnson.

His remarks do, however, fit the interpretation of history that Giles and Jacobi had worked out. To understand how far this is from the "world picture" it is necessary only to contrast it with Tillyard on the same subject: "Shakespeare knows that Richard's crimes never amounted to tyranny and hence that outright rebellion against him was a crime. He leaves uncertain the question of who murdered Woodstock."[48]

The radio curtain raiser to the BBC *Richard II* was given by Ian Richardson, who, with Richard Pasco, alternated the roles of Richard and Henry in John Barton's "radical" stage production. Richardson also failed to adhere to the Tillyardian party line, saying on the subject of Gloucester's death, "Richard had ordered it and so Mowbray from sheer loyalty keeps his mouth shut."[49] He committed further heresies when he suggested that "Richard plucks defeat from the jaws of victory and wilfully destroys himself," and "It's important for Henry Bolingbroke to have had no hand in Richard's overthrow, at least as direct instigator, if he is to maintain the audience's sympathy within Shakespeare's moral framework."[50]

If, in fact, Cedric Messina and the other administrators of the series were bent on "an inclusive and integrated dramatic totality," they seem to have consistently chosen the wrong people for their purposes. David Giles and Derek Jacobi agreed early in rehearsals that Richard was indeed guilty and that his emotion in the first scene is, in Giles's words, "high tension because it is the moment he's been waiting for so long,"[51] with the clear implication that what Richard has been awaiting is revenge. Nor would the two of them have found a defender of Tillyard's orthodoxy in the series literary consultant, John Wilders.

Wilders's wide range of responsibilities included trimming "the texts to fit the two-and-three-quarter hour time slot allotted for productions," plus advising "directors of the series . . . on interpretation of difficult passages, rhythms, cuts, and relevant bibliographical sources" and "holding a 'literary clinic' to help actors make sense of Shakespeare's language."[52] It is probably safe to assume that one reason for John Wilders's appointment to the post of literary consultant was the appearance in 1978 of his book *The Lost Garden,* an elegant study of Shakespeare's English and Roman history plays that strongly attacks Tillyard's thesis.

It is, nevertheless, correct, I think, to see the BBC version of the second tetralogy and especially *Richard II* as productions of the history plays which are very much concerned with history. The background material I have presented up to this point indicates no less. Robert Hapgood said, commenting on *Richard II,* "The best of the Shakespeare Plays histories have been enlightened costume dramas, at ease with their historical ambience yet not at the expense of . . . dramatic strengths."[53]

I also agree with Holderness (with the reservations my discussion so far makes clear) when he says that the emphasis on history is the result of the plays being "produced in 'classic drama' style with predominantly naturalistic devices of acting, *mise-en-scène,* and filming."[54] Extreme stylization of the kind Stanley Wells discusses was ruled out by Messina's house style. At the same time, the emphasis on history and the semidocumentary style that went with it would have pushed many directors (as it later did Jonathan Miller) to consider the historical possibilities inherent in the current play. David Giles and Derek Jacobi created their interpretation within the imposed limits of the BBC Shakespeares, but despite that (and, in fact, partly because of that) they produced a new Richard and an original *Richard II.*

As might be expected in the circumstances, Giles and Jacobi have done their best to maintain the interpenetration that has long existed between Shakespeare's histories and history itself. As Peter Saccio says in *Shakespeare's English Kings,* "far more than any professional historian . . . Shakespeare is responsible for whatever notions most of us possess about the period and its political leaders."[55] Or as J. L. Kirby, himself a professional historian, writes in *Henry IV of England,* "From Shakespeare, of course, we can never escape whether we wish to or not."[56]

More important, though, for this study than the effect of Shakespeare on the writing of history is the impact of history on *Richard II* in its BBC incarnation. David Giles assumed that a modern audience was at a disadvantage because "the first third of the play depends on a circumstance which isn't fully explained in the play and which was close to the Elizabethan audience—the murder of Gloucester. To them it was the beginning of the Wars of the Roses."[57]

While this is hardly a startling position from which to begin,[58] it pushes the performance in definite directions. For example, in 1963, John Gielgud talked of Richard being "only lightly sketched at first in a few rather enigmatic strokes."[59] This attitude pushed to its extreme (as it was by John Neville, playing the role at the Old Vic in 1955)[60] leads to the idea of two Richards—a pre-Ireland and post-Ireland one—the revelations of character in the latter half of the play having no relevance to the actions in the first half.

David Giles and Derek Jacobi took a precisely opposite view. As Giles says, "Derek and I both agree that the key section for Richard is the opening section of the play—the first three scenes."[61] This at once introduces a series of subtextual messages into the performance, which may be expected to alert even audience members who come to the play unprovided with the historical background. Instead of an impartial king attempting to resolve a dispute between two important nobleman—well or ill, weakly or powerfully, as actor, as poet, or as aesthete, according to the nature of the production—we now have a politician, manipulating royal justice to serve his own partly concealed purposes.

In a careful analysis of these subtextual (and in the case of historical information, extratextual) possibilities, John Russell Brown pointed out in 1966 that in the first scene Richard's protestations "may carry subtextual impressions of irony, apprehension or antagonism. Bolingbroke's accusations may seem aimed at the King rather than Mowbray, and Mowbray's confidence to stem from royal support rather than his own innocence."[62]

Brown's words could easily serve as a description of the relevant portion of the BBC *Richard II.* Only one significant element is missing, and Brown picks that up in his comments on scene 3: "Bolingbroke's submission . . . may seem to veil a rivalry with the King himself."[63]

Such a shift in perspective makes for what amounts to a reinterpretation of the motives for various actions in the play (and behind it) and a reassessment of Richard himself. Thus, as Andrew Gurr, editor of the New Cambridge *Richard II*, notes concerning the duel, "Richard cannot afford to have either man win, and therefore chooses to send both into the silence of exile for his own political safety."[64] Such a view of the character is a long way from the picture of a histrionic Richard who stops the fight to make himself the center of attention and is even further from the vision of a political incompetent who makes dim and whimsical decisions. If this Richard belongs in the company of Hamlet and Coriolanus, where Yeats placed him,[65] it is because he too is involved in a battle of mighty opposites. In that case, even his most seemingly self-indulgent moments may shield something more than emotion. Gurr argues, for example, that "Richard calls for the mirror in order to evade Northumberland's insistence that he read the Articles listing his misdeeds."[66] Gurr is not commenting on the BBC *Richard II*, but his words are an accurate description of what happens in the production, nevertheless. In fact, the Richard who emerges from these critical comments, the BBC film, and recent histories[67] is an altogether more dangerous character than a man who, as Theodore Weiss put it, "is Shakespeare's most thoroughgoing study of the absorption in words."[68]

## History as Subtext

The version of history Giles and Jacobi used (and which became a kind of parallel text behind the filmtext) differs from that of Tillyard and other familiar sources in the placing of emphases and the conclusions it reaches. Despite the fact that Giles and Jacobi were contradicting the expectational texts of some of their viewers (including not a few critics), the coherent historical text that was available to them provided a workable interpretation for the play and also fitted in neatly with the BBC emphasis on history. This was true in part because the play is much closer to being historically accurate than many literary critics have realized.

Richard's whole career is seen in this view as a struggle to impose his royal (and therefore divine) will on his recalcitrant subjects. There was an escalating series of clashes between Richard and his nobles. The first—in 1386—involved Arundel and Thomas, duke of Gloucester, and left Richard fuming under the rule of an executive commission for one year. He was compelled to accept this by the threat of deposition, and one chronicle says Richard thought of asking the opposing lords to dinner and murdering them but gave up the idea as unworkable.[69]

The second clash came in November of 1387, when Richard challenged the commission with a royal army in Cheshire and the signatures of many of the country's justices on a document that declared the commission imposed on the king to be not only illegal but also treasonous.[70] Gloucester and Arundel joined with Warwick, swiftly bringing their own troops to London and "appealing" five of Richard's closest advisors (who were supposedly behind the king's dangerous policies) of treason. Caught without an army of his own, Richard agreed to put the matter to Parliament and until that time to "take the case into his own hands."[71]

However, as soon as the three "appellant" lords had withdrawn their army, Richard let his favorites escape and summoned the royal army of Cheshire archers.[72] It was at this point, in December 1387,[73] that Henry Bolingbroke and Thomas Mowbray joined the appellants. The king's men were defeated at Radcot Bridge, and again Richard found himself pressured to agree to demands by the threat of deposition.[74]

It took Richard ten years to prepare his revenge, building up his royal power to the point of tyranny. He now had a formidable force of Cheshire archers, and Parliament had, at his request, redefined interference in the royal household as treason.[75] Bruce suggests that Richard "had never fully recovered from the trauma of the Apellants' revolt,"[76] and the meeting of the five appellants for dinner at this time (and Mowbray's report of it to Richard) pushed him into action. In July of 1397, the three original appellants were themselves appealed of treason. Warwick confessed and was banished, Arundel was executed, and Gloucester, imprisoned in Calais, died mysteriously, almost certainly on Richard's orders.[77]

The next step was to compel Parliament to repeal the general pardon granted after the 1388 Parliament and, in effect, to brand "anyone who had interfered with the king's prerogative, or had persuaded him to do anything against his will"[78] as a traitor. Parliament was forced to agree to what Richard wanted by the presence of four thousand archers with bent bows and arrows drawn to their ears.[79] The repeal of the general pardons put most of the people of southeast England in Richard's power,[80] a power he employed in various profitable ways. He sold pardons, neglected to record the sales, and sold pardons to the same men (and whole counties) again; and, finally, he had blank charters[81] drawn, signed, and stored in chests for later use.[82]

With Richard censoring all foreign mail and "sheriffs . . . being made to swear to imprison at once anyone whom they heard speak ill of the king,"[83] Mowbray told Bolingbroke of Richard's intention to punish them for their part in Radcot Bridge.[84] Remembering Mowbray's hand in the destruction of the three elder appellants, Bolingbroke reported his words to John of Gaunt, who, in turn, reported them to the king. Then, it was simple for Richard to force a quarrel and banish both men.[85]

Giles and Jacobi have made their view of Richard's history clear. Speaking of Richard and the five appellant lords, Giles says,

> One he has executed, one is in the tower, Gloucester has just been murdered, and now of the five only Mowbray and Bolingbroke, the two youngest, are left. Derek and I both agreed that the key section for Richard is the opening section of the play—the first three scenes. He said, "Why is he so angry in the first scene?" and I said, "He isn't— it's just high tension because it is the moment he has been waiting for so long."[86]

Giles goes on to give additional insights into his view of Richard and also his directorial decisions: "it's easier on television . . . because by focusing on Richard . . . and by using a major actress like Mary Morris . . . in a part that's usually skimped over on stage, the audience does gather something of what has happened."[87]

As Giles's remarks indicate, the entire production and not just Jacobi's performance was affected by the historical interpretation (or reinterpretation). Part of the originality of accepting this plausible and well-documented version of history as the blueprint for a production of *Richard II* is that it means treating Shakespeare's play as a serious attempt to set out the facts as well as to get at the truth, an attitude that many critics have been unwilling to adopt. The play is, in fact, more accurate than many critics believe it to be,[88] and this accuracy fitted in neatly with the semidocumentary style the BBC *Richard II* employed.

F. W. Brownlow (among others) finds the play unhistorical, objecting to the view of Thomas of Woodstock as a "plain well-meaning soul" and maintaining that John of Gaunt was never noted for public spirit or high principle. He believes "such changes of character are more damaging to the play's historical truth than are details like the alterations of Queen Isabella's and Henry Percy's ages, because they mean that Shakespeare can never treat properly the political realities of the reign."[89] Saccio is similarly unhappy with Gaunt, since Shakespeare has not followed Holinshed, "who with far greater historical accuracy, depicts Gaunt as a contentious and ambitious baron."[90]

Surely in the special circumstances of 2.1.128 Gaunt ought to be allowed to call his murdered brother a "plain well-meaning soul." "Plain" after all, may be used to describe behavior such as Kent's in King Lear 2.2, where he is repeatedly called "plain" by Cornwall and by himself. Just such plain speaking seems to have been one of Gloucester's faults. Kirby says he "possessed neither common sense nor the respect for the King's estate which had been shown by his brother, John of Gaunt."[91]

But perhaps in Gaunt's last moments, when he himself has been doing some plain speaking to the king, Gloucester's freedom of speech seems more attractive and his critical viewpoint the correct one. It is often dangerous for any critic to assume he knows history better than Shakespeare shows it.[92] As Marie Louise Bruce says about Gloucester, "From a twentieth century viewpoint a curiously unattractive character, at the time his honesty of purpose was to make him seem to many . . . 'the best of men' and 'the hope and solace of the whole community of the realm.' "[93] In that light, John of Gaunt's words are not only historical but also moderate.

The portrait of Gaunt himself is equally easy to defend. Even Saccio admits that he was "fundamentally loyal to his nephew, and remained Richard's faithful advisor throughout the 1390s."[94] Both Kirby and Bruce see him as a moderate influence, whose absence in Portugal allowed more extreme factions to chart the country's course.[95] The critical confusion about Gaunt comes from paying too much attention to his early career and not enough to his later one. His reputation (if not his nature) seems literally to have suffered a sea change. In the summer of 1381, as Kirby says, "John of Gaunt had become the best hated man in England."[96] But by the time he was preparing to leave for Portugal "with the prospect of seeing the last of him for a while everyone liked the duke of Lancaster."[97] On his return to England, as a result of his vast new wealth and his daughters' powerful marriages on the Iberian peninsula, he assumed precisely the role in English politics that Shakespeare gives him. The former hatred of Gaunt "paled into insignificance." He became "a legendary figure admired by nearly all, and with this new image went a new, more sober approach to politics. In England from now on he was to play the part of the most respected elder statesman."[98]

Even in the minor details, Shakespeare's picture is accurate.

The Duchess of Gloucester suspects Gaunt's motives for peace-fully accepting her husband's murder, telling him, "That which in mean men we entitle patience / Is pale cold cowardice in noble breasts" (1.2.33–34). In his campaign of terror, Richard put York and Gloucester in fear of their lives, and they were both "to besmirch the memory of their dead brother"[99] as a result of that fear. It seems safe to say of many of Shakespeare's historical figures what Marie Louise Bruce says of his York, that the portrait "of the bumbling, well-intentioned duke unhappily trying to choose between duty and inclination and in the end taking the only course open to him appears to be remarkably accurate."[100] Though there are clearly elements in the play that benefit from the kind of stylization John Barton's production gave it, there are also elements that can be most easily seen when the emphasis is placed on history and naturalism, as it was in the BBC film.

## Bolingbroke and York

Giles's interpretation of *Richard II* and his emphasis on history has not only produced an effective Richard but also given other characters firmer ground to stand on than they usually have. I have previously mentioned the Duchess of Gloucester, but two other characters were specially important to this production, the Duke of York and, of course, Henry Bolingbroke. In Michael Manheim's words, "Charles Gray brings new dimensions to the character of York, that loved but lightly regarded political weathervane whose rationalizations of his gross betrayal of Richard never make him forfeit the affection his avuncular bum-blings draw from us."[101]

Partly, of course, this is because David Giles and Derek Jacobi have given us a different kind of Richard, but partly too it is because York has been allowed his full part, including the semi-comic 5.3, which is often cut. We thus have the full range of the character from the man who, despite his fear of the king, is pushed by his brother's death into speaking the truth, to the bemused uncle who first berates and then befriends Bolingbroke, and finally to the bewildered husband, father, and subject whose shifting loyalties have brought him literally to his knees.

Stanley Wells says that in the scenes "concerned with Aumerle's conspiracy and his mother's attempts to save him from its con-sequences" there is a not altogether successful attempt "to achieve a subtle fusion of seriousness and comedy for which he [Shakespeare] cannot command the necessary technical resources, so that the comedy tends to submerge the seriousness." But as Wells goes on to argue, "there are good reasons for including the scenes, and the awkwardnesses . . . can be mitigated by tactful acting."[102] One of the strengths of the small screen is evident here because the comedy can be underplayed in a fashion that would not work in a large theater and because York can be pointed out and his character deepened in other scenes in ways that would be difficult if not impossible on stage. For instance, at 4.1.238, "Though some of you, with Pilate, wash your hands," we have a close-up of York bowed over his clasped hands, which he is clearly washing with his own tears.

The same grief emerges in this very different setting as York sits, wearing an informal robe and telling the Duchess the story of Richard's humiliation while she stitches at her embroidery. At 5.2.30, "But dust was thrown upon his sacred head," York's tears begin, and he unsuccessfully searches both of his sleeves for a handkerchief, which the Duchess then supplies. Aldous Huxley says, "We participate in a tragedy; at a comedy we only look."[103] But there is a sense in which we participate more fully in this tragedy of a fallen king because we see it, in part, from the vantage of a domestic comedy. Very few members of Shakespeare's audiences now or at any time will have been firsthand participants in royal intrigues; almost everyone, however, will have experienced the varieties of family tensions. In the context of this naturalistic production, the scenes fit neatly, and the historical footnote of the handkerchief (invented by Richard himself and typical of the attention to historical detail in this film) adds an extra bit of intimate irony.

We are also given a chance to see Bolingbroke from a new perspective. (In this context, it is unfortunate that his reference to his problems with his own son was cut.)[104] At 5.3.64, "And thy abundant goodness shall excuse," he puts his hand on York's shoulder and shakes him affectionately. It is the kind of gesture not often associated with Henry IV, and certainly not with the stiff, self-contained king whom Finch has created. However, throughout the scene Finch manages an undercurrent of exasperation and humor, and at the end, it seems entirely right for him to add the monosyllable "Ha!" to Shakespeare's text while clutching his head.

The praise for Jacobi's Richard usually includes kind comments for Finch's Bolingbroke as well. According to Jack Jorgens he "brought his tough, terse manner from his performance in Polanski's *Macbeth*."[105] For Clive James, Jon Finch was "the revelation of the evening." He went on to argue that if the actor playing Bolingbroke was to do more than look worthy and staunch, "he must play the role on two levels, speaking what is set down for him and transmitting his ambitions . . . by other means." According to James, Finch found those means: "even when he was standing still you could tell he was heading for the throne of England by the direct route."[106] For Michael Manheim also, Finch was a paradigm of political ambition: "Finch's Bolingbroke is a full embodiment of the new Machiavellian ideal in Shakespeare's time."[107]

Finch was probably chosen for Macbeth because "Polanski was insecure about the idea of working with anyone strongly identified as a Shakespearean actor,"[108] and Finch, in his turn, "was understandably insecure when he came to work alongside Sir John Gielgud and Derek Jacobi."[109] But when Gielgud praised Finch's verse speaking at the read through, Finch says, "I couldn't believe it. It immediately made me feel better and I was relaxed during the rest of the rehearsals."[110]

In fact, Finch's limited Shakespearean experience and his lack of drama school training may in some ways have been an advantage for his role in this production. In their *Macbeth* "Polanski and Tynan . . . insisted that the lines be spoken almost as natural speech,"[111] which was a suitable style to bring to the naturalistic BBC *Richard II*. Perhaps an additional advantage for Finch was that he did not bring a firm "expectational text" with him; his Bolingbroke was not already set in a pattern that would have clashed with Jacobi's Richard. As David Gwillim (the BBC's Prince Hal) points out, "Knowing the play . . . cuts both ways: if you have a clear vision of the play that's fine, but on the other hand you can have a *set* vision of the play as opposed to any sense of exploration."[112]

However, despite critical "readings" of Finch's performance that are colored by memories of the dark ambition he showed in Polanski's film, he appears to be a relatively unambitious Bolingbroke. Critical responses to both Finch and Jacobi are here being dictated at least partially by the expectational text: Richard is often weak and so Jacobi's Richard is; Bolingbroke is just as often pointed toward power, and so that must be Finch's direction as well.

There is, though, more to it than that, and while Clive James and Michael Manheim have (I think) got their explanations slightly muddled, I have no serious quarrel with their perceptions. Because of the *strength* of Jacobi's Richard, because Jacobi is playing so thoroughly to the subtext of the conflict between Richard and his cousin, there is a greater than usual political tension between the two of them, which can easily be misread as Bolingbroke's desire for the crown. In fact, Bolingbroke is locked in a political struggle with the king that is far more complicated (and certainly less superficially ambitious) than any Machiavellian desire to charm the people and harm the king on the way to the throne.

The historical reinterpretation of Richard that this production invites also requires a reinvestigation of Bolingbroke, and because of this, Finch's almost unreadable sternness becomes an advantage. Clive James says "there is a good case for asking the actor playing Bolingbroke to content himself with standing around looking worthily staunch."[113] This production makes the case for doing so stronger than usual, and on one level Finch's performance could be described in just those terms. His reactions to his banishment comprise realistic exasperation, not the frustrated ambition he reveals as Macbeth. Even when Richard puts the crown into his hands, he looks as he might have looked if, when they were boys, his cousin king had just given him a favorite toy—there is a mixture of surprise and joy.

On another level, of course, Finch's Bolingbroke is moving purposefully—and even perhaps virtuously—toward the crown. When I say virtuously, I mean to suggest that there are arguments by which he had a right to act as he did. Historically, there was disagreement (and this production certainly emphasizes Shakespeare's references to the subject) as to whether Mortimer or Lancaster was the rightful heir. In the event, the burden of restoring law fell on the adult claimant, Henry Bolingbroke, and much of England saw him as a savior.[114] Whether or not he later felt guilt for taking and keeping the crown (and Shakespeare, history, and the BBC suggest that he did), many Renaissance political theorists would have absolved him of guilt, as Roland Mushat Frye indicates in an extended discussion of the subject. As he says in commenting on John of Gaunt's refusal to act against Richard, literary historians have used "passive resistance as the panacea for too many problems and ills." He points to "the influence of E. M. W. Tillyard and Lily B. Campbell" but concludes that "developments in the history of political thought have made such major advances since the time of Tillyard that reassessments can and must now be made."[115]

Tillyard's thesis requires us not only to ignore theories of politics but also to suppress facts of history. One of the values of this

*Richard II* and of Finch's Bolingbroke is the chance to look at both in a new light. Finch may be especially effective here because he did not bring with him into the production a preconceived notion of the nature of Bolingbroke, because he was not during this performance planning to carry the role forward into the two parts of *Henry IV* and was not therefore affected by the pressure of the other role, and because the part he was playing was rather close to the "usual heroic, rather swashbuckling parts he plays in films."[116]

## Giles, Jacobi, and Richard II

In a production where the acting consistently received greater praise than anything else, Derek Jacobi has equally consistently been praised as the outstanding performer. Jack Jorgens found him "superb at rendering the arc of Richard's development."[117] And Clive James said, "Derek Jacobi gave intelligent, fastidiously articulated readings from beginning to end."[118]

Clive James goes on to point up one of the sources of the strength of Jacobi's performance: "each turn of thought [was] given its appropriate vocal weight by the actor and its perfectly judged close-up by the director."[119] Such a critical comment offers evidence of the success of the Giles-Jacobi partnership and also indicates the value of their shared interpretation. Jacobi, who had played the part of Richard II on radio but not on stage, was probably chosen for the role by Messina because of the triumph of "his television Claudius and his stage Hamlet."[120] And while, as Clive James says, this Richard "managed to make you not think of Jacobi's Claudius,"[121] Jacobi's Hamlet was waiting in the wings and from time to time doing a bit of prompting. While every actor must draw from his own central image to fill the mirrors of his roles, and Jacobi's Benedick, Prospero, Hamlet, and Richard have their overlapping edges, there seems a special connection between Jacobi's active, political Hamlet and his other king involved in a struggle of mighty opposites.

From Derek Jacobi's point of vantage as actor, the part of Hamlet has one of the same difficulties that he found with Richard: "So much has happened in *Hamlet* before the play starts."[122] About the same problem in *Richard II,* he said, "the first three scenes all contain allusions to the death of Gloucester, which happened before the play started." Jacobi goes on to elucidate the problems: "He [Richard] doesn't say very much . . . but the man's got a lot to hide and a lot to lose and a lot to gain from the situation, and it's completely understated by Shakespeare."[123] Given this vision of two characters who must play to the subtext as a means of explaining what has happened before the start of the action, of two men who are striving against great odds to fulfill themselves as kings and who find themselves in deadly political battle as a result, it is not surprising that Jacobi should use some of the same devices. The comparison not only illuminates Jacobi's acting style, but it also helps to explain the Richard that Jacobi as star and Giles as director created.

Thus, faced in both productions with the problem of successfully communicating a subtext, of suggesting that the character he is playing is at once more complicated and more powerful than he immediately appears to be, Jacobi has employed the device of sarcasm. Indeed, for Jacobi, sarcasm is more than a device, it is a whole armory of weapons—broadsword, rapier, dagger, and even shield. His Hamlet is arguably the most consistently sarcastic version of the Danish prince yet committed to film, and his Richard is also to this manner born. Jacobi's sarcasm as a means of emphasis has two major advantages: it sends a message of hostility that is easily read by the audience, and it announces itself as either the expression of superior power, superior insolence, or the two together.

So, in *Hamlet,* Jacobi's "Not so, my lord. I am too much in the sun" (1.2.67) immediately signals Hamlet's hostility toward the king, even (in my experience) for student audiences who have never seen the play before and who do not understand the pun. With "I shall in all my best obey *you,* madam" (1.2.120), which is delivered with all the nastiness of a knife blow and which Claudius is compelled to meet smiling, the battle is truly joined, and the audience settles down to watch the outcome.

The effect Jacobi achieves in *Richard II* is similar, allowing for the difference in his position. Here his attack is softer, less abrasive because he *is* king and his position adds emphasis, but the harsh message is still there. He does, of course, send other messages too. At 1.1.15, "Then call them to our presence," he sounds more eager than apprehensive because this is a confrontation he has been awaiting. Following Bolingbroke's compliments at 1.1.20–21, Richard turns to Mowbray, expecting more of the same, not even commanding the flattery but only waiting for it. The attitude is very much like the one Ian Richardson cultivated for the part. In his words, the sovereign "never needed to ask for anything. . . . I never looked to see if my commands were executed because I knew they would be."[124] That Jacobi bothers to look is the only sign of his tension.

Giles and Jacobi gradually build up the connections between Richard and Mowbray. At 1.1.79, "Which gently laid my knighthood on my shoulder," there is a cut from Mowbray to Richard. At 1.1.84–86, we get the first full flash of Richard's sarcasm in defense of Mowbray (though it can also be taken as an incitement to Bolingbroke, a stirring of the quarrel and a means of pushing it to extremes). At 1.1.100, "That he did plot the Duke of Gloucester's death," there is (as Michael Manheim has noted) a cut to Richard and only then to Mowbray. At 1.1.109, Jacobi's slightly worried reading of "How high a pitch his resolution soars!" suggests that there is something more than a well-pointed camera that links him to Mowbray. There is still more evidence at 1.1.131, "Since last I went to France to fetch his Queen," where a cut to Richard suggests satisfaction on his part and complicity or at least an understanding with Mowbray. In the same speech there is another cut to Richard and an even stronger signal. At 1.1.134, "Neglected my sworn duty in that case," Richard looks at Mowbray in what must (by now) be taken as a stern warning.

Jacobi has, however, sarcastically signaled that there is another, equally important issue. He puts Bolingbroke in his place at 1.1.116–17, "Were he my brother, nay, my kingdom's heir, / As he is but my father's brother's son." The camera cuts to John of Gaunt as a visual explanation of the relationship, but Richard's sarcasm suggests that something more is happening than meets the camera's eye. That impression is confirmed at 1.1.122, when Richard says, "He is our subject, Mowbray, so art thou," with a special emphasis on "subject" that clearly implies that someone somewhere has doubts about that subjection.

Historically, Shakespeare, the BBC production, and Derek Jacobi are essentially right; the issue was uncertain. As Bruce says, "Since William the Conqueror no one as distantly related to the king as the earl of March had succeeded to the throne and the custom of primogeniture had not always been followed."[125] So there was a reason for Richard to remind his audience of what he considered to be the proper order and succession of things. When Roger Mortimer, earl of March, died in Ireland on 20 July 1398, leaving only a child heir,[126] preparations for the combat between Mowbray and Bolingbroke were going forward; Richard had an even stronger reason on 16 September 1398, the day of the duel,[127] to get his dangerous cousin away from the throne.

With such preparation, the second scene will be watched more closely than it often is, clearly the intention of both Jacobi and Giles. Jacobi continues to build on what are now textual as well as subtextual impressions in the third scene. His hand-holding with the queen may be taken as an indication of the health of their relationship and a refutation in advance of the charge of homosexuality; it may also be seen as his indifference to a ritual he has already decided to abort. At 1.3.119, "Let them lay by their helmets and their spears," his decision seems firm, and there is no indication of sudden impulse or the process of thinking to a decision, two reactions at which Jacobi is particularly adept.

In addition, his antipathy for the House of Lancaster, father and son, has come much closer to the surface. The embrace he has for his cousin at 1.3.54 is extremely sketchy, and at 1.3.224, "Why! uncle, thou hast many years to live," he is as close to being sarcastic as he is far from being sympathetic. Almost he anticipates his wish for Gaunt's death. With Mowbray's half-spoken sense of betrayal by the king he trusted (1.3.155, "All unlooked for from your Highness' mouth") and Richard's cynical determination to be rid of Mowbray and Bolingbroke, we are left with a relatively dark public portrait of the sun king.

The public portrait of the king becomes effectively (and viciously) private in 1.4. The scene begins with Jacobi's laugh climbing above and dominating the laughter of his courtiers. It is the first indication we have had that the king may lose control, but, oddly, this seemingly unplanned mirth soon emerges as one more device in the power struggle. Jacobi has forged a link between Richard's insecurity and his attempts to make himself even more powerful than he already is.

Jacobi employs laughter as a weapon in *Hamlet* as well as *Richard II,* and again its use is broader and more obvious in the prince than the king. In *Hamlet,* for example, at 1.2.94, " 'Tis unmanly grief," Hamlet laughs at the king in a thoroughly disrespectful but slightly hysterical and therefore presumably forgivable manner. He tries a similar ploy on the king after the play within the play. At 3.2.275, "Give me some light," the king approaches Hamlet, studies him by the light of a torch, and in response, Hamlet covers his face with his hands and then laughs foolishly. The silly laughter turns to triumph as the king exits.

The BBC *Richard II* describes the setting for 1.4 (their scene 5) as "Interior. A Room in the King's Palace."[128] It is clearly, however, a representation of Richard's famous bathhouse, with the king and his favorites draped Roman fashion. This at once makes a number of suggestions not necessarily present in Shakespeare's text.

At 1.4.11, Aumerle's report of Bolingbroke's "Farewell," there is a cut to Jacobi for an extended reaction shot. Lying on his back with his head over the edge of a table and the camera shooting down at him as he looks awkwardly up, he appears particularly vulnerable, while his long fit of laughter seems a part of that vulnerability. The laughter is, though, both a sign of his uncertainty and one means to his ends, the ridicule and destruction of Bolingbroke and Richard's other enemies. Again, the insecurity and the attempt to gain greater power are presented as cause and effect.

Richard's resentment (or at least his show of it) continues to build throughout the scene. At 1.4.31, "Off goes his bonnet to an oyster-wench," he uses a parodic gesture and sarcastic emphasis to suggest his disgust. By 1.4.35, "As were our England in reversion his," his emotion has reached to royal rage, a danger to his self-control and his control of others and, more than that, an indication of his true feelings and insecurities. At this point Jacobi's Richard disguises himself in the same mask of laughter that his Hamlet uses. It is a means of undermining the seriousness of his own emotion, of reducing the importance of the situation, and as he had done earlier in the scene, of making the very suggestion of ambition in Bolingbroke seem ridiculous, a laughable stupidity. Coming as it does shortly after this, Richard's decision to go to Ireland himself has an air of relief about it. It follows Green's "Well, he is gone, and with him go these thoughts" (1.4.37) and suggests a brief vacation for Richard from his long revenge.

That there is to be no such vacation, that, in fact, Richard's vengeful, insecure nature and central position will not allow it, becomes clear with the news of Gaunt's illness. Jacobi's taking of the news is one of his neatest bits of characterization. From 1.4.59, "Now put it, God, in the physician's mind," he moves from a quiet acceptance of the news to the thought of Gaunt's death, the satisfaction that death will provide, and the use he can make of it. And he does all of this, arcing from stillness to an almost childish glee, with an eye on his courtiers to make sure they share his antipathies and intentions. The strength of Jacobi's performance as Richard is clearly visible here. In a scene that is not too far removed from the melodrama of Don John in *Much Ado About Nothing* and his "Would the cook were o' my mind!" (1.3.68), Jacobi conjures a Renaissance prince and a charming tyrant.

I emphasize that Jacobi's Richard is a legitimate king who maintains himself by tyrannous means, a dispenser of justice who suborns murder, and a man whose power has become so great that it must decline. The tension in the early scenes between the Richard who accepts absolute obedience as his due and the Richard who carefully maneuvers to conceal his crime has already begun to send these messages. Like those other Shakespearean tyrants Richard III and Macbeth, Richard II falls as a result of harshness, not weakness. In trying to grasp all, he threatens too many people and ends by clutching nothing. As A. R. Humphreys puts it, "at the beginning he is decisive even to ruthlessness, and it is his very energy of action which, when ill-directed, endangers his kingdom."[129]

One of the specially interesting facets of Jacobi's performance is that he manages to demonstrate that the Richard in the second half of the play is the same as the Richard in the first half. This Richard has always oscillated between a vision of himself as a divinely supported, all-powerful king and a picture of himself as a nameless beggar. In trying desperately to rise to the height of one, he has fallen almost to the depth of the other.

By 2.1, the family contentions and Richard's tyrannous intentions are very much out in the open. In this production Gaunt's accusation is coupled with the strong memory of the Duchess of Gloucester's, and their two dying voices convict Richard of a crime that his casual acceptance of Gaunt's mortal illness has helped us to believe he could easily commit. The first of several strong reactions to this situation from Jacobi's Richard comes at 2.1.123, where the last line of that verbal assault on Gaunt, "Should run thy head from thy unreverent shoulders," has a regal ferocity that explains his two uncles' fear of him and lets us know that Gaunt's death is near indeed when he dares to challenge the king as he does. At 2.1.145–46, "Right, you say true, as Hereford's love, so his, / As theirs, so mine; and all be as it is," Richard's voice is under control, but his anger is still stinging him into telling the truth without his usual rhetoric. He has calmed down for 2.1.153–55, and we have another of the excellent Jacobi-Giles reaction shots; there is some shock for him in this death he has wished for, perhaps even a suggestion that his wish is the cause, but again we see him thinking, walling himself off from everything but his royal purposes. The message that emerges is a deadly callousness: "So much for that" (2.1.155). He is not to be deflected by his Uncle York's tears or even by what seems to be semirebellion from this most placid of his relatives. There is nothing undecided about this Richard or about his "Think what you will, we seize into our hands

/ His plate, his goods, his money, and his lands" (2.1.209–10). It needs only his casual dismissal of the queen to send him off to Ireland as an unsympathetic tyrant.

One of the advantages of this Giles-Jacobi strategy now becomes apparent: the two halves of the play, pre-Ireland and post-Ireland, hold together. The audience has been asked to work out the nature of Richard before his military voyage, and the clues provided by Shakespeare and the production have proved pretty conclusively what he is.

As I have already pointed out, Jacobi's Richard (and Shakespeare's Richard, for that matter) is clearly identified as a tyrant. For the historical Richard, the use of the Cheshire archers or mercenary troops was one such indication. Shakespeare's Richard repeatedly makes decisions that are enforced by his power as king and not supported by the people or advisers such as York and Gaunt. As a result, Richard's fear of the love the common people have for Bolingbroke, like "Claudius' twice stated recognition of Hamlet's popularity . . . indicates the tyrant's fear of being supplanted."[130] Also like Claudius, Richard surrounds himself with flatterers and wastes the substance of his country, in his own words, on "too great a court / And liberal largess" (1.4.43–44). Gaunt's condemnation of him rises to the height of wishing for his retroactive deposition: "O, had thy grandsire with a prophet's eye / Seen how his son's son should destroy his sons, / From forth thy reach he would have laid thy shame, / Deposing thee before thou wert possessed" (2.1.104–8). In the crime of murder to which Gaunt refers and in the crime of seizing Lancaster's lands just after Gaunt's death, Richard commits the tyrant's unforgivable sin of destroying the order of the commonwealth he is set to rule and preserve.[131]

The rest of the film is (at least from Richard's point of view) a matter of why and wherefores. It is one thing to create and label a tyrant;[132] it is another to explain him, especially if that explanation is, as Richard's must be, something more than the itch of ambition or some other tragic flaw of the flesh.

Richard's return in 3.2 becomes in this production the means to an explanation; the stress of crisis is used to break through to the why of his earlier actions. Part of Richard's complexity (and no doubt one of the sources of the many suggestions that he is an actor-king)[133] comes from the control he exercises over his words and emotions and from the use he makes of them even when they are not in his complete control. Until now Richard has had no reason, either political or personal, to talk about the divine rights of kings. Now his private obsession becomes public; nor can it rightly be called an obsession, an abnormality, except in the intensity of his belief and the insensitivity of his actions. Gaunt and York share his point of view,[134] and even those very practical politicians, Bolingbroke and Northumberland, want Richard's acquiescence and royal sanction for his own deposition. In this production his speeches to the English earth and his dependence on plagues and angels must be seen not as vain posturing but as the misty periphery of his beliefs, a mixture of wishful fantasy and literal expectation. For Jacobi's Richard, like his historical counterpart, the boundaries of the world are immense, stretching from fear of being deposed and becoming nothing to an ecstatic state in which all his royal words could come divinely true. It is the arc of alternation between these two states that Jacobi has managed to travel.

In the context of 3.2, Richard's appeal to God to end Gaunt's life and Jacobi's almost stunned pause when he receives the news suggest Richard may have been willing to believe in the power of his own prayer. His actions through the rest of the production argue a vacillation between faith in his practical political (and, failing that, divine) support and a desperate uncertainty caused by the fear that at long last he will conclusively lose the battle to hold his throne (his identity as person, priest, and king) while holding down his subjects; thus the alternation between hope and despair, frenzied activity and passive suffering in 3.2. A particularly effective collaboration of director and star to demonstrate this occurs at 3.2.63, "How far off lies your power?" when Richard in an anxiety of optimism thrusts his arm out of the frame (at last an effective use of what has happened often accidentally), reaching to Salisbury as to a more than physical savior.

The danger in the man is demonstrated once more at 3.2.129, "O, villains, vipers, damned without redemption!" as Jacobi works himself up to a terribly active anger that ends in the threat of political execution, which he clearly means to carry out. If another revolution of the wheel (always possible while life remains) brings Richard to the top, Bolingbroke will certainly suffer the fate Richard had momentarily intended for Bushy, Bagot, and Green.

At 3.3.132–40, which begins with "O God! O God! that e'er this tongue of mine," the fury of Jacobi's Richard is again obvious and indeed barely contained, but he follows Aumerle's advice that it is wiser to delay to a better time than to force battle now and so die. This is very much the sort of policy Richard has pursued before, and always, in spite of humiliations and threatened depositions,

he has been able to emerge more powerful in the end. No doubt
he hopes beneath all the words of despair that this new deposition
will prove impermanent. One of Jacobi's neatest demonstrations
of this part of Richard's nature comes at 5.5.105, "How now! What
means Death in this rude assault?" He turns his back to the
murderers, reading the line as though he is resigned to die without a struggle. Then suddenly, on the next line, he turns to face
the murderers again, beating them and making use of the surprise to seize a weapon.

The historical interpretation begun in the early scenes carries
through consistently and successfully in the second half of the
play. The tension between Richard and Bolingbroke does not
relax, though the roles are reversed. Jacobi's Richard (like his
Hamlet) is adept at maintaining political pressure even when he is
at a disadvantage.

At 3.3.71, he has already insisted on an obeisance from Northumberland. At 3.3.171–72, with double-edged irony he has called
Northumberland "Most mighty prince" and his hated cousin
"King Bolingbroke." As he marches energetically down a stone
staircase, Richard describes himself (equally energetically) as
Phaethon, a sun king "Wanting the manage of unruly jades"
(3.3.178). This is not self-pity but a simple act of placing the blame
where he feels it belongs; he is a divinity betrayed by baseness, as
his reference to Christ and Judas (where, interestingly, Christ's
situation is found to be preferable, His troubles less severe) makes
plain in 4.1.170. The same point is made in a different way at
5.1.35–36, "A king of beasts indeed: if aught but beasts, / I had
been still a happy king of men." In each of these instances Jacobi's
sarcasm is itself a judgment; he is categorizing and chastising what
he sees as political injustice. His will is still active, still struggling
against circumstance, and though waves of despair wash over him,
he is not yet ready to sink.

Thus, in his encounter with Bolingbroke in 3.3, he repeats and
expands his earlier accusations against his cousin. "Up, cousin, up,
your heart is up, I know, / Thus high at least" (3.3.192–93). In his
fuller accusation, which begins at 3.3.198, he reaches with
"Cousin, I am too young to be your father, / Though you are old
enough to be my heir" (3.3.202–3), an almost exact restatement of
his earlier indications of Bolingbroke's royal ambition. Far from
giving up, this Richard is naming Bolingbroke's crime as his only
immediate means of combating it. Part of the strength of
Richard's conviction of his own divine mission is clearly visible
once we realize that he cannot totally accept the possibility of

being deposed. For Jacobi's Richard, naming the crime—which is also a blasphemy—should almost have the power to stop the criminal, as he has earlier said that his very presence in England will stop "this thief, this traitor, Bolingbroke" (3.2.47).

Perhaps the greatest strength of this production and of Jacobi's acting is the coupling of the sympathy that these scenes usually generate for Richard with a firm conviction in the audience that Bolingbroke is ending a tyranny; the very lines that make us pity Richard's loss of power show us how dangerous he has been and would be again in wielding it. This is especially true in 4.1, where we seem to see Richard breaking down, stripping away the layers of pretence that have surrounded his essential personality, but at the same time we perceive (in this production at any rate) his political maneuverings and his outmaneuvering of both Bolingbroke and Northumberland, who must win by force what Richard has kept them from gaining by any other means.

Jacobi's Richard takes command of the scene immediately on his entrance, and his bitter reading of the biting lines, his taunting emphasis at 4.1.181, "Here, cousin, *seize* the crown," show him to be an exceptionally dangerous adversary still.[135] He does everything that can be done in the circumstances to undermine Bolingbroke. He is compelled to give some small support to the new king, but he retracts everything he says both before and after he says it. Jacobi believes that though Richard is at "rock bottom" in the deposition scene, "he gives a marvellous account of himself." Jacobi sees Richard as an actor thinking, " 'If I've got to go, I'm going to go in style,' " an attitude he says he found "fascinating. . . . All the emotions are absolutely real for him—but he can switch it on."[136] This is an explicit statement of what we have earlier seen Jacobi's Richard do, that is, turn a real emotion, fear or doubt, for instance, into a weapon in a political situation.

Indeed, much of Bolingbroke's silence seems enforced by the energy of Richard's speech, and only that withdrawal into stillness keeps the new king from being made to look ridiculous. Northumberland too, who tries to force Richard to read a list of his crimes and, in fact, claps the king on the shoulder just after 4.1.220, like a buff-jerkined officer apprehending a malefactor, is repeatedly baffled. Richard first turns against him the accusation of deposing a true king then delays with "Mine eyes are full of tears, I cannot see" (4.1.243), at which point Northumberland casts his eyes up to heaven in frustration. At last Richard tears the list of crimes from his hands and throws it to the floor. The request for the looking glass is another tactic of delay and another opportunity to display the perfidy of his enemies.

The end result of the historical, naturalistic interpretation that Giles and Jacobi have created has been a more coherent and complex protagonist than is sometimes the case. This Richard is a legitimate king whose insecure position, echoed in his oscillations between confidence and despair, makes him a tyrant. His belief in his divine right to power and his fear lest he lose all are at once terrifying and pathetic. His insecurities—internal and external—force him to reach for absolute power and finally mean his downfall. In the desperate attempt to make himself perfectly secure financially, militarily, and therefore personally, he has threatened and alienated most of his supporters. Bolingbroke does not succeed because of his own superior ability or because of Richard's incompetence but because he offers an alternative to tyranny. The production succeeds because it offers a consistent and believable Richard who is set in an understandable historical context.

# 4

# The BBC First and Second *Henry IV*

## Factors Shaping the Productions

Many of the tensions and forces that shaped the BBC *Richard II* were also present in the two parts of the BBC *Henry IV*. The restrictions on budget and the corresponding constriction of rehearsal and shooting schedules had not changed, nor had the naturalistic house style, with its semidocumentary emphasis on history. However, the battle scene in *1 Henry IV* offered an additional difficulty. Richard Last expounded the dilemma: "How do you make the battlefield scene in studio Shakespeare convincing without the assistance of Cinemascope and a cast of thousands?" He conceded that his suggested solution, "some form of stylised combat," might "in the context of a naturalistic production . . . create more discrepancies than it overcame."[1]

Though many reviewers shared Richard Last's opinion that the problem of the battle scene had not been solved completely, few saw as clearly as he did the complexities that had prevented its solution. David Bevington said, "Cedric Messina chose to demystify Shakespeare in a generally sturdy, but uninspiring, interpretation, marred by low-budget naturalism and unconvincing studio filming techniques (especially in the battle sequence)."[2] Samuel Crowl blamed television itself: "The small screen just can't contain or capture its massive energies. . . . *1H4* can't be squeezed into a series of medium close-ups."[3]

However, as I indicated in my discussion of *Richard II*, Giles was limited more by the absence of funds and the presence of the house style than by the nature of the television medium. John Wilders suggests in an unpublished lecture that "Shakespeare is signalling to the director from his grave" and that a television director who analyzes a scene and understands its form "can also discover how to use his cameras, where to place them, and can thereby make his audience more aware than they would be in the theatre of Shakespeare's mastery of scenic construction."[4]

This account by a distinguished scholar and actor suggests that television has the capabilities not only to deal with all of Shakespeare's scenic structures but to perform that task more effectively than the theater can. But this assumes that after the director has correctly "dissected" the scenes, he will then have the technical resources to do what his dissection tells him is necessary to vivify the script in television terms. For David Giles and his BBC team the situation was different. Caught in the net of naturalistic filming, their "biggest problem," according to Giles, "was finding a style that would also encompass the battle"[5] when they did not have the money to film a battle in the same way they could film the Boar's Head.

Their solution was, in effect, to continue the policy of *Richard II* and give up the long shot. Set designer Don Homfray explains that they used a very shallow depth of focus: "A character is in focus, but perhaps even six inches behind him is out of focus."[6] This device was used for all exterior shots, with fog added to the battle scenes for good measure—hence the critical complaints about low-budget naturalism and the inaccurate assumption that television is exclusively the medium of the medium close-up.

This concentration on small events during something as large as a battle may perhaps explain features of the BBC productions that annoyed Maurice Charney. He believed that Giles was preoccupied with Henry IV's leprosy and fixated on the symbolic wound. Charney notes that "Hal receives a nasty, festering gash on the right side of his face that is never allowed to heal."[7] Pointing to the Hal-Hotspur and Romeo-Tybalt duels as examples, Charney draws the conclusion that "the BBC seems fascinated with violence as a new way of interpreting old texts."[8]

Certainly David Giles's comments on video gore do little to dispel this impression. As Henry Fenwick reports him, " 'David and Tim . . . have the most marvellous fight, really gory, and Tim's death is horrific, extremely nasty.' He chuckles with appreciation."[9] Clearly this version of the Hal-Hotspur fight was an attempt to get some show of violence into a sequence that was pretty much the proverbial three men and a boy in armor.

Unfortunately, the fight that the two actors spent "hours and hours rehearsing"[10] is little more than the cliché of rolling about on the ground until the hero dispatches his adversary with the expected upward thrust to the stomach. Richard Last called the attempt at gory realism an anticlimax: "Tim Piggott-Smith gasped out Hotspur's dying speech . . . through a mouthful of blood, after a Western-style roll in the dust which sounded like a crate of sardine-tins being shaken up."[11] Good special effects also cost money.

The difficulties caused by insufficient rehearsal and filming time make themselves felt in the BBC *1 and 2 Henry IV* as they had in *Richard II*. Though most of the characters remain within the frame for most of the time, and there is nothing like the sloppiness of the first three scenes of *Richard II* anywhere in the two Henrys, there are still more examples than a careful director would permit in ideal circumstances.[12]

There are also other problems. Although long shots have been pretty much eliminated from the production, there are a few left, and some of them are troublesome. At the opening of 1.3, Henry IV is so far down a long table that he is barely visible. Hotspur and Kate have the same problem at 2.3.77; they are both at such a distance from the camera as to be unclear.

However, as in *Richard II,* there are the deft touches that prove the rough spots to be the result of haste, not lack of skill. In the first scene of *1 Henry IV,* lighted by stained glass, accompanied by faint strains of monks singing, Henry IV and his advisers stand like pieces on a chessboard. The framing and use of close-ups (with the exceptions I have already recorded) are crisp and, in one instance at least, imaginative and visually and thematically effective. During Henry's talks with Westmoreland, the two of them are often close together, sharing effective two shots at 1.1.28, 1.1.33–46, 1.1.49–52, and 1.1.68–77. But Henry is also able to step back and look in other directions, which, coupled with clever close-up work, makes him appear to be alone, a technique employed between 1.1.77 and 1.1.95, "This is his uncle's teaching, this is Worcester," where there is a cut from Henry alone to Henry in profile with Westmoreland standing beside him that (despite what we know of the scene and the two shots we have already experienced) makes it seem as though Westmoreland has sprung from nowhere. It is a visually interesting moment, reminiscent of some of Peter Hall's camera work in *A Midsummer Night's Dream,* and thematically it suggests the danger and suddenness of the Worcester-Percy rebellion.

There are nice touches elsewhere too, including 2.4.212, "So, two more already," where Hal and Poins sit together on a wooden bench in a corner like two innocent, expectant schoolboys waiting for a story. And earlier in the same scene, at 2.4.145, "Zounds, ye fat paunch, and ye call me coward, by the Lord I'll stab thee," where Poins and Bardolph stand on either side of Falstaff with knives drawn in a nicely visual balance of attack and defense, dislike and affection. Equally effective is Falstaff's relatively static soliloquy in 2.4. The fat knight speaks most of his lines through a haze of smoke from a cooking fire. With his ruddy face, Anthony Quayle is the unmetaphored metaphor of the "roasted Manningtree ox" (2.4.451–52).

David Giles has also managed an entertaining, mildly symbolic sequence with—of all things—tables. In 1.3, Henry and the Percys are met together at that extremely lengthy table which I have already listed as part of the furniture in one of the problem long shots. Henry is, of course, at the head of this table. In 3.1, there is another conference and another, smaller table, this time with Hotspur at the head and Glendower roughly in the place Hotspur had earlier occupied in relation to Henry. This table, too, is a space for wrangling. In 4.1, there is a yet smaller table with Worcester at one end (in Henry's place) and Hotspur (who has seemingly lost his preeminence) at the other. In 5.5 is the smallest table of all, like the one employed by Bolingbroke and York in *Richard II* for the sentencing of the favorites. This table too is a prop for a tribunal, where Henry sits alone to give judgment on Worcester, the first of the guests to have left that much longer (though not much friendlier) table, where all of this began.

Another point that should be made in David Giles's favor is that he has done a much better job of opening things up to the camera in *1 and 2 Henry IV* than he did in *Richard II*. Apparently he has been willing sometimes to deny a part of Messina's house style and interpose himself a bit more obviously between actors and audience. One indication is the increased use of reverse-angle, over-the-shoulder shots, a strategy that was pretty much confined to the "arty-crafty" shooting of Richard's prison soliloquy in *Richard II*.[13]

T. F. Wharton, justifying his "institutional" choice of three Royal Shakespeare Company (RSC) productions and the BBC production for his text and performance study of *1 and 2 Henry IV*, said, "In the end, I have preferred . . . to use a good production rather than a bad one."[14]

Apparently, the BBC Henrys can successfully be matched against their stage counterparts. In fact, Michael Church suggests that the BBC films are superior to RSC stage productions, pointing to a BBC audience of "millions . . . across the globe and down the years" and to the BBC's job of demystifying Shakespeare and breaking down psychological and social barriers: "The RSC have done sterling work in taking the Bard to new audiences, but as . . . [the BBC *1H4*] showed their approach is often mannered in the extreme."[15]

But despite praise for the nonmannered BBC films and the fact that the naturalistic historical strategy Giles had employed for *Richard II* worked well, providing a platform for tense, dense, and fresh performances, that same strategy created problems in the two parts of *Henry IV,* as the critics' dissatisfaction with the battle makes clear. It is ironic that the attention to historical subtext which had helped to energize a play as emblematic and formal as *Richard II* should have caused difficulties in two plays that were seemingly so much better suited for it.

However, *Richard II* is essentially closer to history (provided that history has not been rewritten by Tillyard) than the two parts of *Henry IV* are. Falstaff throws his enormous, unhistorical shadow over the whole of the two plays, and the frolicsome prince who joins him in the tavern is not much like the religiously bigoted,[16] politically adept young man who ran the country when his father's illness incapacitated him mentally as well as physically.[17] As a result, details such as the introduction of Henry IV's "leprosy" focus the attention of the audience on material that is more distraction than elucidation.

The idea that Henry IV has, as Finch says, "got leprosy and syphilis,"[18] unlike the historical subtext on which the BBC's *Richard II* depended, cannot be readily supported from recent histories. The suggestion of leprosy appears in the *Brut*[19] but is rejected by modern historians.[20] To diagnose Henry's illness as syphilis gives an entirely misleading picture of his life and character. As Marie Louise Bruce puts it, "Sexual continence was a characteristic that set him apart from his relatives."[21]

A parallel problem, also caused by paying more attention to small, realistic details than to the larger issues of the play, comes in the filming of the Gad's Hill robbery. Martin Banham points out that this important scene "should be riotous and ridiculous, and above all . . . clear." He finds instead that it was "a rather hurried scuffle" and contends that it is "a scene that unless treated in an entirely unrealistic way fits most awkwardly into the medium."[22]

Again, the medium (and the realism it supposedly dictates) comes in for its share of the blame, but Orson Welles's version of the scene, shot in autumnal sunlight, plays beautifully on large and small screens. Admittedly, the First Carrier says, "I think it be two o'clock" (2.1.35), and, therefore, presumably the scene must be shot in the dark. However, there are at least two ways around the difficulty. First of all, semidocumentary or not, it is necessary to read all the text. There is no indication of the hour when the thieves encounter their victims, and there must be at least enough light for Falstaff to correctly distinguish that the prince and Poins are wearing buckram suits, as Poins tells us at 1.2.181 and Falstaff recounts at 2.4.191–92. Falstaff's excuse that "it was so dark, Hal, that thou couldest not see thy hand" (2.4.222–23) will be even funnier if we have already watched the encounter in the bright light of dawn.

The second possibility involves remembering that both stage and screen conventions allow night scenes to be as well lighted as necessary. There is, for instance, no difficulty at all in seeing what happens in the final scene of the BBC's own production of *The Merry Wives of Windsor;* none of the comic effect is lost, and everybody can easily discern that the fairies are not fairies and the boys are not Anne Page. Giles himself does the night scene in *Henry V* without difficulty or loss of detail. It is, then, possible to do a "naturalistic" night scene and still maintain the effect that was originally designed for the daylight of Shakespeare's stage. But I think Martin Banham is right when he says David Giles has not managed to do so in *1 Henry IV*.

Finally, though, the central interpretation that emerges from the two parts of *Henry IV* (and *Henry V*) has more to do with Hal and Falstaff than with history. As I pointed out in the previous chapter, David Giles did not know when he directed *Richard II* that he would also be the director for all of what might readily (in view of the BBC project) be styled the Henriad.[23] Indeed, Messina seems to have had even larger plans, saying, "Whether he will carry on to *Henry VI*, I don't know. I think it would be right and proper."[24] In the event, of course, neither the producer nor the director carried on to *Henry VI*,[25] but the sequence of three plays he was immediately committed to obviously had an impact on David Giles's decisions.

The last three of the four plays were shot as a unity. For example, *1 Henry IV* begins with a flashback to Richard's death, and in *2 Henry IV* "before the play opens we see, in flashback, King Richard II handing the Crown to Bolingbroke," then "Bolingbroke (now King Henry IV) at his prayers," and, finally, "Prince Hal in mortal combat with Hotspur on Shrewsbury field."[26] As a result, we are able to watch the development of Bolingbroke, Falstaff, and Hal from play to play. Our Henry V has also been our Hal and has had to come to terms with the shift on film. As John Wilders says, "I think that certainly to see the two parts of *Henry IV* and *Henry V* as a sequence makes an enormous difference."[27]

Another extremely important factor in shaping the productions was the presence of Anthony Quayle, one of this century's best-known Falstaffs, director as well as star of the 1951 Stratford productions. Certainly the version of Falstaff that emerged from the films belonged as much to Quayle as the version of Richard had to Jacobi. It is a measure of the success of the films and of Giles's skill as coordinator as well as director that Quayle's Falstaff exactly suits this Prince Hal and even fits with Jon Finch's idiosyncratic Henry IV.

## Jon Finch as Henry IV

The chorus of praise for Jon Finch in *Richard II* was muted as he moved into *1 and 2 Henry IV*. The focus of most of the critical comments was Henry's leprosy and the gestures Finch used to emphasize it. Wharton provides a vivid description of Henry's illness, with his face "progressively invaded by a scarlet and yellow crust around his mouth, nose and cheeks" and his glove and sleeves stained as if by seepage. He concludes that "the medium of television was able economically to draw attention to a central symbol of the play, by its capacity to close in on detail."[28]

Nevertheless, most reviewers did not share Wharton's tone of mild approval. Samuel Crowl says Finch compensated for his lack of facial expression by giving "his king an embarrassing and irritating series of hand gestures as his sole means of displaying Henry's care, concern, guilt and insecurity." Crowl sees "the stain of Henry's usurpation" as "an overpowering image," which undermines the generous and optimistic elements in *1H4*.[29] Such heavy emphasis on Henry's guilt seems to contradict the BBC *Richard II* and makes it difficult to match that Bolingbroke with this Henry IV. However, the BBC *Richard II* was not filmed with the three Henrys in mind, and the transition is a large one for any actor.

For Maurice Charney, Henry's malady "gives a peculiar twist to the character of Henry IV and actualizes his guilty conscience in a way unlikely to have been envisaged by the author."[30] One reason for the decision to focus on Henry's disease may be found in Henry Fenwick's comment that "Finch is a very physical actor, and it was in the ageing and sickening of Henry that he found most of the challenge and most of the difficulty."[31] However, even given the brevity of television reviews, it may be fair to say that when many comments on a performance focus disapprovingly on hand gestures, something is wrong.

There were other uncomplimentary things said about Jon

Finch's performance. The natural style of speaking verse he had brought from his role as Macbeth and modified for Bolingbroke became what T. F. Wharton called "a highly stylised and stagey delivery of his lines. The words were chanted out mostly in pedantic monotone."[32] Russell Davies was unhappy with the casting of Henry IV because Finch was "starchily declamatory beyond the call of regal duty. His lecture to the Prince was a rant."[33]

In addition to chanting and ranting, Finch has also done a bit of screaming. In *2 Henry IV* at 3.1.17, for instance, "A watchcase or a common 'larum-bell?" he reads the line with an echoing shriek, a representation presumably of the alarum-bell itself. Between the visual distraction of his gestures and the aural distortions of his oddly stressed delivery, however, there is still room for an interesting if idiosyncratic characterization.[34]

David Giles saw Finch's version of Henry IV as "edgy and dangerous," a judgment echoed by Tim Pigott-Smith, who found the counsel scene in *1 Henry IV* stimulating to play "because of that paranoiac at the other end of the table."[35] Again, this does not fit well with Finch's Bolingbroke from *Richard II*, though, in fairness, the sequence of plays is remarkably complicated, and there is room for a Bolingbroke who honestly takes the throne and then guiltily suffers for his action. It is perhaps the range of variation in Finch's performance, from an all-but-innocent Bolingbroke[36] to an obsessively guilty Henry IV, that makes it difficult to see the one as resulting from the other.

Samuel Crowl described Finch's Henry as an "inadequate performance,"[37] and even if one sees that judgment as too harsh, clearly Finch's Henry is the weakest of the major roles in the BBC *1 and 2 Henry IV*. There is, however, something to be said both for the conception of the role and for the way it works into the overall interpretation of the two parts of *Henry IV*. The illness itself, though perhaps overplayed and overstressed, offers interesting insights. Samuel Crowl talks about a "ritual cleansing" in *1 Henry IV*.[38] What actually happens is that we watch Henry washing, drying, and applying ointment to his hands and arms. The term "ritual" is appropriate because all of Henry's movements are careful, concentrated, almost religious in their intensity, and obviously often repeated. Further, Henry is in need of "ritual cleansing" because the disease he has is traditionally "unclean" and because this horrible illness has supposedly (at least according to his enemies) been imposed on him as a punishment for his sins and the sins of the land he rules.

This raises the issue in a way that most productions do not of the king as a scapegoat. The idea of scapegoats is certainly not foreign to this play, nor is the idea of Bolingbroke's being destroyed by the burden of kingship anything unusual. As James Winny puts it, "The struggle imposes strains upon him which drain his previously buoyant energy and wear him down to the point of exhausted collapse."[39] For C. L. Barber, since Bolingbroke's taking of the crown could be considered a duty undertaken for the sake of England, he is "almost a sacrificial figure, a king who sins for the sake of society, suffers for society in suffering for his sin, and carries his sin off into death."[40]

D. J. Palmer makes a similar point when he says of Hal that "in losing his father he has also cast off the old man."[41] The very concept of casting off the old man has overtones not only of casting off the old Adam, the sinful nature, but also of replacing age with youth, soiled with fresh. In mythological terms, as James Frazer points out, it is a combination of functions: the god or king "was killed . . . to save the divine life from the degeneracy of old age; but, since he had to be killed at any rate, people may have thought that they might as well seize the opportunity to lay upon him their sufferings and sins."[42]

This version of Henry as a worn-out king fits with Henry's own picture of Hal (which is in many ways only a reflection of his self-image). Thus, because he feels himself to be old, he sees Hal as the incarnation of youth, impatient for power and the death of the father, which must precede it. At the same time, since he suffers guilt for his actions, he has a paradoxical image of Hal as an irresponsible wastrel (a reincarnation of Richard) sent as one more of his painful punishments—and incidentally unworthy to succeed to the throne, replacing and, in effect, killing that good king, Henry IV. In these terms, Hotspur is a good heir, an acceptable son, *because* he is a rebel and has therefore disqualified himself as a legal successor.

The BBC production adds an extratextual (but historical) tension to the already difficult relations between father and son. David Giles found it very interesting that "Hal was one of the hostages Bolingbroke gave to Richard when Richard went to Ireland. Richard treated Hal very well when he could have been extremely nasty." Giles saw this as a partial explanation for "Hal's reaction against his father."[43] In fact, the relationship between Hal and Richard was, if anything, warmer than Giles suggests. A year after Henry IV's death, Richard II was reburied at Westminster Abbey, where, as commanded by Henry V, "who had never ceased to love him more than his own father, Richard joined his queen . . . in the great bronze tomb adorned with the insignia of kingship."[44]

The BBC production of *1 Henry IV* indicates this tension unmistakably in the very scene of the "ritual" cleansing, 3.2. During the king's recounting of his earlier conduct, "Had I so lavish of my presence been" (3.2.39), Hal stands behind him with the cold countenance of a judge, not the shamefaced appearance of a truant prince. At "I did pluck allegiance from men's hearts, / . . . Even in the presence of the crowned King" (3.2.52, 54), Hal turns to his father with a look of such pointed accusation that Henry, even in the midst of chastising his son, is forced to feel guilt. As Giles describes the end of this scene, it "should really finish up with Hal crying and Henry being the headmaster, but it ends completely the other way round: Henry becomes so involved with his guilt for the death of Richard it's he who's crying and Hal who's steadying him."[45]

As T. F. Wharton points out, "The traditional portrayal of Henry IV has been in terms of anguished guilt." He calls John Gielgud's performance in *Chimes at Midnight* "the classic example."[46] And while Jon Finch's portrayal certainly fits this pattern, a comparison of the two performances turns up some important differences. Wharton describes Gielgud's king as "at once ennobled and soured by his burden of conscience. The voice was majestic, but the face betrayed the dyspeptic sufferings of a man for whom life has turned bitter.[47] While Gielgud's Henry can also be perceived as a scapegoat, visually associated with the gallows on which other rebels hang, he maintains a kind of royal control, a *gravitas*, that seemingly belongs to Finch's Bolingbroke but not to his Henry IV. The rubbings, scratchings, and twitchings of a king before his court that are the center of Finch's performance suggest at once a man whose physical and psychological sufferings are so great that he cannot control himself. At the same time these indecorous motions suggest a king so self-absorbed, in fact so self-obsessed, that he ceases to consider the effects of his own actions on those around him. The control Gielgud's Henry exercises allows him to maintain his authority over son and kingdom in a way that seems impossible for Finch's character.

Interestingly, T. F. Wharton found in the productions he examined that "the king emerges as a figure who is tightly bound up with his own obsessions."[48] He goes on to comment that the BBC production "ran entirely true to form" in this respect, with the king emerging as "a figure of harsh remoteness."[49] Thus, despite the heavy emphasis on Henry IV as a scapegoat, as weak and diseased internally and externally from the very first scene, Finch's performance can be fitted into the general pattern of Henry IVs. His Henry is less fully characterized than usual, more a collection of mannerisms than of matter, but the historical and mythological overtones emerge perhaps more clearly as a result of the overemphases.

## Anthony Quayle's Falstaff

Critical reactions to Anthony Quayle's Falstaff were favorable, as might be expected, for his third performance in the role, the first having been the "now fabled production with Richard Burton as Hal, when Quayle was director at Stratford on Avon" in 1951.[50] There was even a certain tendency to treat the BBC performance as an extension of the earlier stage versions. For Judith Cook, Anthony Quayle was her "favourite Falstaff . . . both on stage and, more recently, on television."[51]

There is certainly some justification for this because, clearly, the animating conception behind the BBC's Falstaff belongs to Quayle, and his version of the fat knight is one of the best examples in the BBC Henriad of the actor as auteur. That the performance which emerged on the television screen conformed to Quayle's ideas of what Falstaff should be like is easy to demonstrate. He says, for instance, "I have this very strong feeling . . . that he was desperately aware of his own failings and shortcomings."[52] In fact, Quayle himself is very much aware of Falstaff's weaknesses. He says, "He's a monster. He's a desperate character and infinitely lovable."[53] He goes even further in his discussion of Falstaff's stabbing of the dead Hotspur: "It's horrible. . . . In that sequence he's a rat, a great fat rat."[54] Richard David found this conception in Quayle's 1951 performance: "As Falstaff, Anthony Quayle commanded the two absolutely essential qualities: a wholly winning gusto, and real, unpardonable wickedness."[55] The BBC Falstaff also emerges as a character with a dark side; at times he might prompt members of the audience not to echo Quayle's description of "infinitely lovable" but to repeat Robert Speaight's comment about the fat knight's rejection, "Falstaff is not so lovable—is he indeed ever lovable?—that we cannot bear to see him go."[56]

According to Maurice Charney, Quayle's BBC Falstaff "convincingly expresses the character's doubleness and ironic conception of himself."[57] For Richard Last, "This Falstaff recognized

his own ignobility."[58] Such critical reactions seem to validate Anthony Quayle's words about the role, since they suggest that he has
been able to present the Falstaff he describes. Michael Church
said, "Anthony Quayle's Falstaff compels joyful assent. This is the
one justified indulgence in David Giles's low-key direction."[59]

There were, nevertheless, some criticisms of the performance.
Maurice Charney found that "by the end of Part Two . . . Falstaff's
energies are so distressingly diminished that we are over-pre-
pared for the melancholy rejection scene."[60] I would suggest that
this diminution of energy is a direct result of the very "doubleness" which Charney himself describes; Falstaff's own darkness
begins to collect around him and weigh him down. For Quayle,
the turning point is Falstaff's stabbing of Hotspur. He says,
"That's the crucial point where the relationship between Falstaff
and Henry falls apart."[61] I would also suggest that in a production
where Henry IV's illness is so graphically displayed, his nonroyal
counterweight, that other counterfeit and scapegoat, is unlikely to
remain obviously healthy. Further, in productions that emphasize
Hal to the extent that these do, Falstaff and the minions of the
moon must dim as the sun of Henry V rises.

Another criticism of Quayle's Falstaff comes from Samuel
Crowl. He was troubled "by unnecessary interjections ('ah . . . er
. . . oh-ho . . . harumph . . . hmmmm') as though the quickest
mind in the west needs to fumble for words in repartee with his
own student."[62] T. F. Wharton sees this characterization quite
differently: "He seemed to fill all the available space of the small
screen, not only physically but vocally—the lines themselves being
given a sonorous orchestration of snorts, growls, snuffles and
hisses of breath."[63]

I would suggest that on one level, the snorts and snuffles are an
attempt to make Falstaff's very formal speeches seem more natural and improvisational for the naturalistic television production
in which they appear. Significantly, they are not a sign that Falstaff
is unable to think and speak with extreme rapidity but an indication of his nervousness as a performer. Wharton has missed the
connection between the two patterns, though he did see them
both. He says, "Always there was the flicker of anxiety between the
joke and the laugh."[64] In the words of Russell Davies, "Falstaff's
insecurity—that moment of facial panic after the uttering of a
joke before the reaction set in around him—was perfectly
caught."[65] Anthony Quayle has also talked about Falstaff's uncertainty, and he connects it with the fat knight's darkness. "He says
to himself if that is what I have become, then that I will be. I will go

beyond all limits, and he has the wit and skill to back it up. But somewhere there's a terrible grief inside him."[66]

The grief and the anxiety come together in the performance because it is only the performance that protects Falstaff from the consequences of the evil he perceives inside himself. When he fails to please his audience in the same way that—secretly—he fails to please himself, he knows that some sort of catastrophic end will be at hand. The BBC production prepares us for this by showing us several of Falstaff's unsuccessful performances, even when it is necessary to ignore stage directions in order to make them unsuccessful.

In fact, almost all of Falstaff's appearances in the role of brave soldier are undercut. I do not mean to suggest that Shakespeare has left a great deal to undercut in the first place, only that the BBC has undermined the mines already dug. For example, Falstaff is deprived of the "blow or two" he strikes before running away from Gad's Hill. The same thing happens at Shrewsbury. The stage direction says Douglas "fighteth with Falstaff," but the only blow Quayle's Falstaff strikes is one against his own shield.

There is nothing unusual in such deflations: Orson Welles has his fat soldier running away and poking his sword comically back over his shoulder at Gad's Hill, and he eliminates Douglas altogether. But the pattern carries over and becomes more obvious in *2 Henry IV.* Falstaff's only successful military encounters are against Pistol, a braggart soldier so wound about with cowardice that he is ready at the first breath of opposition to roll himself downstairs, and Coleville of the Dale, who is defeated by the weight of Falstaff's reputation and the sight of that great belly in armor. After the encounter with Pistol at 2.4.212, "I pray thee, Jack, be quiet. The rascal's gone," Falstaff is left swinging his sword with his eyes shut tight. Surely this suggests not only cowardice but also a temporary stupor, if he is not able to recognize that this Pistol (unlike Percy) has no gunpowder about him. Even the valor of Falstaff's name is taken away at the beginning of 4.3. Falstaff is worriedly hiding himself in the trees when Coleville backs over a tripwire that the fat knight's Page (who was added to the scene for this purpose) has set, and thus Falstaff's only prisoner falls down instead of delivering himself up.

This not only suggests that Falstaff's performances can fail, it also takes away any small measure of value that might be attached to his military reputation or any minuscule mitigation of his cowardice. Anthony Quayle even deprives him of the possible courage in 2.4.499–500, "I hope I shall as soon be strangled with a halter as another," with a bit of special, facial pleading to Hal. It might be argued that this makes him darker than he needs to be and also that one Pistol in the play is enough. In effect, the actual Pistol in this production becomes something less than he might be in order to make room for the fat knight on a sort of sliding scale of cowardice, a result that did not please everybody. In Maurice Charney's words, "Falstaff's companions, especially Pistol, are so overwrought that they seem more like circus clowns than meaningful comic characters."[67]

It would be misleading to suggest that this is all a matter of making room for Falstaff. In fact, it is at least partly the business of remaking the play in the light of the late-twentieth-century British and American dislike for war and warriors. As Tim Pigott-Smith puts it, Hotspur "ends up slung head down across Falstaff's back—the most humiliating image we could find. We worked very hard on the fights, trying to take them away from the noble image."[68] Thus, not only Pistol and Falstaff but also Douglas and (as Tim Pigott-Smith suggests) Hotspur are played in less admirable ways than they have sometimes been. Tim Pigott-Smith's Hotspur begins with bluff, youthful impatience, but what starts out as a kind of charming anger ends up seeming a desperate bluster. Most of his lines immediately preceding and during the battle are spoken as a species of tough talk, an attempt to reassure himself and intimidate everyone else. John Cairney's Douglas is, if anything, a less subtle version of the same phenomenon.

It is no wonder that Hal's "It is the Prince of Wales that threatens thee" (5.4.41), delivered in a straightforward tone with no touch of bluster, comes as a welcome relief and makes both Douglas and Hotspur seem to be almost the caricatures of themselves Hal has described in the tavern. Nor is it surprising to find Samuel Crowl saying, "Tim Pigott-Smith's Hotspur is appropriately red-headed and fiery but fails to rival our affection for Hal."[69] In this interpretation Hotspur dying with his mouth full of blood is entirely consistent: he has been speaking blood and thunder throughout the play; now time has turned the thunder to silence, and only the blood remains.

And in this interpretation (to bring the argument full circle) Falstaff, whom Anthony Quayle sees as "absolutely in antithesis"[70] to Hotspur, is appropriately a player acting the role of coward as Hotspur is a blusterer acting the role of hero. It is Falstaff's misfortune that the roles he has elected (and been selected) to enact are part of a play with a limited engagement. As Anthony Quayle says, "Shakespeare seems somewhere to have decided to go on to write the heroic, nationalistic play of *Henry V* and he's going to turn Hal . . . into the national hero. . . . He cannot have Falstaff hanging round his neck."[71]

This uncertainty (plus the fat knight's self-disgust) sets up the fundamental anxiety in all of Falstaff's performances. T. F. Wharton describes him as a performer whose high energy and spirits were merely part of his assumed character and was, as a result, "subject to all the anxieties of his trade. He was a man dependent on his audience, and forever having to trick them and to win their response."[72]

The point is driven home in a number of ways in the production. Wharton finds his first example in the play extempore in the tavern scene.[73] However, much of Anthony Quayle's performance (including his extratextual mutterings and his more-than-Falstaffian cowardice) can be seen in these terms. And both 2.4.235, "What upon compulsion?" and 2.4.268, "By the Lord, I knew ye as well as he that made ye," are indications of Falstaff as performer. In the first case, he has found a desperate (but characteristically entertaining) means to delay long enough to think, and in the second (or rather just before he delivers that line), we see Falstaff thinking desperately, and then he sniggers, having hit a solution.

An even clearer indication of Falstaff's dependence on approval than his suggestion of the play extempore is 2.4.378, "Shall I?" when he openly looks around at his prospective audience for their permission and encouragement. Their reaction is enthusiastic, and Falstaff really is (temporarily) "Content" (2.4.378).

The audience is, of course, directly involved in this performance in other ways, and many of the signals they send are loaded with proleptic irony or foreshadowing or just plain warnings to Falstaff. It is Mistress Quickly and not Falstaff himself who supplies his name (in a small, high voice that is a reminiscence from the same moment in *Chimes at Midnight*) at 2.4.425. The whole audience assents to Falstaff's question at 2.4.434, "Depose Me?" and there is such boisterous agreement from the audience during Hal's catalog of Falstaff's vices that it is hard to hear the words. Falstaff gets a foretaste of pity from Hal at 2.4.459, "Wherein worthy, but in nothing?" and the seriousness of this rehearsal for the real thing is driven home when Hal sits silent and motionless at its conclusion. He actually seems angry to be interrupted by Quickly in the midst of his dark thoughts, reading "Heigh, heigh, the devil rides upon a fiddlestick! What's the matter?" (2.4.487–88) with more irritation than any other speech in the two plays.

T. F. Wharton correctly points out that the encounter between Falstaff and the Lord Chief Justice in *2 Henry IV* 2.2 is another example of the fat knight as performer. The audience joins in, and this time even "the Lord Chief Justice has been drawn into the performance. . . . His whole manner indicated his pleased awareness at being stooge and collaborator in a comedian's matinee."[74] What Wharton does not point out is that Falstaff goes dancing off at the conclusion of the scene, waving his stick like a circus baton. There is a special appropriateness about that stick, which is at once a symbol of Falstaff as performer and Falstaff as a vulnerable, ailing, old man—the very infirmities that compel him to perform. It is also particularly appropriate that his first duet should be with Hal and the second with the Lord Chief Justice, the man Hal chooses as a father in preference to Falstaff.[75]

Samuel Crowl maintains that "Quayle's performance is most interesting when director Giles has him identify and confront the camera-as-audience."[76] I would suggest that at least part of the strength of Quayle's performance in the soliloquies comes from the fact that they are merely an extension of Falstaff's other performances, his attempts to cajole approval. The intimacy of the television camera is enhanced by the feeling that Falstaff is suddenly meeting the television audience in the same way that he meets the other characters, that the television audience has suddenly become part of the performance, an experience more often thought of in terms of live theater.

A particulary good example of the process is in *2 Henry IV* 4.3. "I would you had the wit. 'Twere better than your dukedom" (4.3.88–89) is Anthony Quayle's closest approach in the two plays to vitriolic, Jacobi-style sarcasm. Falstaff is clearly hurt by the encounter with the impermeable, unamusable Prince John, and his long speech about sack is a way of cheering himself up by talking to a more sympathetic audience.

The roles of Falstaff and Hal and the way their relationship develops were partly shaped by the portions of Shakespeare's text the BBC chose to omit as well as by the film text they actively created. By far the most important omission from the two productions was the prince's question, at 3.3.135–55, "Sirrah, do I owe you a thousand pound?" and Falstaff's answer, "A thousand pound, Hal? A million! Thy love is worth a million, thou owest me thy love" (3.3.139–41). This exchange is especially important not only as one of the turning points of the scene but also as an indication of the complex relationship that exists between the prince and the fat knight. For Orson Welles and Keith Baxter it was the occasion for a hug; it is likely that Anthony Quayle and David Gwillim would have been colder and less demonstrative, but that, in the circumstances, can only be speculation. The lines ask and partly answer an important question that this production has chosen to omit. It is a deliberate reduction in the warmth of the relationship between the two that makes the coming rejection more bearable.

In a similar manner, David Giles and Anthony Quayle have decided to reduce the duration and therefore the warmth and impact of Falstaff's last performance, to ensure that it is a failure with the television audience in somewhat the same way as it is with the royal one. After all, it is necessary in the course of a Henriad for Hal to move on to *Henry V.* Anthony Quayle says, "I think the audience must love Falstaff to the end but they must also say: 'Hal had to do that, he really had to!' "[77] For David Giles, "Part 2 is very much the death play."[78]

Pushed in among a crowd that is held back with a rope, Falstaff shouts to his new king, but the shouts are difficult to hear, and one might wonder why Hal bothered to stop in the first place. Once he does stop, the camera is almost constantly on the young king. The camera turns to Falstaff for "My King! My Jove! I speak to thee my heart!" (5.5.47). There is then a cut to Hal and, next, a cut to Falstaff seen over Hal's shoulder. This shot indicates (if any proof were needed) that the scene could have been filmed much differently because, though Hal is looking upscreen at Falstaff, three-quarters of his face is visible. With a slight modification of the camera angle, the reactions of fat knight and new king would have been simultaneously available.

Instead, there is a cut back to Hal, full face and staring straight ahead, the posture he maintains for most of his next speech, which begins now with "I know thee not, old man. Fall to thy prayers" (5.5.48).[79] There is a brief cut to Falstaff at 5.5.49, "How ill white hairs become a fool and jester!" and there is also the obligatory cut following "Know the grave doth gape / For thee thrice wider than for other men" (5.5.54–55), so that Falstaff's brief smile can cue Hal's next line.

In addition there is a significantly placed cut to Falstaff at 5.5.63, "The tutor and the feeder of my riots." Even this last cut to Falstaff during the speech that proves mortal to the fat knight comes on Hal's cue, "my riots," rather than on the threat to Falstaff, "on pain of death."

In "Shakespeare, the Telly and the Miners," David Margolies complains that in the BBC rejection scene "the camera focuses on the old man's greasy face . . . a real abandoned old man, an actuality instead of a representation."[80] However, greasy or not, real or representational, there is very little of Falstaff's face on the screen until after Henry V and his procession have passed by. Then, again relatively briefly, we see Falstaff in tears[81] before he is carried away to the Fleet and replaced by a stiff-faced Lord Chief Justice and a chuckling Prince John.

Anthony Quayle describes Falstaff as "a great Lord of Misrule."[82] At the end of this production, he is cast off and cast out like that kingly scapegoat, Henry IV. He has become "the real man who personated Saturn and when the revels were over, suffered a real death in his assumed character."[83] It is interesting that Frazer describes the situation in terms of an actor who dies in the role he has assumed. That idea seems also to be clearly behind Anthony Quayle's conception of the character of Falstaff, a performer who survives only while he holds his audience's attention and then perishes in the unsavory persona he has created.[84]

C. L. Barber shares this perception of Falstaff as Lord of Misrule, describing part 1 as the reign of Carnival and part 2 as his trial and expulsion.[85] But for Barber, as for many other critics, the expulsion, the conclusion of the ritual, does not entirely succeed.[86]

It seems to me that the conclusion of the BBC *2 Henry IV* should be considered with these issues in mind. Though it may be argued that the process has darkened and diminished Falstaff, the justification is in seeing the last three plays of the second tetralogy as a Henriad, the education of a king and the creation of a hero. David Giles puts it in just these terms, saying about part 2, "It is also, when viewing the three plays as a continuity, the one which crucially affects the audience's vision of the action and of the 'hero,' Prince Hal."[87]

The rejection of Falstaff becomes another in a series of tests for Hal, and it is his face, struggling with emotion, turning to look straight ahead or slightly down but not at the fat knight, Hal's face becoming at last the face of a ruler who controls himself and therefore his subjects, that the scene is really about and that the camera must focus on. For Cedric Messina the change was there: "By the end of Part 2, after the rejection of Falstaff, David Gwillim seems a totally different person."[88]

There is a danger of seeing the rejection of Falstaff as the acceptance of Henry IV, but in Anthony Quayle's words, "Henry has two fathers and neither of them are any good for him. Both of them . . . act as fathers and both of them fail him as fathers."[89]

There is a sense in which Hal must reject the rebel Bolingbroke at the same time he rejects the rebellious Falstaff: both scapegoats must be banished; they have both touched the same pitch. As Leonard Tennenhouse points out in *Power on Display: The Politics of Shakespeare's Genres,* "it is significant to find Richard describing Bullingbroke in language more appropriate for a Falstaff than an English king" and, a few lines later, "the figure of carnival is associated with Henry."[90]

## David Gwillim's Prince Hal

Critical responses to David Gwillim's performance were as diverse as the critics' opinions of Prince Hal himself. Maurice Charney attacked Gwillim's Hal and Henry V as not only "awkward" and "supercilious" but also "proprietary" in his attitude to the crown and patronizing toward Falstaff. From Charney's perspective it seemed as though all of *1 and 2 Henry IV* had been "sandwiched between the 'I know you all' soliloquy . . . modeled on the villain's self-address to the audience—and the catastrophic 'I know thee not, old man' speech."[91]

Charney's objections point to several things that have become clear during the discussion of Anthony Quayle's Falstaff: the idea of Hal as hero of the Henriad, the subordination of Falstaff to the prince, and Hal's awareness of the role he must play as king. While I do not share Charney's negative response, I think his irritation has proved a fairly accurate guide to what is happening on the screen, or at least that the violations of Charney's expectational text (which prompt his hostility) serve as indications of the performance text which is actually present.

However, I think his reaction to Hal's first soliloquy is, quite simply, wrong. Whatever the speech may be intended to do, it is highly unlikely that Hal's telling us he is not a villain is designed for the same purpose as the speeches of Richard III and Edmund, which tell us they *are* villains.[92] Besides, in this production the speech is nothing of the sort. Hal reads the speech as though he's just thinking it for the first time, finding himself as he defines his companions. As Samuel Crowl puts it, "Gwillim's Hal genuinely seems to discover himself . . . as he thinks his way through the notoriously dangerous 'I know you all' soliloquy. The lines seem immediate and fresh."[93]

If there is a danger for this Hal, it is not in being a villain but in becoming the unmitigated opposite. As Peter Saccio puts it (faintly echoing part of Charney's irritation): "Hal seemed to be thinking so often of Westminster that I wondered why he'd gone to East-cheap at all."[94]

The problem may be tracked to conflicting visions and versions of Hal's opening soliloquy. James L. Calderwood calls him "an interior playwright" who "will counterfeit unkingliness himself so that in a belated recognition scene his suddenly revealed royalty will shine forth the more goodly to his English audience."[95] The underlying question is, to what extent is Hal a developing character in his own drama? Is he a young man who changes and grows as we watch him or is he the most successful of Shakespeare's machiavels, a king sprung fully armed in deceit from his own forehead?

John Wilders suggests in his introduction to the BBC *2 Henry IV* that "perhaps what is offensive about Hal is his lack of spontaneity, his ability always to calculate exactly what he is doing and to carry out to the letter the plans he makes for himself."[96] But that is only one way of seeing Hal, and as Wilders makes clear in *The Lost Garden,* in a discussion of the conflicting images Shakespeare provides of his characters, "it is doubtful whether Hal himself knows wholly what he is doing."[97]

Samuel Crowl perceived Gwillim capturing Hal's "essence as mimic and mocker" with a series of "mischievous smiles" that "almost seem to twinkle as Hal dances his way along the narrow path weaving among playboy, pariah, and prince."[98]

T. F. Wharton, on the other hand, found the smile empty and the face "opaque." For him Hal had a "skin-deep attractiveness" but a weak identity and pallid impulses. At last, "his voice subtly changed and took on something of the stilted rhetorical air of his father's, again enhancing the sense that there was almost no such person, no such identity as 'Hal.'"[99]

Each critic is describing not what was on the screen but the vision of the play he brought with him, and the contradictions in their responses are at least partly the result of conflicting expectational texts. It is, of course, necessary to go back to the films to determine who is right. The process of checking the filmtexts is particularly important in the case of a character as complicated as Hal, who can be altered so greatly by the director's interpretation and actor's presentation.

As John Wilders told me in a personal interview, the role of Henry V depends greatly on the personality of the actor playing the part. David Gwillim has "a certain natural enthusiasm and charm and energy and youthfulness. . . . Those qualities are not necessarily in the script, but if you happen to have them, you make him a much more likeable character than he need be." This description of David Gwillim and Gwillim's Hal/Henry would suggest that Samuel Crowl is closer to the truth of the BBC performance. Indeed, the very idea of a Henriad, of a prince developing into a heroic king, would seem to include the idea of a sympathetic character in the central role. The subordination of Falstaff to Hal and the general darkening of the fat knight in these productions are other indications of the emerging central interpretation.

But simply to identify the BBC Hal as a sympathetic character who develops into a heroic king is not to eliminate his complexities. Certainly the Hal Shakespeare wrote is a performer. And equally certainly, the Hal David Gwillim acted (like both his fathers) is a performer. Hal performs, for instance, his one-person version of the domestic life of the Percys. Just before 2.4.107–8, "Give my roan horse a drench," Hal runs his sleeve roughly across his mouth and nose, assuming the identity of that tough, taciturn warrior, Hotspur, but making it clear in the process that he is playing the part of a man who is himself playing a role. He turns the same kind of mockery on Falstaff at 2.4.263–65, "What trick, what device, what starting hole canst thou now find out to hide thee from this open and apparent shame?"

He pulls faces here just as he has pulled faces during his impersonation of Hotspur and as he will shortly do during his humorous interrogation of Bardolph and Peto: "You are lions too, you ran away upon instinct, you will not touch the true prince; no—fie!" (2.4.300–302). Nevertheless, despite his chiding of hypocrisy, he can lie with a straight face or play the part of the good young prince as he does at 2.4.525, "I think it is good morrow, is it not?" when he has a smile as bright as the sun he compares himself to for the Sheriff. He is, then, an expert performer who uses his skills at least in part to mock the performances of others and also in part to deceive others.

It is, however, dangerous to deduce from this that Hal is merely a collection of roles, a hollow waiting to be filled with the luminosity of kingship. I have previously mentioned the sympathy he shows for Falstaff at 2.4.487, as he looks ahead to the inevitable rejection, and his silent and almost surly contemplation of a separation he does not seem to want. There is another point in this scene where we see Hal without any of his masks, although, paradoxically (or perhaps naturally), David Gwillim's Hal shows his deepest emotions with his face all but motionless. At 2.4.370–71, "Art thou not horribly afraid? Doth not thy blood thrill at it?"

Hal is turned downscreen from Falstaff, away from everyone, looking straight into the camera. His face becomes entirely immobile, a mask (or what might easily be perceived as a mask if we did not know the incredible mobility of his face in disguise) in which only the eyes change—and they brighten.[100] What is there is not fear, though it could be read that way. It is not a Hotspur-like eagerness for battle either, though it might be taken for that as well. Keeping in mind that it is all too easy to read too much into an expression, I would say it is Hal looking at the future with a double edge of anticipation and dread. Whatever may be precisely contained in that look, it is not the expression of an absence, of an unmoved mover passing over the shallows of his life.

There are other points in David Gwillim's performance where Hal the performer disappears and Hal the vulnerable boy who is finding his way is clearly visible. At 3.2.158–59, "And I will die a hundred thousand deaths / Ere break the smallest parcel of my vow," Hal is all solemn seriousness, answering the real emotion he has perceived in his father after the long and painful scene in which Henry IV has accused him of taking up Richard's role as wastrel and David Gwillim's Hal has, by means of facial expression and subtext, accused his father of stealing Richard's place as king. Hal's vow generates real warmth from the king, an unusual happening for Jon Finch's Henry IV. There is real feeling between them too after Hal's battlefield rescue of his father. There is also warmth for the dead foe and the dead friend when Hotspur and Falstaff lie side by side.

Because of Hal's distrust for and relatively harsh judgment of his father (made unusually plain and clearly explicated in this production), the prince's sympathy for the king has an especially strong element of basic human emotion about it, apart from judgment and reasoned actions. As Cedric Messina says about Hal, "In Part 2 he is feeling things that he thought were foreign to his nature up to that time: he has decided he will take on the responsibility of being heir to the throne, and his rejection of Falstaff is terrible to see."[101] Hal's problem is not just his responsibility to the kingdom, it is also the difficulty of finding that he has sympathy, grief, and love for a man he greatly distrusts and has partly abandoned. This is another connection between Henry IV and Falstaff.

It is perhaps this conflict as much as anything that accounts for Hal's weariness in *2 Henry IV*. In the BBC production the tension is apparent in the prince's relationship with Poins. Peter Saccio describes it as probing each other's masks: "Poins's edginess, his hinted bitterness . . . a fine cameo of the awkwardness entailed in

being Hal's semi-confidant."[102] Equally important here is the awkwardness of being Poins's semiconfidant, and, in fact, Poins becomes a representative for Hal's other frustrations, for his difficulties in reconciling his conflicting responsibilities and emotional
responses.

David Gwillim connects the two, feeling that Poins has had to
bear an unfair share of the burden: "I do think his dealing with
Poins is very cruel. His dealing with Falstaff, on the other hand,
destroys Falstaff but there's no intention to be cruel; there's just a
statement of truth: 'I can't associate with you.'" Though Gwillim
sees this as "awful and painful for everybody," he believes "it's
what has to happen." In the end, he says, "Certainly I don't see
Hal as a shining knight; I do see him as ruthless." And Henry
Fenwick adds, "But he seems to imply, is that so bad when it leads
to the creation of the character of Henry V? And is not that a
major part of Shakespeare's point?"[103]

Shakespeare's point or not, it is very much behind this BBC
Henriad. David Gwillim's Hal is not simply good or bad, sympathetic or callous, warm or cold; he is a human combination of
those qualities who can lie to the Sheriff to save Falstaff's life one
minute and coldly order Poins to pick the fat knight's pocket as a
joke the next. But these varied beads of humanness hang on the
string of youthful inexperience. He speaks his first soliloquy as a
discovery, a new idea about himself and the world, and far from
being the wholly made machiavel some critics take him for, he is a
boy whose boast of "I know you all" is more an expression of what
he doesn't know than what he does. The BBC has made the two
parts of Henry IV the story (on one level at least) of how Hal
grows up, how he prepares to be Henry V. He has the usual
youthful intolerance for the follies and crimes of his elders and
the posturings of his contemporaries. He also has a youthful taste
(which he shares with that other youth, Falstaff) for jokes and play
and general fun.

He fits into this BBC production with its scapegoats as the
young hero who will revitalize the sick land, acquiring in the battle
that signals the end of his childhood a scar of identity like the one
Odysseus carries. It is a wound, incidentally, that is very similar to
the one he himself inflicts on Hotspur at the same time. By the
end of 2 Henry IV he has accepted the larger responsibility of
kingship (and the quest involved in war with France).[104] In effect,
Hal's performance and quest does not end until the conclusion of
Henry V, and consequently this evaluation must be concluded in
the next chapter.

# 5
## The BBC *Henry V*

### The Central Interpretation

In addition to the usual factors that went into making the BBC Shakespeares in the first two seasons and under David Giles's direction, *Henry V* was shaped by the presence of the Chorus, the position of *Henry V* as the fourth of four plays, and the importance of Henry himself, a constant presence in any production[1] but here made even more central because this Henry is the main figure in an epic, a Henriad during which Hal grows up and becomes king.[2] In fact, the central interpretation that emerges from this film is Hal's transformation from boy to king. He could not have been played simply as Henry V without to some extent disavowing the BBC productions that had gone before.

As a result, the film focuses on Hal's earlier life and on his past and present emotions in a way that is essentially foreign to many productions of *Henry V*. It is, for instance, a radically different approach from Olivier's, where we first meet the actor-king as a fully formed personality and where, despite the interpolation of a Falstaff scene from *2 Henry IV*, it is hard to imagine Olivier's Henry V as a boyish Hal.

### The Chorus and Other Factors Shaping the Film

*Henry V* is easily the most stylized and theatrical of the films in the second tetralogy. In David Giles's words, "If you do a realistic *Henry V* then you must cut the Chorus, and if you cut the Chorus you don't do *Henry V*."[3] The stylization was also necessary from Cedric Messina's more pragmatic point of view: "We couldn't reproduce all those castles! And thank god [*sic*] the battle of Agincourt isn't actually in the play."[4]

However, the major impact of the stylization was on scene design. Don Homfray (scene designer for all three Henry plays) describes his work on the film as two-dimensional and theatrical, prompted by the Chorus's repeated apologies for his medium. He talks about "lights coming up and people walking into scenes, lights going down and the scene is changed. We're using turning towers, rather as you might in the theatre . . . starting the scene with a master shot like an auditorium from the audience."[5] The most extreme example of such theatrical scene design comes at 2.4, where the French sit in a sort of parliamentary chamber, which is draped in a bright blue fabric decorated with fleurs-de-lys.

In one sense the concentration on the theatrical has resulted in a separation between this production and the other plays in the tetralogy. Unlike the two parts of *Henry IV,* which began with flashbacks to preceding plays, *Henry V* starts with the Chorus against a black screen. At line 18 of the prologue, "On your imaginary forces work," the floor of what appears to be a stage becomes visible. This expands until we can see two figures in addition to the Chorus, and finally, the Chorus moves between two trains of actors, divided like the two kingdoms. After this, we return to the black screen.

The Chorus works as an alienation device. At 1.2.305, "Be soon collected, and all things thought upon," Henry V begins throwing tennis balls to his courtiers. As the scene ends, the Chorus, standing before a stone wall, catches a tennis ball and starts his second speech. As he finishes line 40 of this second prologue, "We'll not offend one stomach with our play," he finds himself facing Bardolph's ruddy face. The Chorus appears startled by this, and then, as though Bardolph's presence has been his inspiration, he gives his last two lines, a nice visual explanation for what does, in fact, sound like an afterthought. For the beginning of the third act, the Chorus, who has been sitting among the French courtiers, stands up, throws off a blue cloak (which in this production marks him as French)[6] and begins to speak. A close-up gives him a black background.

This sort of alienation does not extend to the other characters except during the first prologue, with the entire cast "onstage," and at 1.1.95, "Then go we in to know his embassy," when the king suddenly becomes visible on his throne but seems to have been sitting there throughout, head down, awaiting his cue to speak and move.

The impact of the alienation effect on the overall production is minimal except as it reinforced the interpretation that was already uppermost. From Don Homfray's point of view, "*Henry V* is . . .

nothing to do with social history, nothing to do with the state of England, it's to do with idealism and heroism."[7] In this production that meant even more weight upon Hal and his transformation into Henry V.

The less naturalistic sets (or at least the director's impression that they were less naturalistic—many of them were similar to what had been used in the earlier plays) may have produced a feeling of greater freedom in relation to camera movement, a greater willingness to indicate the director's presence. In any event, there are fewer difficulties with characters out of frame in this production than in any of the others,[8] and one scene (2.2) demonstrates a kind of precision that is a surprising achievement on a six-day shooting schedule.

Another of Giles's achievements is a visual strategy of emphasizing profile shots as indicators of high tension and even as pointers to meaning. For instance at 1.1.76, "Upon our spiritual Convocation," Canterbury and Ely face each other in profile, their birdlike secrecy heard as well as seen in whispers between the nearly touching beaks of their noses. At 1.2.221, "Call in the messengers sent from the Dauphin," we have Henry's questing profile as he makes up his mind to action. There is a return to this decisive profile shot at 1.2.296, "When thousands weep more than did laugh at it," a kind of visual echo for the violence of Gwillim's delivery. There are also multiple uses of profile shots in 2.2. The production, which has used double profiles to such good effect, ends with one last example—Henry and Katherine kneeling before an archbishop while bells chime—an image that Paul Cubeta says "freezes the marriage in figurines of unusual beauty, as though for eternity while the Chorus tells us of what 'small time' is left this star of England."[9] And the profile shot, which has in the BBC *Henry V* been associated with politics and an archbishop in 1.1, with the decision to make war in 1.2, and with treason and betrayal in 2.2, visually reinforces the message from the Chorus, despite (or perhaps precisely because of) the beauty of the image.

By and large the preparation of the script appears to have been a matter of careful thinking and painstaking cutting, a matter of taking out lines here and there and, most often, of shortening the rhetoric of speeches (such as Canterbury's exposition of the Salic law). Perhaps the most noticeable omission is the truncation of Henry's threatening speech before Harfleur, so that most of the horrific details disappear. This is the result, no doubt, of the popular critical assumption that Henry's Harfleur speech is an example of the unpleasant, violent part of his nature (or at least of the unpleasant, violent war he is willfully waging). As Cedric Messina puts it, "The speech he makes threatening the people of Harfleur is absolutely awful!"[10] From this point of view the cuts in the speech essentially defuse it as an explosive obstacle in Henry's path on the way to successful kingship. However, given the success of the scene with the traitors, another emotionally charged episode in Hal's development, the shortening of Henry's threats before Harfleur may have been a mistake. Note, for instance, Branagh's success with the speech in his 1989 film.

Two negative pressures on the BBC *Henry V* may perhaps have had some effect here. The first is the impact of the Olivier film itself. David Giles admits to being haunted by it, "All you can do is push those images back and try to see the play fresh."[11] The result is, no doubt, a conscious and subconscious attempt not to do what Olivier did, a situation that undoubtedly cancels some possible options and inhibits the exploration of others.

Another negative pressure is the unquestioning assimilation of certain standard critical approaches, such as the opinion that the Harfleur speech (in which Shakespeare very likely contradicted his sources to make Henry appear more merciful and, incidentally, got the history right) shows Henry in a bad light. An example of this process is the refusal to believe that the Chorus is telling the truth. David Giles argues that

> The Chorus is a wonderful mine of misinformation! He says something like "The French are in a terrible state," and then we go to them and they're not in a terrible state at all—they can't wait to get into battle. He says Henry goes around the camp and fills everybody with hope and joy, and then we see what happens is that he has a terrible argument with Williams.[12]

There is certainly a case to be made on the other side of this argument, and if the play had been looked at in an entirely fresh way, the production might have changed as a result. The Chorus tends to paint things with bold strokes, and "The French . . . shake in their fear" (2.prologue.12–14), even though he may mean no more than that the French are cowards for trying to use the mechanism of assassination, is not an example of Anglo-Saxon understatement. Nevertheless, the French have bribed Scroop, Cambridge, and Grey to assassinate Henry, just as the Chorus says. The French king's description, "This is a stem / Of that victorious stock; and let us fear / The native mightiness and fate of him" (2.4.62–64), chimes nicely with what the Chorus tells us. If the French are eager to fight, they do not quickly show it. The Dauphin fails to come to Harfleur, and the army that the French finally browbeat themselves into meeting (and which they outnumber five to one) is a poor, ragged force, much reduced by fighting, travel, and disease.

The Chorus's description of Henry, "With cheerful semblance and sweet majesty" (4.prologue.40), cheering up the troops, is a little harder to square with the night wanderings we actually witness. However, in his proper, kingly person, Henry is both cheerful and cheering, with a kind word for everyone and the Crispin's day speech when it is needed. What he actually says is "I and my bosom must debate awhile, / And then I would no other company" (4.1.31–32). Unfortunately for his purpose, he is accosted by Pistol (Olivier makes the sense of intrusion and unwanted company very clear in his film version), interrupted by the cross-talk act of Fluellen and Gower, and challenged (in more ways than one) by Williams. This does not necessarily contradict the version of events we get from the Chorus (we see quite a bit of King Henry encouraging the troops); rather, it indicates that the Chorus does not know (or has not told us) about Henry's adventures in disguise.[13]

## Other Films in the BBC Henriad and *Henry V*

For Messina, Giles, and many members of the cast, one of the most important influences on the shape of their *Henry V* was the fact that it was the fourth play in a series of four. Henry Fenwick talks about Brenda Bruce, who had played Mrs. Quickly for the RSC but found the BBC role new "mainly because of the extra dimension given by playing the part through all three plays."[14]

As Cedric Messina puts it in discussing Hal, "One of the marvellous things is to see the growth of the character and the actor."[15] David Giles has similar views: "You need to see all three plays . . . because if you do you cannot possibly take Henry at his face value in *Henry V*."[16]

There are, indeed, a number of connections to and explications of *Henry V* in the earlier productions. The kiss Pistol rather surprisingly gives Mistress Quickly in *2 Henry IV* and which (unexpectedly) she seems to enjoy provides some preparation for the marriage of the two in *Henry V*. The look of accusation that Hal directs at his father in *1 Henry IV* 3.2.54 reinforces the sincerity of his protestations in *Henry V* at 4.1.297–99, "Not today, O Lord,

O, not today, think not upon the fault / My father made in compassing the crown!" For this Henry V that fault has long been felt, the subtext in the earlier plays suggesting that Hal cared for Richard II as well as for Henry IV; and when he reports that "I Richard's body have interred new" (4.1.300), we may take it as a gesture of private affection and restitution (which, historically it was) as well as public policy. The ironies of the first three productions continue interestingly into this one. Richard the tyrant has in a sense not only made Bolingbroke a scapegoat for both their sins but left Bolingbroke's son to apologize to God for them.

Another example of looking into the dark backward and abysm of the two parts of *Henry IV* comes at 4.1.168–70, "some, making the wars their bulwark, that have before gored the gentle bosom of peace with pillage and robbery." This is a thoughtful passage for Henry V, in any event. In fact, David Gwillim pauses for thought between Williams's argument and his own answer. But there is a special sense of reminiscence in the way he speaks the words that makes them apply quite obviously to Bardolph, Nym, and, behind them, to the shadow of Falstaff. As David Gwillim says about another passage that conjures up the same memories, "when you're told of Bardolph's death, doing the three plays together makes it mean a lot more . . . it makes it more obvious that Henry's task is more daunting than it seems."[17]

Messina points out the value of this moment in Gwillim's performance and television's ability to emphasize it, "you can see his early years going before his eyes. In the theatre that scene goes for very little, but in this production there is a great big close-up."[18]

## Hal into Henry as Central Interpretation

Concentrating in this production on *Henry V* as the conclusion of the Henriad, the transformation of Prince Hal into King Henry,[19] also places an emphasis on the new king as a private person. He is the Hal we know and remember from the earlier plays, with his old emotions brought to a new situation; hence the importance of Bardolph's death and the deaths of the traitors, which Messina comments on: "For a young man the painfulness . . . of finding out that somebody who is a bosom friend is as traitorous as a snake is overwhelming."[20]

Perhaps for this reason *Henry V* 2.2 is as well and imaginatively filmed as any scene in the tetralogy. It begins with the Duke of Bedford coming downscreen, chuckling uneasily with a nervous falseness very different from the superior and sarcastic chuckles we remember from him as Prince John at the end of *2 Henry IV*. When he arrives downscreen, he makes part of a three shot reminiscent of the traitors in *1 Henry IV* who put his father on the throne. Henry V and the new group of traitors (who really represent a revival of the old rebellion against Henry IV) are visible for most of the time upscreen.

In this production, the very name of Scroop must stir memories that might well be absent from a *Henry V* which stands alone, just as Henry's smiling manipulation of the traitors must remind us of Hal's games in the tavern with Falstaff. It is part of the strength of this scene and of David Gwillim's performance that we do not see an implacable king deftly catching traitors but, instead, a boy becoming a king, who is bewildered on his way by treachery and betrayal.

The scene picks up emotional and visual intensity as Cambridge, Scroop, and Grey kneel to receive their "commissions." The king appears to leave at 2.2.70–71, "My Lord of Westmoreland, and uncle Exeter, / We will aboard tonight," but actually stands behind them where he is clearly visible to the audience. The three rise to read the documents the king has given them, then turn around in consternation to find themselves facing Henry just before 2.2.71, "Why, how now, gentlemen?" The shot of Henry is made neatly over the shoulders of the traitors, a device that will be repeated and enlarged on shortly. At 2.2.73, "Look ye, how they change!" there is a cut to the three in profile, relating to the profile shots that run through the production.

At 2.2.76–77, "I do confess my fault, / And do submit me to your Highness' mercy," the three traitors are back on their knees, a repeated visual effect with very different significance. That this is not for Henry merely an exercise in successful political manipulation is obvious as soon as the crime of treason is named, but the actual intensity of his reaction does not emerge until 2.2.93–94, "But O, / What shall I say to you, Lord Scroop," where his voice is almost tearful. At this point, Scroop is in profile, while Henry is standing, looking down. At 2.2.96, "Thou that didst bear the key of all my counsels," Henry stands behind Scroop, who is still kneeling. Neither can see the other, but both are full face to the camera.

At 2.2.98, "That (almost) mightst have coined me into gold," Henry turns profile so that briefly the two of them seem to make a Janus figure, visually signaling both the treason and intimacy that are the subjects of this scene and making another of the effective images with profiles that distinguish the production. The precision achieved in this scene is indicated by the fact that Henry turns profile on the word "almost."

There are rather substantial cuts in the lines that deal with fiends and demons, but at 2.2.127, "Show men dutiful?" Henry, in a quick motion, arrives on his knees behind and below Scroop. Now, he is looking up at Scroop while both remain full face to the audience. This form of humility seems at once to demonstrate and enhance Henry's pain and, if anything, to make Scroop's guilt seem the greater before a king who can genuinely feel affection and betrayal. This move of abasement seems to be passion, not an actor's calculation of position. Henry does not get up until 2.2.142, "Another fall of man," and then he begins to rise (as one would expect in this carefully crafted scene) on the word "fall."

Once Henry is on his feet, the Janus figure is recreated, and at 2.2.144, "And God acquit them of their practices!" we have the three profiles again. Then beginning with Grey's words at 2.2.165, "My fault, but not my body, pardon, Sovereign," we have an over-the-shoulder shot of Henry, where the camera moves past each traitor's back and the helmet of a man at arms before coming around for a close-up of Henry. The delicacy of the timing can be judged from the fact that the close-up arrives on 2.2.174, "Touching our person, seek we no revenge." We have the three profiles again at 2.2.176, "Whose ruin you have sought, that to her laws," and this painful scene for the young king ends in subdued, almost tearful tones, not the ringing boisterousness Olivier employs as his Henry sets out for France. There is, however, a bit of extratextual support for this Henry V, an indication of affection from his loyal subjects, in two shouts of "God save the King!"[21]

David Gwillim manages to suggest that Henry V needs such reassurance. He has, in addition to his boyish voice and face, a nervous habit of nodding his head, like a lecturer who hopes by that means to convince his class to agree with him or at least to pretend his jokes are funny. In 3.1, we get a very different brand of heroism from the usual "Once more unto the breach" speech.

At 3.1.8, "Disguise fair nature with hard-favored rage," Henry has both arms outspread, and his voice cracks on the word "disguise," an effect that signals both his youth and his uncertainty. Olivier's comment on what should be happening during this line (and the one before it) is "Stay in control but begin to feel the excitement. Then change the intonation."[22] Clearly the interpretations are dissimilar.

At "That hath not noble luster in your eyes" (3.1.30), David

Gwillim's Henry is panting with the exertion of running up and
down the set and leaping about, waving his arms. Olivier's comment for this line and the one following is, "Moving up the ladder,
pace, excitement, almost flying,"[23] advice Gwillim's Henry is in no
condition to take. His performance here is considerably less self-
possessed than the one he gave at the Battle of Shrewsbury. That
very cool hero seems to have become a relatively nervous com-
mander. In a sense, we are seeing an insecure Hal we never met
(but may have suspected) in the tavern scenes.

That this production has its own context and terms of reference, its own center and central interpretation, can be demonstrated by looking at an unsuccessful commentary and examining
the reasons for its failure. Martin Banham ascribed Gwillim's
unease during the "Once more unto the breach" speech to quite
different causes from the ones I have been exploring, maintaining
that Henry "was diminished in scale and impact" and further
weakened because "he didn't have anyone to talk *to*. A few actors
on a small set on a small screen do not a Harry make!"[24] He
amplifies this later, saying, "And back at the breach itself, no one
looked more lonely and embarrassed than poor King Henry urg-
ing on invisible troops to an indistinct objective via an improbable
scaffold."[25]

In addition to an overhasty reading of the filmtext, Banham has
the problem of setting out to prove that television Shakespeare
requires live audiences and should be filmed on reconstructed
versions of Shakespeare's stages.[26] He is also working with an
expectational text based firmly on Olivier-like stage performances
and on the Olivier film itself. He says that our memories of the
film "(in contrast to the compressed scale of the television production) include the thrill of the splendidly recreated Globe Theatre
. . . and the essentially filmic . . . battle scenes."[27] I have no argument with his estimate of the Olivier film, but it seems to me there
is a very real danger here (as usual with a firmly fixed expectational text) of failing to examine the new production on its own
merits.

While it is true that both the producer and the director were
very much aware of the limitations their budget imposed on them
in terms of spectacular effects for the battles, it is hard to explain
the uneasiness of this Henry V as Gwillim's own despair in the face
of an inadequate army and insignificant sets. It is still harder (with
the Olivier film itself as evidence) to credit the assertion that a
heroic Henry V requires a stage audience to activate his heroism.

If there is an influence on Gwillim in this scene external to the flow of the play and the production, it is likely to be the desire to avoid imitating Olivier (which may well be one of the sources of Banham's annoyance). Henry Fenwick says that Gwillim "faces the daunting task of following Olivier . . . bravely and shrewdly: 'It isn't a question of finding amazing new interpretations,' he says. 'But audiences change.'"[28]

More important, though, is what the production itself and Hal/ Henry's own carefully nurtured characterization require. To play the scene with heroic confidence would suggest that this inexperienced Henry V, having been emotionally harrowed by the treason of near friends, had somehow in his brief sea journey not only recovered from betrayal but also arrived without experiment or uncertainty at a perfectly polished style of military rhetoric.

David Gwillim's performance has suggested from *1 Henry IV* on that while Hal is a very good actor, he is also a very youthful one whose roles tend to be explorations, a means of acquiring an identity as well as a way of passing the time amusingly. Hence the seriousness with which Hal ends the play scene in the tavern: he has put on the role of king and looked ahead at the consequences. He may begin *Henry V* 2.2 with the kind of smile he had ready to deceive the Sheriff or entrap Falstaff, but the end of the scene is not boy's play, and we see the kind of emotional intensity and personal commitment that the Battle of Shrewsbury and his father's illness and death had earlier drawn from him.

This explains a Hal/Henry whose voice cracks and who has run and shouted himself out of breath. Undoubtedly in the process he looks uneasy and awkward. He is meant to. To suggest that David Gwillim could not keep his voice from cracking or restrain himself from panting or that if those things had happened accidentally and against the intentions of actor and director, the scene would not have been reshot is to argue that the production was out of control. When, instead, Gwillim's actions as Henry fit the characterization he has been building through three plays and that both Cedric Messina and David Giles have endorsed in print, it seems fair (and logical as well) to examine the production on its own merits and in its own terms rather than as it does or does not conform to the particular theory the critic happens to be advancing.

Henry's confidence increases as the play goes on. This is clearly visible because David Gwillim's Henry handles most of his challenges more calmly and with better control than he did his "Once more unto the breach" exhortation. The measure of Henry's growth is that he is facing larger challenges. But he is still Hal/ Henry, still in some ways adapting boy's play to his role as king.

Three episodes on the night before the Battle of Agincourt demonstrate the stage Hal has reached on his journey toward the completed Henry V. At 4.1.84–85, "Though it appear a little out of fashion, / There is much care and valor in this Welshman," Henry laughs with real delight. And admittedly, the BBC has given him something visible as well as audible to laugh about. Fluellen is wearing a helmet covered with greenery as camouflage. He enters, crawling, with a blanket draped over himself and exits, also crawling, with Gower creeping along beside him while the two of them share the blanket, more like Trinculo and Caliban than anything military. That Henry is able to find a value other than a good joke in that spectacle is perhaps a measure of his increased sympathy for those around him.

Nevertheless, that he has not become a sort of soldier-saint or even an English version of Machiavelli's perfect prince is abundantly clear from his handling of the confrontation with Williams. As I pointed out earlier, he has a long pause to think just before 4.1.150, "So, if a son that is by his father sent about," and a look of remembering old acquaintances when he talks of highway robbers who have turned soldier. But he loses control when Williams directly (though unknowingly) challenges his honesty. At 4.1.224– 25, "Well, I will do it, though I take thee in the King's company," the king rises angrily and is held back from a physical confrontation (as is Williams) by those around him. This is no twisting of meanings for the sake of a future joke but real (if temporary) anger, as a result of which he acts without thinking. It is no doubt the result of cumulative stress, of the looming battle, of Williams's moral questions, and of the memory of old, lost friends who were entitled to call him coward with impunity. In any event, it becomes a brief release for Hal, who is finding the job of Henry V (even in disguise) rather hard going. He can, in his disguise, allow himself to be angry, a luxury the king cannot often afford.

It also serves another function in this production. Henry's easy anger seems more like Hotspur than Hal. It is perhaps a suggestion of the similarities between them, just as the scar on Henry's cheek is a reminder of the man who gave him the wound and (also in these BBC productions) of the similar wound Hal inflicted on Hotspur. David Giles evidently sees the two as nearly equal. He says in commenting on understanding Henry the man in *Henry V,* "All through Part 2 Hal has much less to do with Falstaff and is obviously coming to the end of his companions because nobody measures up to Hotspur—whom he killed in Part I—at all."[29] It is an interesting kind of preparation for the Crispin's day speech, which is a more rational, better controlled version of Hotspur's lines "I rather of his absence make this use: / It lends a luster and more great opinion, / A larger dare to our great enterprise" (*1H4* 4.1.75–77).

The authority of David Gwillim's Crispin speech and the conviction it conveys to David Buck's Earl of Westmoreland, who has been standing shaggily and stolidly by since the first scene of *1 Henry IV*, suggest that Henry is now in complete accord with his men and almost complete command of himself. There are residual uncertainties, demonstrated by the head-nodding mannerism, among other things. There is exasperation with Montjoy at 4.3.92, "Good God, why should they mock poor fellows thus?"; simple determination at 4.6.36–38, "The French have reinforced their men. / Then every soldier kill his prisoners! / Give the word through"; and the announced emotion at 4.7.57–58, "I was not angry since I came to France / Until this instant." But all are within the bounds of kingly control; there is no panting for breath, and Henry's voice holds firm. Only his announcement of the unexpected, divinely assisted result has an air of astonishment about it: "Where ne'er from France arrived more happy men" (4.8.128). The line is delivered, as might be expected in this production, with Henry in profile. His decision has proved a success and a reassurance.

The last act of *Henry V* has troubled both critics and producers. Arthur Rank, for example, thought that Olivier "should have cut the 'unimportant' scenes like Henry's wooing of Katherine,"[30] and many critics see it as one last hypocrisy from that princely hypocrite, to pretend to woo what his negotiators are inevitably winning for him even as he speaks.

There is, however, another way of approaching the scene. Leonard Tennenhouse points to Shakespeare's use of the "iconography from the comedies" to demonstrate that Henry truly possesses France: "Only with such dramatic language . . . could he . . . transform the violent contests of chronicle history into a tableau of stasis and hierarchy."[31]

The iconography of the comedies functions especially well in this BBC *Henry V* because David Gwillim's Henry has been from the beginning an embodiment of youth. The emotion he demonstrates when he is betrayed and the uncertainty that never completely leaves him suggest that Henry's wooing of Katherine is real. Certainly David Gwillim's reading of 5.2.288–89, "You have witchcraft in your lips, Kate," suggests a young lover and not a playacting conqueror. Further, the very uncertainties of Gwillim's Henry in other circumstances tend to support the awkwardness he claims as a lover. Clearly with the casting of Jocelyne Boisseau as a fairy-tale Katherine, the visual distancing of the earlier garden scene, Hal/Henry's own youthful struggles to grow up through this and the two earlier BBC productions, and the overall emphasis on what scene designer Don Homfray calls "idealism and heroism,"[32] this Henry V may be seen as honest in his wooing. After all, the princess in the fairy tale is supposed to fall in love with the royal stranger (even in cases like those of Nausicaa and Dido, where the motif has moved far from its starting place), not merely marry him as an act of political policy.

The end result of this developing of Henry V, through what David Gwillim calls the "chrysalis" of Hal,[33] is a king who is complex because he has a history made from those earlier history plays but who is in some ways simple as well and for the same reason. If we see in Henry's eyes that he remembers and mourns for Bardolph and Falstaff, if the director has given us visual evidence that Hal is bound to Hotspur, we are forced to see layers in the man that we otherwise might miss. As David Gwillim says, "If you watch only *Henry V* he may seem just the archetypal hero, whereas if you've seen the situation in *Henry IV Parts 1 and 2* you know it isn't like that at all."[34] On the other hand, there are simplifications. If we know that Hal felt sympathy for Richard's fate and condemned his father's action, we also know that his prayer the night before Agincourt is sincere, and the ambiguity many critics find in that moment disappears for this production. Finally, the BBC's Hal/Henry emerges as a consistent character through the course of the three plays, and in a real sense he is the center of the central interpretation that David Giles and company have created.

# 6

## Laurence Olivier's *Henry V*

### The Film and Audience Expectations

In some ways the central interpretation of Olivier's *Henry V* is easier to find than the central interpretations of the BBC films examined in earlier chapters. Olivier is an auteur[1] who says, "Filippo Del Giudice . . . left me with complete artistic control, including every bit of casting."[2] He unselfconsciously notes that he played his "roles of director, producer, leading actor, script and film editor with gusto and sincerity."[3] Though he describes himself here as script editor, he was, in fact, cowriter (with Alan Dent) of the filmscript. As Harry M. Geduld puts it in his *Filmguide to "Henry V,"* "In most respects, it was Olivier's inspiration rather than team work that was to determine the quality of the film."[4]

In the circumstances, it is not necessary to search for a shared interpretation emerging from the cooperation of director and leading actor within a framework imposed by a producer, as it was with the BBC productions. There have, however, been other difficulties that have previously prevented accurate readings of the filmtext. Chief among these difficulties are the impressionistic criticisms of the film, the failure of critics to examine the film and its shooting scripts in detail, and finally, the misleading expectations critics brought to their viewings of both the play and the film—three problems that, of course, overlap. A detailed analysis of the film and its scripts would correct false impressions, while a more accurate (or at least less rigid) expectational text would have a similar result.

There have always been critics who disliked *Henry V* and its title character. William Hazlitt, for instance, saw Gadshill and Agincourt as two examples of the same disease: "Falstaff was a puny prompter of violence and outrage, compared with the pious and politic Archbishop."[5]

Some modern critics have been uncomfortable with such a hero or with the concept of heroism itself and have searched Shake-speare's subtext for more palatable messages. Unfortunately, re-evaluations of the play that find an ironic text under the surface have also tended to see Olivier's film as failing to realize more than one part of the play. Ralph Berry's summary is typical of this attitude. Though he admits that everything in the film is "stated or implied in the text," he maintains that "the secret play" has "been cut out with surgical intelligence and precision. And it is the 'other' play that has exercised its fascination over a later genera-tion."[6]

This is, I think, at best an underinterpretation and at worst a misinterpretation of both the film and the play. It goes back (among other places) to the essentially simple choice Norman Rabkin offered in *Shakespeare and the Problem of Meaning*.[7] His argument, which purports to open up a new possibility, actually locks *Henry V* into a closed system, allowing the play to be about a good king and a just war or a political machiavel and an unjust adventure or (his famous rabbit-duck conclusion) both together.[8] The play is thus forcibly tied to whether or not the prevailing sentiment in its audiences is for or against war, and in Ralph Berry's words, "What happens to that text in future will no doubt be determined less by directors than by history."[9]

The belief that the film and the play behind it are essentially about war is bolstered by the fact that Olivier made his film during wartime as a propaganda vehicle. However, an examination of Olivier's work on other films that were also regarded as serving a propagandistic purpose contradicts this naive assumption. Olivier's artistic preoccupations before and during the filming of *Henry V*, his own comments, and changes between drafts of the film's scripts and the film itself offer additional evidence for a more accurate assessment of the film's central interpretation.

To begin with, it is worth noting that an extremely wide range of materials was deemed helpful to the British war effort. Lord Lothian, the British ambassador in Washington, told British actors in the States, "You are here in America on legitimate business. Yet what would Germany give to have such a corner as you actors have in the making of American pictures for the world market?"[10]

In Hollywood, Alfred Hitchcock was directing Olivier in *Re-becca*, in "what was to all intents and purposes a British picture. To complete it to the best of his ability was the only thing he [Hitch-cock] could do, and also the most telling."[11] Hitchcock was cer-tainly not the only actor or director to make such a decision. Alexander Korda came to Hollywood in 1940 with Churchill's support and possibly at his request to make "films which would project British values and the British way of life for American audiences."[12]

Olivier confirms this government connection in his autobiography, saying that his telephoned offer of help to Duff Cooper, then minister of information, produced a telegram that read, "Think better where you are Korda going there."[13] The value of such projects was publicly recognized when the director "was put on the Black List by the Nazis and on the Honours List (for a knighthood) by Britain in 1942."[14]

While *Henry V* is more directly applicable to the events of the time than *Rebecca* or *Pride and Prejudice,* it does not, like Michael Curtiz's *Casablanca,* present Nazis as villains nor does it offer obvious stand-ins for the Nazis as the same director's *The Sea Hawk* does.[15] As Ralph Berry notes, "the propagandist elements are muted: there is, at bottom, no enemy."[16] Harry M. Geduld suggests that many critics who disliked the film's "partially propagandist purpose" would not have noticed it "if the film had been made at any other time."[17] Raymond Durgnat, diligently looking for parallels, finds Olivier obscure, "whether France here = France our ally, to whom Churchill had . . . proposed 'marriage,' or Germany our enemy whom we mustn't hate for ever, is quite ambiguous."[18]

Olivier's own comments and the changes between the shooting scripts and the film indicate that he did not see *Henry V* as dealing primarily with war and violence. Olivier says that he "showed no bloody gashes. The bright medieval costumes tended, too, to emphasize the formal elements and patterns of the battle." In fact, he says that to match "the film's overall style the battle should have been fought on green velvet—and that, clearly, was impracticable."[19] There is abundant evidence to support Olivier's statements, though that evidence has hitherto remained unexamined.

As I noted in the introduction, there are two extant shooting scripts for Olivier's *Henry V;* the later version is titled "HENRY THE FIFTH" and labeled directly under that, "Shooting Script." The earlier script is titled *"William Shakespeare's 'Henry V.',* Revised Treatment for Technicolor Film by Alan Dent & Laurence Olivier." No doubt one reason these scripts have previously remained unexamined was the former difficulty of making detailed comparisons between a filmtext and its sources, a problem that the technology of the videocassette has solved.[20] Perhaps another reason is that British film studios usually do not keep shooting scripts,[21] and many critics may simply have assumed that no shooting scripts survived. There is also a published release script,[22] which has, of course, been studied before, though the release script has sometimes been used by critics not as an additional text to be compared with the filmtext but as a substitute for the film itself.

A clear pattern of development and change emerges between the two unpublished scripts and also between the later or shooting script and the film. The earlier script is, as might be expected, much the briefer of the two, and its material is usually expanded as more detailed descriptions and precise ideas are substituted for the earlier material. For example, scene 23 of the earlier script, the beach at Harfleur, says,

> Amid the confusion of parties still landing, boats and stores still being beached . . . an engagement is already in progress. . . . Henry has led one or two unsuccessful attempts to gain a small cleft in the rocks. He returns to rally small groups of men.[23]

In the later version of the script, this becomes scene 64 and begins with the camera tracking over a wave and then onto a cannon being hauled up the beach. A flight of arrows strikes the face of a cliff on camera left; a group of four or five English archers run in camera right and move down into a gap, some of them firing arrows back camera right as they run left. Before they get offscreen, a second flight of arrows comes down, "and one or two of them fall and are dragged off by their comrades." Additional English archers run to the gap from screen right; though one or two shoot arrows, most simply "scatter." Henry makes his entrance "on horseback. He jumps through the gap, turns, looks back then moves quickly out of picture right followed instantly by a shower of arrows."[24]

By the time this scene reached the screen, almost all of the direct violence had been removed. There were still English soldiers retreating, some of them did pause to fire arrows, and one of them even fell on the sand, but there were no arrows being fired at them, no one was obviously injured, and the man who fell might simply have slipped or been exhausted by the strenuous exercise. In the words of the release script, "CAMERA TRACKS FORWARD as English Infantry appear round the cliff breach in retreat. Henry rides round on horseback."[25]

As he gave his material its final shape for the film, Olivier consistently reduced the violence; indeed, he almost eliminated it in many cases. The best examples of this process come, as might be expected, in the Agincourt battle sequence.[26] There were a number of instances of explicit or strongly suggested violence in the shooting script that were dropped entirely from the finished film: "The blackout is shattered by a gun-flash and explosion" ("SS," 111); "Tracking & Panning from the cannon muzzle to disclose gunners falling about deafened by the noise" (111); "Inside the tent the priest is still kneeling at Mass when a sword is seen to cut through the tent from the outside from right to left. A horse, upon whose back ORLEANS may be seen, plunges through the gap, upsets the altar, and the priest and others . . . fall away" (114); "as the horse passes the page we see Bourbon bring down his sword and strike him" (114); "two frightened boys come into the picture. . . . Bourbon is seen to . . . charge into camera towards the boys. As he rears his horse to plunge down on the boys they disappear. . . . Two boys facing camera right looking absolutely terrified as false hooves come down on them" (115); "The priest is lying dead in the tent and through the opening we see the horsemen galloping away" (115).

There were also cases where Olivier kept a particular shot and the concept behind it but filmed it in a less violent fashion than the one described in the shooting script. For instance, in the encounter between Henry and the Constable, "Henry's head and crown on right of screen, sword on left of screen comes down and slices away part of Henry's crown and denting helmet" (119). The release script describes this accurately as, "The sword crashing on Henry's helmet."[27] There is no actual damage shown. Another example from the same duel reads, "Henry's sword cutting Constable's wrist and Constable being forced to release sword from his hand" (119–20). To use the release script's words once again, "Henry's sword knocking the Constable's sword out of his hand."[28] The blow is struck directly on the sword hilt, so that once the Constable's sword falls away, there is a flicker of time when it seems as though the flat of Olivier's sword is striking the Constable's open hand.

If there is no clear sense of an enemy in the film, if there is no exact parallel with Germany, if war and its attendant violence are subordinated to other concerns, it is because Olivier has deliberately made it so. As he writes in *Confessions of an Actor*, "All active fighting was done by suggestion, apart from the final blow delivered by me, backhanded with mailed fist to the visored jaw of the Constable, which marked the end of the battle."[29] There are, of course, swords striking other swords, and several Englishmen drop from trees onto or near French knights,[30] but if these things are not counted as "active fighting," Olivier's statement may be taken as accurate. Not one arrow in the famous flight is shown striking anything (though some horses rear with arrows already sticking out of them), not one man is shown being killed onscreen, and the only blood the audience sees is in the mouth of the dead boy, who has been killed (offscreen) along with the luggage.

Olivier has also been careful to downplay the violence even in nonbattle scenes. For instance, the earlier script has "Enter Fluellen and Gower. The extent of the after-battle looting is obvious. They are both tricked out in pieces of finery that we recognize as having belonged to Bourbon and Orleans." During Fluellen's encounter with Pistol (who is wearing the Constable's breastplate and carrying the Dauphin's gold helmet), Pistol suffers a bloody nose ("RTTF," 55). The shooting script adds to this, "Fluellen . . . gives Pistol a terrible bang over the head with the [sword] hilt. . . . He . . . clutches his forehead down which a little blood is seen to trickle." (131). In the film, however, only Pistol is wearing looted armor, and though he still receives a blow to the head and another to the face, neither one causes him to bleed.

Cutting the report of Bardolph's execution (threatened or already carried out) may be another example of the same process. Olivier has been criticized both for the number of lines he cut from the play and for the particular elements he chose to remove. Bardolph's execution is one of those elements Olivier is supposed to have removed in order to keep Henry's heroic luster gleaming as brightly as possible. However, the complete incident of Pistol's appeal to Fluellen and Fluellen's report to Henry is to be found in the earlier script ("RTTF," 29–31), and it appears again in the shooting script (63–66) with the addition of various camera directions, including one that indicates Olivier's emphasis for the scene: "Camera pans him [Henry] round to include Gower, Jamy and MacMorris in the right of the picture. He makes his speech to these four—so that they form a little semi-circle round Henry who has his back to the camera" (66). Henry's speech is, of course, his statement of the policy that "when lenity and cruelty play for a kingdom, the gentler gamester is the soonest winner." In light of Olivier's other changes and given the fact that this scene was retained through both scripts, it might well be argued that Olivier eliminated it as a part of his policy of subordinating war to other issues in the play and not as a means of keeping Henry's reputation spotless.

Olivier's own statements about his intentions in the battle scene provide evidence that his changes were not random and that his script choices were painstaking. In another context, he describes the care he took in shaping his material: "I mapped out every moment first and knew exactly what every shot was going to be. I couldn't afford to reshoot, so I designed every angle in advance, knew every move, every cut; all were pretimed and pre-planned."[31] Geduld provides evidence to confirm this, citing Olivier's "cutting ratio" (film wasted compared to the film in the final print) as "about 1.25 : 1—whereas in Hollywood at that time a ratio of 15 : 1 was considered economical."[32]

Olivier's artistic concerns and experiences in the time immediately before and after the outbreak of war provide a clue to the other issues he emphasized in *Henry V*, while he was, at the same time, deemphasizing war and its violence. Following his experience with Wyler in *Wuthering Heights*, Olivier had come to see acting on the stage as "unnatural and unsatisfying." He confessed to Vivien Leigh that though he had previously been unaware of the problem, he now believed "that audiences in the theatre swallow dialogue and acting conventions that on the screen would draw howls of derisive laughter."[33]

Additional film experience did not cause him to change his mind. His 1940 production of *Romeo and Juliet* with Vivien Leigh used a circular stage, "setting the action free to flow with the continuity and logic of a film sequence."[34] Having adapted his British stage acting style to films, Olivier was attempting to reverse the process with *Romeo and Juliet* as his experimental vehicle. However, not everything in the production was naturalistic. As he tells it, his legs were padded, his stomach was corseted, his nose was puttied, and his hair was covered with a black wig.[35]

Though *Romeo and Juliet* was a failure, the mounting of a naturalistic (yet romantic) production with a completely disguised Olivier at its center was typical of his style through much of his career. As Foster Hirsch summarizes it, "Beginning with an almost childlike interest in disguise and artifice, the actor probes deeply. . . . Putting on a mask himself, he unmasks the people he plays."[36] Olivier was probing not only into the characters behind the masks but also into the nature of the masks themselves, hence his experimentation with a blending of stage and film styles and his delight with the fluid medium of film itself. In his words, "How I loved the problems! How I loved the medium's ingenuity! How I loved the medium! Wyler's medium, mine, William Shakespeare's." He saw his main difficulty as finding "a style which Shakespearean actors could act and yet which would be acceptable to the audience."[37]

Given this background, it is not surprising that Olivier should find in *Henry V* the metatheatrical and metacinematic issues with which he himself had been struggling or that his central interpretation should be shaped in large part by those issues. As he says, "In *Henry V* more than any other play, Shakespeare bemoans the confines of his Globe Theatre . . . and all those short battle scenes, in a lot of his plays are frustrated cinema."[38]

Olivier's description of battle scenes as cinema is interesting in the light of his handling of Agincourt. I have earlier quoted his statement that "all active fighting was done by suggestion." On one level this means that war and its violence are likely to be subordinated to other issues. On another level it makes the battle itself a cinematic demonstration of how to create an image in the minds of the audience without showing it. Thus, the battle scenes are doubly subordinated and become a commentary on filmic art. In fact, while Olivier was consistently reducing the violence he showed and changing the nature of the violence that finally reached the screen, he also expanded parts of the film to raise metatheatrical and metacinematic issues. Because of the changes he made in the battle scenes, he was able to achieve both of these goals simultaneously. Ultimately, Olivier's battle scenes are, like their Shakespearean theatrical counterparts, an illusion. And Olivier, like his source, has drawn attention to the illusion from the beginning.

Of course, the use of the Globe Theatre as setting for part but not all of the film was the initial signal for the issues Olivier meant to raise, with the Chorus present at the end and beginning, "where Shakespeare put him. And in the Globe as Shakespeare had him. . . . The goddamn play was telling me the style of the film."[39]

André Bazin says that Olivier made "his film out of a play by showing us, from the opening, by a cinematic device that we are concerned here with theatrical style and conventions."[40] A few lines later he adds, "The film exists so to speak side by side with the theatrical presentation, in front of and behind the stage."[41]

The first clear reference in the film to metacinematic questions was added by Olivier between the shooting script and the screen. The earlier script has "The Swan Theatre is to the extreme left, the Hope in the centre, and the Globe to the right. The camera should very gradually concentrate on the last" ("RTTF," 1). The shooting script is essentially similar: "camera starts to descend towards the Hope and Globe Theatres: still descending, it turns right, bringing the Globe Theatre into greater emphasis by centering it as it turns" ("SS," 1). In the film itself, however, the audience is deceived at the same time that it is led by the camera. As the release script puts it, "CAMERA TRACKS BACK to reveal the City in extreme L.S. then TRACKS in to centre first the Bear Playhouse and then the Globe Playhouse."[42] In Sandra Sugarman Singer's words, the camera compels "us to focus on the wrong theatre."[43]

Olivier added or modified a number of incidents between the two scripts and between the shooting script and the filming to sharpen the references to metatheatrical and metacinematic issues. The earlier script has the general statement, "Throughout this Theatre sequence, it should be made plain that there is far more intimate interplay between actors and audience than can be imagined in today's theatre." ("RTTF," 2). It also contains specific bits of business such as "At the mention of Sir John Falstaff the audience give a joyous cheer," and there is the corresponding groan of displeasure at the reminder of his banishment ("RTTF," 3). On the Archbishop's line, "is it four o'clock?" the script continues, "A bell obligingly chimes four" ("RTTF," 4). These examples are unchanged in the shooting script (5–7).

In the film itself, the audience responds much more often, with laughter, with boos, and with jeers,[44] so that the Archbishop and Ely seem to be part of a double dialogue, the one that Shakespeare wrote for them on the stage and the one that Olivier wrote for them with the audience. Perhaps the two most important additions to this scene, which came between the shooting script and the filming, are the applause that the two actors playing the Archbishop and Ely receive when they enter and an offstage difficulty in getting the bell to ring four times. "The prompter gets up from his chair and peers through a grille in the door at the side of the stage. BELL RINGS THREE TIMES THEN A FOURTH."[45] Both of these additions (like the deceptive camera at the beginning of the film) force the movie audience to think about dramatic and cinematic conventions.

The entrance of Olivier as Henry changes from "On a last magnificent flourish of trumpets King Henry and his courtiers exit on to the stage" ("RTTF," 5) to "King Henry appears from the left and stands for a moment in profile shot." He is followed by the camera as he comes out onto the stage, but no reaction is indicated for the audience ("SS," 7–8). Finally, in the film we have Henry pausing in profile and coughing, with a look of extreme nervousness. Only then does he move onstage to be greeted by applause, which he takes by bowing to various sections of the audience.

An interesting adaptation of theatrical convention to cinema appears first in the shooting script: "On the words 'Are now confin'd two mighty monarchies' Chorus indicates the two entrances . . . the left one bearing an English insignia (prop) and the right one a French one" ("SS," 3–4). In the film, the English and French insignias are inscribed on the inner stage curtain, which the Chorus closes at the end of his speech. Sandra Singer sees this as a pattern running through the film. Every French entrance or exit is "Screen R" (even in the Globe), "while the English, in their quest move ever eastward, L to R."[46]

Even more important is the use of the curtain as a signaling device. It does double duty as a visual indicator and as a reminder of stage conventions. One other change between script and screen is clearly made to introduce a curtain and its theatrical associations. In the shooting script, Mistress Quickly "looks . . . towards first floor window, camera pans up to this window. . . . Within a light . . . finally dies away. . . . FADE OUT" (35). In the film this becomes, in the words of the release script, "Mistress Quickly looks L. up to Falstaff's window. CAMERA PANS . . . to centre on the window. The curtain is drawn across it as we: FADE OUT."[47]

Two other additions between script and screen help to draw the audience's attention to cinematic and theatrical issues. The earlier script says, "The Ambassador of France and Mountjoy enter, together with attendants and servants" ("RTTF," 7). The French Ambassador remains unidentified in the shooting script (17), but in the film, he is the Duke of Berri, introduced here and thus much more likely to be noticed in his later scene when he holds the *Très Riches Heures du Duc de Berri,* visual source of much of the film.

The other addition is a minor bit of Pistol's costume—a leek. When he first appears on the Globe stage, he is wearing it in his hat. But as Sandra Singer notes, he is still wearing it after the transition from the Globe as an indication "that though the film *seems* to be telling us that we are now expected to perceive the Henry story as less art and more 'real,' the art is still very much with us."[48]

There are yet more additions between script and screen to be noted. One is Katherine's visit to the Globe Theatre at the end of the film, which I shall discuss in detail in this chapter. The other additions might almost be taken as a personal statement by Olivier about the nature of disguise and of acting on stage and before cameras. As Ian Johnson writes, Olivier played (in addition to Henry) nine small parts, which include "the youth who summons Mistress Quickly to Falstaff's death bed, the harassed French court messenger, the sly addressee of the Constable of France the night before the battle, and the French knight's attendant the next morning."[49] It seems clear both from Olivier's statements and from his sequence of script changes that he meant his *Henry V* to emphasize metatheatrical and metacinematic issues and that he shaped the battle scenes to serve the same purpose.[50] It is also clear that any reading of Olivier's filmtext must take this material into account.

## Expectational Texts and Olivier's Script

It might appear that the innovation and success of Olivier's *Henry V* would protect it from critical attack or at least ensure that such attacks would be based on careful readings of the filmtext. Among many other firsts, it was the first Shakespeare film to be made in color, the first to achieve both critical and commercial success, the first to reverse the usual close-up pattern at the climax of a big speech, the first to use period artwork as the inspiration for scenic design, and, of course, the first to look behind the scenes and pose questions about theatrical and filmic conventions. It was also the first film that helped to form the critical background of a Shakespeare play.

Even Gorman Beauchamp, an extremely hostile critic, writes, "In only one instance that I know of, however, has a film been taken as a validation of the dramatic effectiveness of *the play itself*— Olivier's *Henry V*."[51] In Beauchamp's case this may sound a bit like pumping up a balloon before pricking it, but Marsha McCreadie points out that "the longevity of influence of Laurence Olivier's 1944 film was evidenced in both Terry Hands's and Joseph Papp's *Henry V*."[52] Olivier's influence is also clear in Branagh's film.

The critical impact has been equally long-lived. Both Michael Manheim in "Olivier's *Henry V* and the Elizabethan World Picture" and Graham Holderness in *Shakespeare's History* argue that Olivier's "film and the theories of Tillyard can be associated with the same impetus."[53] But Manheim finds that "the work of art— has outlived the scholarly interpretation,"[54] and Holderness maintains that the film's interpretation is more complex than it is often taken to be and that Olivier's "aesthetic devices" have been seriously underestimated: "to see the film as concerned simply to offer a 'straight' patriotic version of *Henry V* is to interpret selected parts rather than the film's significant whole."[55]

However, both the propagandistic war film Olivier is supposed to have made and the shortened version of the text he used seemingly violated the expectational texts of some reviewers and critics. One of the earliest of the many difficult choices Olivier had to make was how many lines to cut. Incredibly, C. Clayton Hutton claims in *The Making of Henry V*, "no word has been altered or deleted: that would be sacrilege."[56] But Harry M. Geduld's figures in the *Filmguide to Henry V* reveal that of the 3,199 lines in the original, Olivier "retained only 1,505."[57]

Olivier maintained that "the film was always in danger of being too long,"[58] but Gorman Beauchamp, among others, takes exception to his editing: "Olivier has systematically and tendentiously gutted *Henry V*." Beauchamp calls the result a "pasty patriotic ragout."[59] Clearly, he has found what his expectations prepared him to find. But as I have previously noted, the assumption that only obviously patriotic films could serve (or were thought to serve) a propagandistic purpose is contrary to the facts. Further, there is no indication in Olivier's comments on the making of the film that he chose to include or exclude material on the basis of what would produce the most patriotic result. On the contrary, the only examples I have found will bear the opposite interpretation. There are two cases where Olivier omitted material that could easily be seen to have a patriotic application. The first, which I have already mentioned, is Henry's speech that includes the line "when lenity and cruelty play for a kingdom, the gentler gamester is the soonest winner."

The second case involves Fluellen's encounter with Henry after the Battle of Agincourt. The earlier script had followed Shakespeare's text from 4.7.94–115 without alteration ("RTTF," 53). The shooting script contains a change of two significant words from Shakespeare's text and the earlier script. Instead of "All the water in Wye, cannot wash your Majesty's Welsh blood out of your pody, I can tell you that: God pless it, and preserve it" ("RTTF," 53), the shooting script has "God pless your majesty." The camera direction that accompanies this is, "As he says this Exeter enters from tent with crown which he places on Henry's head. Fluellen kneels at the side of the King and finishes his speech" ("SS," 126). During the process of revision between shooting script and screen, when Olivier was subordinating the war and violence in the film to metacinematic and metatheatrical issues, he cut the entire encounter with Fluellen.

If Beauchamp's assumptions are correct, it is hard to explain these changes. Olivier's account is far more consistent with what happens in the scripts. He appears to have seen himself not as an exponent of British patriotism but of William Shakespeare: "I was particularly anxious to maintain purity of intention. . . . I felt myself to be an agent of his [Shakespeare's] imagination."[60]

Arguments similar to Beauchamp's have been marshaled by many critics, and one of their main points is that Olivier has deliberately removed all ambiguities from the play in order to make it a more effective vehicle for England's national interest. It is obvious that if one is willing to cut more than half the play, a great many lines must vanish from somewhere. Nevertheless, it is possible to maintain that what is left of the text is still a fair representation, that this filmtext of a history may claim to be something more than merely Olivier's version of *Henry V,* and that, finally, despite the lopping of branches, the shape of the tree remains.[61]

The contention over the details of the play begins with the first scenes. In Geduld's words, "Critics interested in Olivier's adaptation of the play can, justifiably, object to the distortion of I.i and I.ii by turning much of it into comedy."[62] What Olivier has actually done is to place the first two scenes and everything up to the move to Southampton in Shakespeare's Globe. Using models and the tracking, questing camera, which is so much a part of his film style, Olivier created a performance within a performance, layers of reality and unreality that are positively Shakespearean in their complexity.

The device of the Globe Theatre creates what Foster Hirsch calls a "documentarylike texture,"[63] establishing a recognizable genre for the audience at the opening of the film and also serving "as a cushion for the poetry: the theatrical framing softens the difference between theater and film while frankly acknowledging it."[64] It also, undoubtedly, distracts some of our attention from the words themselves. Dale Silviria maintains that even in 1.1, which is played essentially straight, "the noise and general business of the Globe's audience serves to shift our attention from wholly upon Canterbury's meaning to a double awareness of the words and the crowd's reactions."[65] The result of this is "our experience and affective responses juxtapose to Agincourt not the suspect words of two shady clerics, but a performance by a couple of inadvertently humorous actors."[66]

Such comments begin from a largely untested critical assumption that the first two scenes of *Henry V,* if given full weight, would have told Shakespeare's audience and still will tell modern audiences that the clerics are corrupt and that Henry is intent on pursuing an unjust war. However, when the BBC *Henry V,* unlike many modern stage productions, did those scenes without extra-textual humor and with the majority of the lines intact,[67] the result came much closer to being an endorsement of Henry and his policies than an attack on either. Canterbury and Ely emerged as faithful if not entirely straightforward servants of the church who believed that helping a noble king to achieve his legal claims (and incidentally saving church money from Parliament) was both morally and politically correct. In this light, Henry's reiterated questions about the rightness of his course and his concern for the harm it may cause can make him seem a careful and concerned ruler.

In fact, Gary Taylor argues that having created suspicions about the motives of Henry and the Archbishop in order to ensure the audience's careful consideration of the issues involved, Shake-speare works to alleviate those suspicions. "The Archbishop *may* have ulterior motives, but Henry's claim seems valid nevertheless; Henry *may* be looking for a fight, but not necessarily *this* fight or any fight he cannot morally justify."[68]

The simple switching of part of the second scene into the comic mode will not destroy its effectiveness. Terry Hands's 1975 RSC production was played straight for the first half of the Salic Law speech. Then the complex genealogical precedents were spoken at extreme speed, making them essentially unintelligible. Thus, when "the Archbishop—returning abruptly to a slow and clear delivery—called this legal chaos 'as clear as is the summer's sun' . . . the audience laughed."[69] But as Richard David reports, that particular version of the Salic Law speech "was more pungent and intelligible when presented (in full, too) by a dapper salesman in gent's lightweight suiting than by an archbishop in full can-onicals."[70] Obviously, these scenes have their problems for a modern audience, but they can be played in various ways and still support Henry.

Olivier's additional distancing of the second scene has a number of advantages for a modern audience. It uses the very difficulty of what Silviria calls "a damn-near unplayable scene"[71] as an approach to the play.[72] The actors function as actors, eliciting sympathy for their blunders and engendering admiration for their skills. It also keeps the audience focused on theatrical and filmic issues. Anthony Davies maintains that Olivier's "comedy of incompetence" contains an indication that the film will not be a simple photographic record of a stage performance. "The brief moments

. . . during which the camera is wholly focused on the stage action are interspersed with sound-track signals which keep alive our consciousness of a dual role."[73]

At the same time, the ambience of Shakespeare's London, of Merrie England, has been established, and it is this, plus the presence of Olivier-Burbage, that provides the first emotional sanction for Henry's decision. Silviria says that the Globe and the English theatrical tradition are honored: "Above all, there is Shakespeare himself; on one level the film is nothing more nor less than an offering to Shakespeare."[74]

Sandra Sugarman Singer suggests "that the performance we were witnessing might be seen as the first performance of *Henry V* on the stage of the Globe."[75] No matter whether the year Olivier gives is correct or not, he may well have intended an even larger event. Robert Speaight says that if "the Globe opened its doors with the first performance of *Henry V,* that would have been the most historic occasion in the annals of the English theatre."[76]

In fact, Olivier substituted a historical justification that is more effective in a contemporary context than the one Shakespeare provides. One of the interesting ironies is that Shakespeare himself has become the center of that justification, receding into the mists of history that his play was meant to explore. James Agee's paean to the film testifies to just this element of its success: "I was persuaded . . . that every time and place has since been in decline, save one, in which one Englishman used language better than anyone has before or since, or ever shall."[77] Dale Silviria describes this as "an England of the mind."[78] For Orson Welles it was "Merrie England . . . a conception, a myth, which has been very real to the English-speaking world . . . the age of chivalry, of simplicity, of Maytime and all that."[79]

If there is a part of the film Olivier consciously shaped to help the British war effort, it is this England of the mind, this homage to Shakespeare, rather than any specific deletions from or additions to the text. But those elements would have been a part of Olivier's film no matter when he had made it. His shifting of styles and his probing of illusions are a valiant attempt to re-create Shakespeare's *Henry V.*

The artifice is immediately apparent; the opening scenes are filled with "tricks," for instance, the camera that focuses on the wrong theater, which I mentioned earlier. As Sandra Singer points out, the model of London is "a joy, but it's too good to be true, and . . . that's exactly what it wants to be."[80] The multiple focus in the opening scenes—London, the Globe, the audience, the actors, the backstage world—places the performance of the play in a frame, distancing it from reality so that we are viewing it through a double window. Through the first we peer into the England of 1600; through the second we watch a play while at the same time watching the audience; thus, we are at once members of that historic audience and participants in our own aesthetically and intellectually distanced time. Harry Geduld sees Olivier filming the scenes in the Globe from the free viewpoint of the camera, not the confined view of the theater audience: "Olivier paradoxically uses the theatre scenes to expose the limitations of theatre."[81]

The film audience is compelled to adopt the questing, questioning viewpoint of the camera, to look behind the characters at the actors and behind the scenes at the machinery, to look, in effect, through a twentieth-century lens and then to use that same lens to peer into a mirror. As a result, the transition to Southampton, though it is an opening out from the limitations of the stage, is also another invitation to test what is happening.

Almost immediately Olivier encourages us to do so. The Chorus has helped in the transition not only with his speech but also by pulling a curtain across the proscenium arch. The curtain turns to a kind of gauze and literally dissolves to a medium long shot of Southampton, as the release script has it, "exactly as depicted on the curtains."[82] This mixing of filmic and theatrical transitions, the dissolving of one artificial backdrop to reveal another, slightly less artificial backdrop, coming as it does after the audience has already looked behind the scenes in the theater, turns what had been a metatheatrical comment into a meta-cinematic one. That the film scenery behind the stage curtain is truly a device for revealing the artifice in both mediums is clear. As Geduld says, "Olivier introduces us in one short scene, to the various styles . . . in the rest of the film."[83]

And having had the connection between a curtain and an artificial scene to come made thus clear to us, we are much less likely to miss the device when it is repeated. In fact, "three of the four curtains which at one time or another cover the proscenium of the inner stage of the Globe are painted to represent scenes which will appear later in the film."[84]

Following Henry's brief appearance in Southampton (the traitors and all their lines have been deleted from the script), the camera moves off again, this time to the Boar's Head Inn and the first night scene, where it can peer not only behind the scenes but also behind the text.

This is yet another place where Olivier has been criticized for painting *Henry V* entirely in the bright colors of patriotism. Michael Quinn believes the conspirators' scene is cut to prevent "unfavourable comparisons between Scroop's treatment of his friend Hal and Hal's treatment of his friend Falstaff."[85] But in going behind the text of *Henry V* to the text of *2 Henry IV,* Olivier has at another point emphasized rather than smoothed over one of the dark places in the play. As Foster Hirsch states, "His treatment of Falstaff is especially somber."[86]

While the voice of the unseen Chorus urges us to "Still be kind, / And eke out our performance with your mind" (3.prologue.34–35), "the camera comes to rest on what looks momentarily like a Dutch or Flemish interior painting by Pieter de Hooch or Van Eyck."[87] Dudley Andrew calls it a "Vermeer setting with its single light source warming the profile of Mistress Quickly,"[88] and it does indeed have the inwardness, the sense of peering into a private space, of a Vermeer painting.

Mistress Quickly goes out, and the rejection of Falstaff is enacted as the fever dream of a pallid, shrunken old creature. There is no kindness in the king's mind for his old companion's last performance. Even Falstaff's memory cannot "eke out" anything of warmth or forgiveness. Olivier's juxtaposition of this scene with the Chorus's words has indeed constructed another irony of mirrors, as one mind remembers the unkindness of another, one actor is cast out by another. Hal is not seen, but his voice echoes hollowly from offstage, as it will the night before Agincourt, when he talks (unwillingly) to Pistol, much like the cold echo of his own mind against itself, which is the voice-over soliloquy on that same sleepless night.

The presence of Falstaff has many functions. The connection with the earlier and better-known play and the physical presence of this greatest of all English comic characters may help the audience to feel at home despite Falstaff's deflation and his pain.[89] Additionally, Olivier is probing at the limits of theater as he shows us a room that stage productions are not "allowed" to present. Ironically, we must also see "the Falstaff sequence as a little play which we enter through the proscenium of the window frame and which ends with the closing of the curtains,"[90] the curtain, be it noted, that Olivier had added between the shooting script and the filming. Thus, again we have the work of art within the work of art, the frame within the film. And there is, of course, more. This dark deathbed scene provides a corrective for the bright colors and a reminder that even energy such as Henry's does not bustle in the world forever—the little play encompasses the ending of the larger work that surrounds it.

Equally important is Falstaff's symbolic role as scapegoat. He has replaced Lord Scrope, that other "bedfellow," and we do not need to compare Scroop's treatment of Hal with Hal's treatment of Falstaff. Indeed, as A. R. Humphreys indicates, the two incidents of Falstaff and Scrope are of the same kind, public humiliations "and for the same reason, that the fault committed affects Henry's public station, and the world must understand this."[91] Olivier has simply substituted one incident (the more theatrically resonant one) for the other.

What we have is an old man reported to be sick and then observed to be dying, while in the scene between Hal says, "Set free the man committed yesterday, / That rail'd against our person." And "We doubt not now / But every rub is smoothed, on our way."[92] Hal's isolation is complete enough, the political destruction of a friendship clear enough without the addition of Lord Scrope.

Gary Taylor points out that "isolation is the structural principle behind most of the first three Acts" and that the Falstaff material has been stretched out so that it is "immediately juxtaposed with all but one of the main political scenes of Act One and Two."[93] Olivier has simply, despite the odd weightlessness of his Falstaff, made him carry more weight than usual.

Geduld has trouble with this performance, saying that it contains nothing to remind us that "the character was once the most engaging of all knaves. . . . Perhaps Olivier expected . . . Falstaff's former character to be suggested by George Robey's reputation as a stage comedian."[94]

From a purely practical point of view Olivier probably wanted an unfunny Falstaff who would not whet anyone's appetite for more "fat meat," thus distracting the film audience as his name does the theatrical one from the main business of the play.[95] Graham Holderness says the closed curtain is the end "not so much of Falstaff's life, as of his role. Has the king destroyed him because he cannot tolerate such theatrical competition?"[96]

There is a nice symmetry in seeing Falstaff as both a political and theatrical threat. Indeed, if one considers the possibility that he can also threaten the film, it is hard to resist the idea of Olivier (producer-director-star), who is playing Burbage (shareholder-star), who is playing Henry V (king and therefore a producer and "star of England") all rejecting Falstaff because of the various dangers he represents. However, in the circumstances a bright, jovial Falstaff would have gone counter to the thematic strategy as well. He is a scapegoat for both Scrope[97] and Bardolph, and his "death scene, a still picture bearing the weight of serious dramatic energy, rhymes with Henry's midnight soliloquy at Agincourt."[98]

Whatever the motives of Olivier-Burbage-Henry, we are not allowed simply to sentimentalize the Boar's Head crew. Hal's rejection of Falstaff is still a necessity for a king, and Pistol makes that clear as he leaves for France with a phrase that might be made the motto for the lot of them: "Let us to France, like horse-leeches, my boys, / To suck, to suck, thy [sic] very blood to suck!"[99] Nor are we left to believe that the fairy-tale ending brought about by English victory and French reconciliation has changed all things and all men for the better. Pistol still has the bitter lines: "Well, bawd I'll turn, / And something lean to cutpurse of quick hand. / To England will I steal, and there I'll steal."[100] At our last sight of him, he is wearing the Constable's armor with stars on it and is carrying a stolen piglet and cockerel.

Clearly, though Olivier has deemphasized explicit violence in his *Henry V*, he has made no attempt to remove the dark colors from the film. Graham Holderness is not the only critic who has pointed to the shadows in its texture. Jack Jorgens says, "The splendid charge descends to a grim, unheroic standoff of hundreds of soldiers mired in the mud."[101] And though no one is killed onscreen, there are corpses lying on the field of battle when all is over. Both Williams's speech (reassigned to Court) about "legs and arms and heads chopped off in a battle" (*HV* 4.1.138) and the Duke of Burgundy's listing of the woes of France are retained and given special point. The Duke of Burgundy's catalog gets both a visual illustration and a musical accompaniment. Court's words are emphasized by his own youth and innocence and by the fact that when his two friends walk off into the night, he stays behind with the king, Court sleeping while Henry broods over the problem the boy has presented. Like Olivier's script changes, his use of light and dark material and his attempt to remain true to his Shakespearean original must also be taken into account in any reading of the filmtext of *Henry V.*

## Olivier's Central Interpretation

In the process of exploring the boundaries of both theater and cinema, Olivier has deliberately touched extremes of unreality. He does this, for instance, in the heavy, stagy acting at the Globe and in the film's succession of artificial sets based on the *Très Riches Heures du Jean, Duc de Berri*. Both of these examples of artifice are, however, firmly bound to the story Olivier is showing. This is, after all, a Shakespeare play, and Shakespeare, "our bending author," was a player on a stage more or less like the one the film re-creates.

The same sort of glancing, reflexive acknowledgment of a source occurs with "The Duke of Berri reading at a lectern."[102] He is holding a magnifying lens (is there perhaps a suggestion of the camera's eye peering at these same illustrations and enlarging them into sets?), and Olivier has seen to it that we know him already as the ambassador who brought the treasure of tennis balls to Henry. The book he is reading is the visual source for the scene in which he is standing, just as British stage tradition informs the acting, and the filmtext is one more variation in Shakespeare's *Henry V*.

Not even the "realistic" parts of the movie are free from this footnoting. Eisenstein's *Alexander Nevsky* was one inspiration for the battle scenes, but Olivier also used Uccello's *Battle of San Romano*.[103] And there is at least one unmistakable reference to Michael Curtiz's *The Adventures of Robin Hood*, when the English drop from trees onto the French.

The self-aware stance that Olivier had adopted as director and that he had compelled his audience to share allowed him to turn the weaknesses of earlier Shakespeare films into his own strengths. The artificiality of blank verse echoed convincingly in the Globe, and the more naturalistic style of acting outside the theater seemed by comparison natural indeed, just as the elimination of stage make-up and costume established their film equivalents as closer to reality. The massive (and massively unbelievable) black-and-white castles that had haunted George Cukor's *Romeo and Juliet* and Paul Czinner's *As You Like It* (and no doubt Olivier as well as he tried to play Orlando to Elisabeth Bergner's Rosalind)[104] turned to flowing colored shapes like a medieval tapestry or the "separate panels of a colorful, ornamental diptych."[105] To use Dudley Andrew's words, "the play of color and false perspective serves as an orchestra shell for the Shakespearean verse."[106] Olivier said he meant "the actors to dominate, to feel confident and sometimes to dwarf the scenery."[107]

The Chorus is also a part of this filmic, theatrical pattern, and, as a result, most critics who have not perceived the pattern have had difficulty explaining why Olivier not only kept the Chorus but expanded the speeches from six to ten. Silviria notes, "Paradoxically, the viewer's awareness of Chorus's guide function grows greater *after* the film leaves the Globe, when the . . . exhortations to our imaginary forces [are] no longer necessary."[108]

I suggest that it is precisely in the "realistic" scenes that Olivier is most in need of the Chorus, and that if the Chorus had not already existed in the play, it would have been necessary for Olivier to import him from a different source. This is one more seeming paradox in a long list. Here at last is the techology to go beyond the obvious limitations of the stage, to explode the Wooden O outward until it contains the world it could previously only suggest. Here too is a play where Shakespeare was supposedly indicating the constrictions of the theater, where he seems almost to have foreseen the coming of film and to be pointing out in advance the sort of naturalistic adaptation he wanted for his work. Yet Olivier has not only kept and stretched the limping device of the Chorus, he has also added a host of other tricks, which immediately proclaim both their art and their artificiality.

However, Shakespeare did not need the Chorus either, at least as a means of enlarging the scope of the Wooden *O*. The space that had accommodated the first tetralogy and three-fourths of the second hardly needed renovation in order to make room for *Henry V*. It has been suggested that this play is episodic or epic, or that Shakespeare had lost interest in it, and thus the Chorus is merely the contrivance of convenience. This is part of the critical climate that dismisses *Henry V* as minor Shakespeare, the unsatisfactory and shadowy sequel to the substance of the Falstaff plays. As E. M. W. Tillyard puts it after listing the many problems Shakespeare supposedly faced with Hal/Henry, "No wonder if the play constructed around him shows a great falling off in quality."[109]

It seems to me that one of the major values of Olivier's film is the practical refutation it provides for such theories. It can indeed be taken as a validation of *Henry V*. Both the play and the film are at pains to intellectually distance their audiences from the material they present while at the same time asking more emphatically than usual for imaginative and emotional participation.

One of the mechanisms of this distancing and some of the reasons for it can be seen if we examine what passes for realism in the film. Peter Davison points out that the battle scenes work "not so much because what we see is like it really was . . . as because we are accustomed to such scenes in historical film-dramas."[110]

Emrys Jones says of Shakespeare's histories, "The historical events are rearranged into a highly stylized form in the interests of drama."[111] The same thing is true of the film. From the use of miniatures, which Olivier probably knew from working with Hitchcock and which "idealised the film and further strengthened the fairy-tale quality,"[112] to the frequent intrusions of the Chorus and the dreamlike choreography in the battle, all is convention. As I have previously noted, Olivier's violence is the suggestion of actions; the audience is made to imagine what happens rather than allowed to see it. The battle scenes themselves become another example of filmic convention, another illusion that Olivier's camera questions even while creating it.

After practically demanding that his audience be aware of the art behind his film, of the cross-references and interconnections, Olivier has provided a great many patterns for them to grasp. Henry, for instance, has become a secondary playwright for the play, a director for the film, the character identifying yet again with Burbage-Olivier behind him. It is therefore appropriate that Harfleur is a victory won by Olivier's voice, a human trumpet that opens the gates. In the same way, Henry's role on the night before Agincourt, his disguise, clearly marks him as an actor, while the wandering tour of inspection he conducts smacks of a director nervously checking small details before an opening.

We are also meant to connect the film's two night scenes, the death of Falstaff and the doubts of Henry. There is the same off-camera voice, this time addressed to Falstaff's substitute, Pistol, and then, in the first use of voice-over for a soliloquy, to Henry himself. There is also a clear indication of both stage and screen convention in the sharp contrast between the dark, doubting night and the day that ends in victorious sunshine.

Olivier has made the night seem longer by the nature of his cutting. From the point where he dons his disguise to the shift back to the French camp, there are no obvious jump cuts, no sudden juxtapositions of contrasting locations to shock the audience into an awareness of change. It is all a slow, hesitating movement from one dimly visible place to another, from one question to the next, with the camera briefly taking over Henry's role, as Pistol, searching for him, peers into the lens.

Olivier provides a deliberate contrast to this immediately before the two armies join in battle with a series of crosscuts between the English and the French, the French advancing while the English archers prepare to fire. One of the film's many felicities (and another of its metacinematic footnotes) is that Olivier has here used an exactly opposite film technique to secure the same effect—an unbearable sense of suspension, of delay. He has also, sitting astride his horse "with sword poised"[113] for the signal that will release the arrows and the tension, reemphasized his role as director, as creator and controller of tensions.

Dudley Andrew says the battle restores "a sense of 'movie life,' of watching life as given through film. Here the hyperbola comes nearest the axis of realism."[114] But this is true only because Olivier has previously moved so far from the conventions of realism. Agincourt is primarily a shifting of banners against a painfully blue sky. Everything is swathed in color—the knights themselves, their tents, their horses; this is closer to being a festival and tournament than an encounter of deadly rivals. Though Olivier did not succeed in filming the battle on green velvet, in some ways the style he created had similar effects. And if there is any sense of unease, much of it is washed away by our foreknowledge and our firm trust in the director and star who is also the king.

Singer identifies two genres operating in Henry's Battle of Agincourt, "the Chivalric Romance and its descendant, the American Western."[115] One of the indications of this derivation is Olivier's single combat with the Constable; it is a showdown, and it is also quite literally white knight against black knight.[116] In this context it is important that the Constable is the most important figure in the French cavalry charge.

"The montage seems the work of Harry's hands, as is the mise-en-scène. At its climax . . . he finally plants himself in the center of this deep space and throws his last opponent."[117] As I noted earlier, Olivier considers his backhanded blow to the Constable's jaw the only active fighting that was not done by suggestion. Henry's location at the center of the frame indicates yet another pattern.

> Henry circles the Globe stage during his "mock" speech; he is then encircled by his men for the rousing speech at Harfleur and the St. Crispin's Day speech at Agincourt, and by the men of both armies during his combat with the Constable. When he is victorious in that battle, his horse circles the circle of men before he rides back toward his camp.[118]

All of this, of course, like the Chorus, makes it hard to suspend disbelief, to pretend that the camera is an open window onto reality. We have been presented with a tapestry of colors and castles, with an adventurous and victorious king and with a beautiful princess, in short, with a fairy tale. But we are constantly reminded that it is a representation, that the historical persons are stage actors and that behind them again are film actors; we are never allowed to forget that we are an audience watching and to some extent creating the spectacle that unrolls before us. Not only our imaginations but our expectations "eke out" this text. Shakespeare's Henry and Olivier's Henry are our own cultural mirrors.

And despite his cuts, Olivier also suggests the dark reality of violence in this world. In a proper melodrama (and in most chivalric romances and Westerns) the villain is justly punished in the ultimate conflict with the hero. But Olivier's battle with the Constable of France, despite appropriate costuming, is not a similarly clear reestablishing of order and justice. The Constable, when Henry's victory seems certain, has ridden back into the battle, presumably to face him. Shortly after, Bourbon, Orleans, and their attendants ride in the same direction, leaving the Dauphin behind, watching from a hill. Bourbon, Orleans, and company stop suddenly and go a different way. In the English camp they set fires and murder the boys; it is the only action in the film that is at once cowardly and violent. "When they return to the hilltop, the Dauphin has ridden away in fear. Olivier holds the shot of the retreating Dauphin for a comparatively long time." It is the last we see of any of them, and we are offered no explanation. "Of course, Orleans, Bourbon and their companions are to blame. But that they are, rather than closing or containing the event, only opens the limitless ponderings upon the dark nature of men in war."[119]

Silviria says, "Firing the decorative pavilions suitably emblematizes the blow to an ideal world vision dealt by the killing of the boys."[120] Henry and Fluellen might have joined together in their definition of proper military behavior and discipline, but neither of them can do anything about what both perceive as a "war crime." Fluellen cries and Henry becomes angry, but in this context of the tarnishing of the heroic ideal, the Welshman's grieving and Henry's killing of the guiltless Constable in a fair and courageous fight seem curiously beside the point, symbols whose meaning has been blunted, just as Henry loses his sword and wins with a backhand blow of his mailed fist.

Singer identifies the Constable as "the auspicious opponent . . . whose defeat brings honor to the victor."[121] But such a conclusion reminds us of the history behind the shifting story; "its very appeal introduces an element of head-shaking and wistfulness."[122] Olivier's king, like Shakespeare's, appears powerless before the mystery of human evil.

I seem to be supplying a great many negatives: the film (and by extension the play) is not primarily about patriotism or war; there is no clear enemy provided. Olivier locates despicable evil in men who have seemed to be honorable before their action and who simply disappear afterward. Perhaps, however, the duel with the Constable might be taken as a small part that represents and helps to explain the film as a whole. Henry's courage and success, his defeat of a worthy challenger, is a positive value set against the negative of the murdered boys. It does not cancel that negative or even attempt to set it right by punishing the culprits; it simply offers an alternative value. Indeed, nothing in the film (or the play) suggests the possibility of effective restitution or fair punishment. From Henry's ominous words about the tennis balls to Falstaff's pathetic death and Burgundy's long, illustrated catalog of the ills of France, no one seems to get what he deserves, and justice, whether human or divine, looks more like chance than anyone's design.[123]

Significantly, Henry is not abandoned as Bourbon and Orleans are. He is the champion of his troops, and he fights inside a circle, supported by an audience. Also significantly, he remains in the film, to be supported not only by his men but also by the stage audience and the film audience beyond them. One of the main functions of the Chorus is to remind us that Henry-Olivier is giving a performance, creating a thing of the imagination, but the Chorus, who addresses us directly, also compels us to remember that we are part of that performance, that it will not work without *our* imaginations.

Thus, Henry's victories (like those of Talbot) are not so much the result of his own strength as of the strength he draws from his soldiers and his other audiences. The isolation he suffers at the time of Falstaff's death disappears during his long night's watching. As James Agee said, it "establishes the King's coming-of-age by raising honorable . . . old age (in Sir Thomas Erpingham) in the King's love and esteem to the level of any love he had ever felt for Falstaff."[124]

As both king and actor Henry has come to terms with himself and his audience. James L. Calderwood says, "Harry has not been elected by the Lord. He has had a corporate majesty founded on shared English culture."[125] In Dudley Andrew's words, "For Olivier and for us the king is not some individual privileged by birth to lead, but a human being, like us, who leads, as we might, on the strength of his moral and psychic well being,"[126] and, as the Chorus reminds us, by the strength of his and our imaginations. He is a peculiarly appropriate historical subject for myth and fairy tale, and the structure Shakespeare created and Olivier kept makes his composite identity clear. Olivier's film might be called a remythification, a reenergizing of the imagination, the sharing of a dream. In Jack Jorgens's words, "In *Chimes* we witness the decline and death of Merrie England. *Henry V* is a vivid recreation of it,"[127] or at least of the shared dream it represents.

Olivier has one last situation (and a series of devices) to summarize his points. The situation is, of course, the wooing of Katherine. I have already mentioned Katherine's identity with the fairy-tale princess, but there is also a naturalness in Henry's courtship of her and her response to him that both contrasts with and reifies the artificial setting where they find themselves.

Henry-Burbage-Olivier has one more part to play. The king who has found himself to be a diplomat and general now takes on the role of the tongue-tied and therefore straightforward lover. He is a plain, blunt man, a soldier who might win a wife by some physical exploit but never by charming speech. This is, of course, ridiculous, and all of Henry's audiences from Katherine outward know it. Henry is performing for her as he has been (and is) performing for us. His rough French and exuberant English ask for the love and agreement he now has the power to demand. It is yet another demonstration of the power of shared imagination.

Jack Jorgens notes that the marriage of Henry and Katherine "also represents a marriage of styles—theatrical and illusionist, film realist and painterly—in the film as a whole."[128] Olivier has made this "marriage of styles" unmistakably clear, and at the same time he has found a visual and structural illustration of the power of image and imagination. Backstage at the Globe there are two boys preparing to play the parts of Quickly and Katherine. In fact, Freda Jackson plays Mistress Quickly throughout, with appropriate changes of make-up.

Katherine, however, is represented (very briefly) by a boy within the Globe and by Renée Asherson outside it. This gives Katherine a special significance to begin with, as though she has taken on an extra kind of reality. Olivier heightens this effect by carefully juxtaposing her scenes with Henry's, making her appear to be almost the realization of his dream.

After watching the English army enter Harfleur, Henry looks at the country ahead; this dissolves to the French palace and then dissolves to the "Garden Terrace,"[129] where Alice and the Princess Katherine enter. Henry has been looking to his right while Katherine looks to her left. During her French lesson, she makes a circuit of an enclosed rose garden and ends by looking "up to the horizon"[130] again. The walled garden is here (as it often is) a symbol of virginity, a particularly appropriate juxtaposition with a scene that, as Gary Taylor points out (in commenting on the Terry Hands production), shows "Catherine as more willing, sexually, than she would appear to be."[131]

Katherine is linked to Henry not only by his looking toward her and her looking in his direction, but also by the circle she makes, a motion associated with Henry in the film. There are, as one would expect, other connections. Walton made use of the Auuvergne Bailero as background music for Katherine and for "the Duke of Burgundy's poetic elegy for the ruined condition of France. The logic of the music says that . . . Katherine and France stand for the same elusive entity."[132]

Not surprisingly, the images that support Burgundy's catalog of disasters are part of a circular movement of the camera that starts from a window of the palace and returns to it, actually viewing the palace itself in the process. The two scenes are thus joined by the musical theme and the motion within them, while one of their subjects is both a connection and a contrast. Katherine's perfect garden (Eden) is compared with the ruined garden of France, the one suggesting what the other has been and may be again. And in the process Olivier has suggested (as he has done in various ways before) that the camera can view its own starting place, examine its own images.

Katherine's waiting, like Burgundy's, can be seen to have an element of impatience to replace the desert of war with the arts of peace, the martial with the marital. As often in Shakespeare, marriage brings a suggestion of wholeness, of restoration. During part of Henry's wooing of Katherine, for example, his voice is heard from offscreen, as it was with Falstaff, with Pistol, and in his soliloquy. This is (for the film, at least) his final doubt, and it is quickly resolved. The union with Katherine is an indication that Henry's own deserts may (in Benedick's words) "be peopled." As Silviria puts it, "If Falstaff's death is ever ameliorated in our minds, it is because Henry . . . loves the beautiful and wise Katherine."[133]

The last of the circles in the film, the final completion of patterns, is the return to the Wooden O itself. And here something extraordinary happens with Katherine. Silviria says that "Henry's adventure can be seen as a struggle to reclaim some sort of Eden" and that "in Katherine and Burgundy we begin to meet citizens of this new demi-paradise."[134] Olivier's filming suggests that the working imaginations of actors and audience have briefly realized this reclamation, as the "real" Katherine appears on the Globe stage.

As might be expected with critics writing before (or at any rate without) the videocassette, there are varying accounts of this scene. Harry Geduld appears to have missed the moment entirely: "Henry turns . . . wearing the crude make-up in which he first appeared in the Globe Theatre scenes. Then the camera pans to the right and shows a boy made up as Katherine."[135] He is undoubtedly following the release script, which reads, "CAMERA PANS R. to show a boy made-up as Katharine[136] acknowledging applause."[137] However, the release script is sometimes misleading and occasionally wrong (it misspells Renée Asherson's name, for instance). It is, after all, only the imperfect record of the text, not the filmtext itself.

Silviria says that when the film cuts to Katherine in close up, "what startles is the obvious wig and its curls. And while the actual individual is—I *think*—Renée Asherson, the thought flashes by that what we really behold is one of the boy actors."[138]

The most accurate account, however, is Singer's. At first she sees not a boy-Katherine but "the French, story-book, imaginary Katherine," who is not in her fifteenth-century costume but is wearing "a Renaissance gown, her hair a wig of descending waves. She, too, wears make-up, and she smiles and acknowledges the audience response." Next, a cut to a medium shot "shows us the same Henry, but the heavily-made-up figure next to him is not actress Renée Asherson."[139]

Anthony Davies disagrees, saying, "No print available for viewing . . . has shown the transition to be as Singer describes it." He also notes that "the published film script includes none of the complexities which Singer claims to be part of the film's deliberate artifice."[140]

Of course, the release script does not deal in complexities.[141] The descriptions in the unpublished scripts are interesting. The earlier script has, "When they . . . have turned towards us, then only—when we come into a close up—do we perceive the wigs, make-up, materials and props of our Elizabethan players" ("RTTF," 63). There is, however, no mention of a boy actor. This script suggests that Renée Asherson was to appear in the Globe. The shooting script indicates a full-length shot "in which we can plainly see that Henry and Katharine, at this point played by the boy actor, from the Elizabethan theatre are dressed in Elizabethan clothes" (149). When the camera reaches a full-length shot, Katherine is played by the boy actor, and this is what happens in the film. But there is a shot that the shooting script does not have and the release script does not record. I suggest that given Olivier's other changes between shooting script and screen, it would be surprising if he had not somehow added a filmic/theatrical reference here as well.

As Silviria sees (and says), "repeated viewings of *Henry V* show that beneath the white wedding robes Olivier and Asherson have already donned their Elizabethan apparel."[142] Though he does not specify what he means, it is clear (from my own repeated viewings) that there are high Elizabethan collars under the flowing robes. When we see Renée Asherson in the Globe, she is wearing such a collar, but her gown has a low neck, emphasized by a double strand of pearls. This is a close-up, close enough to show the color of Asherson's eyes. Next, there is an obvious cut to a medium shot revealing a boy as Katherine but in a different gown with a higher neck, without pearls or other jewelry. The camera then tracks back without a break, and Chorus enters left to shut the two of them behind the proscenium curtain. I offer the Katherine–boy actor controversy as an excellent example of the value of the videocassette in the study of filmtexts.

Sandra Sugarman Singer regards Asherson's brief appearance in the Globe as "perhaps Olivier's most crucial statement. In these two simple shots . . . many of the major issues—art, time, history, reality, theatricality—which have arisen during the film, appear and coalesce."[143] She also finds it "interesting that this singular and arresting moment is never mentioned in the criticism that deals with this film."[144]

It is not only interesting, it is also natural. Since both the release script and Geduld in his film guide (probably following its lead) missed the "moment," the only way for another critic to discover what is really happening is to watch the film closely and repeatedly. In the present context there is a special irony to so many critics missing this specially important part of Olivier's message. Too often film performance is treated like its stage counterpart, as a memory that cannot be again consulted.[145]

Ironically, a film in which Olivier has brilliantly captured the ephemeral feeling and the imaginative unity between audience and actors of a stage production has been treated in criticism almost as though it *were* a stage production. The brief glimpse that Singer finds so powerful is part of Olivier's return to the Globe. There is no reason why the medium shot should reveal a boy Katherine except to remind us that the brief arc of Henry's star is at an end and that it has been a performance we and Olivier-

Burbage have made together. When the Chorus closes the curtain on the two of them, Henry makes a slight gesture of surprise or annoyance; he does not emerge again, even after the conclusion of the play.

Despite his pruning of Shakespeare, Olivier has recreated the text of *Henry V* on film. He has sacrificed much of the luxuriance of the original's foliage (to continue my earlier metaphor), but the trunk and limbs have not been deformed or dwarfed. Like the play, Olivier's film is about the stage itself, about illusion, about history and myth, heroes and dreams. It presents (but does not offer simplistic explanations for) love, evil, courage, isolation, and the unity of shared imaginings. It makes possible a revised evaluation of the play itself, suggesting that it is not exclusively or even primarily about war and that the speeches of Henry and the Chorus have more to do with theatrical than patriotic victories. Dudley Andrew sums up the film thus: "Olivier has joined . . . the fragile momentary inner life of every viewer to the continuity of cultural life in history." He points to cinema's "reproduction of painting, drama, and music" and concludes, "Seldom has cinema participated in a more massive ideological undertaking. Seldom has it seemed . . . more worthwhile."[146]

The conclusion to John Wilders's book *The Lost Garden* chimes interestingly with this estimate of the film; "Henry . . . was not the New Adam nor did he recover the lost garden, but he did for a time, achieve 'the best garden in the world' and that, under the circumstances, is the most we can expect."[147]

Olivier's film presents determined courage and inexplicable cruelty, ruined and restored gardens, tapestries of sound and color, and briefly commands our belief in the images, imaginings, and the people behind them. It is a filmtext that deserves and repays careful study. More than that, it helps to demonstrate the complexity and validity of film interpretations of Shakespeare and the importance of a scholarly approach to films.

# 7

# Orson Welles and *Chimes at Midnight*

## Shaping of the Film: Welles as Auteur

Of the three directors whose work this study examines in detail, Orson Welles has the strongest claim to the title of auteur. Francois Truffaut calls him one "of the ten greatest cineastes in the world."[1] Like Olivier, Orson Welles combines the trinity of adapter, director, and star. But even more strongly than Olivier, Welles saw himself as an artist whose medium was film. As Dudley Andrew says, "Orson Welles . . . knew the *auteur* theory in advance."[2] As Charles Higham phrases it, "Welles was making his films as a novelist makes a novel or a poet makes a poem."[3] There is no question that he saw himself as an independent creator, a maker of new works of art. He said in a 1966 interview, "I like to make films in which I can express myself as *auteur* rather than as interpreter."[4] His feeling of artistic control is emphasized in the way he describes his treatment of his subordinates: "At the beginning I tell them . . . know you are going to be a second-class citizen."[5]

His insistence on control did not mean, however, that he was afraid to experiment in the exploration of the film medium. In fact, improvisation and alteration were part of his attempt as an artist to realize his intentions by the most effective means. Describing his filming, he says, "The thing isn't working. Then you must change, and the change does everybody good."[6] In Charles Higham's words, "He demanded unlimited time, the capacity to improvise, the trick, common to all artists, of weaving in and out of a theme according to his own instincts."[7] This fluidity is part of the medium and part of Welles's effective use of it. The tentative becomes permanent when the right performance is transferred to film and edited into form. Welles said, "I will work and work for a moment in an actor's performance."[8]

Nevertheless, the "moment in the actor's performance" was very much under the control of Welles as director. Often it would be shaped by him in ways the actor was not aware of until the film had been completed. After the release of *Chimes at Midnight,* a friend of John Gielgud's told him that one of his best moments came as Hotspur lay dead and Gielgud looked at Falstaff, then to Hotspur's corpse, and finally at Prince Hal. John Gielgud says, "We never did the scene at all. . . . Orson said . . . just look down there, that's Hotspur's body, now look up at me.' I never even saw Orson made up as Falstaff." But, he willingly concedes, "the clever cutting" made the scene "enormously effective."[9]

The decisions about the dubbing and editing of *Chimes at Midnight* were made by Welles, and the work—with the exception of one track cut in a studio with a door "so small that Welles could not get through it to see what was happening"[10] was supervised by him. Thus, the final variation of *Chimes at Midnight* is the form intended and largely created by its auteur. Welles's technical virtuosity is attested both by film critics and fellow actors. Robin Wood, for instance, describes the opening shot of *Touch of Evil* as "perhaps the most astonishing virtuoso crane-cum-tracking-shot in the history of the cinema."[11]

Another instance of Welles's mastery is his innovative and painstaking use of the sound track, a result, at least in part, of his earlier work in radio. Francois Truffaut points out that "*Citizen Kane,* no doubt by the richness of its sound track, made us finally disgusted with dubbing."[12] Phyllis Goldfarb hears the same skillful use of sound in the later films,[13] where sound is used in many ways, including "the negation of reality. What we hear no longer works in conjunction with what we see. Eisenstein might have called it harmonised counterpoint."[14]

Dudley Andrew points to Welles's use of dialogue overlaps and microphone placement to create "a veritable audio space in which events take place." The techniques were clearly adapted from radio and amounted to a "spatializing of the sound track. . . . Touted for his expressionist visual sense, Welles' most signal moments come to us from devices realized on the sound track."[15]

The care with which Welles created his films justifies an equally careful reading of them. Welles always wrote and rewrote his scripts in the process of imposing his own vision on them. However, he shaped and reshaped the material that became *Chimes* for most of his career, partly because of his fascination with Shakespeare and perhaps more importantly because he found that the material of the second tetralogy illuminated his own life. Interpretations of *Chimes at Midnight* must take into account the extent to which Welles saw himself (or his friends and family) in the characters of the film. Robin Wood finds a pattern in all Welles's films, but it is expressed "completely and perfectly" in *Chimes,* "where Welles's interest in the *Henry IV* plays is primarily an interest in the Falstaff/Hal relationship."[16]

Orson Welles created his first version of the material that was to become *Chimes* when he was at the Todd School for Boys. Beginning with *Richard III,* Welles added "fragments of other plays so that the result was decidedly a most personal . . . concoction."[17] In addition to this early assault on both tetralogies, there were three more or less distinct adaptations of the second. The first two versions were stage productions: *Five Kings* in America in 1939[18] and *Chimes at Midnight* in Ireland in 1960.[19] In both, Welles played Falstaff, chose essentially similar materials (with more of *Henry V* in *Five Kings*), and rearranged his text almost constantly.[20] Robert Hapgood says, "*Five Kings* was in a continual state of redefinition, especially of ruthless cutting, during its time on the road."[21] Charles Higham notes that "just before the opening in Philadelphia he radically shifted all the positions of the cast."[22]

The film of *Chimes at Midnight* was the third of these adaptations, a fact that any interpretation of the work must take into account. The relationship between Shakespeare's plays and Welles's film is more complicated than many critics have realized. What Welles did has been described as mixing scenes from the second tetralogy and *Merry Wives* to make a story about Falstaff. It would be more accurate to say that he mixes lines from those plays to make his own scenes. In the first tavern scene, for instance (scenes 5, 5A, and 5B for both the shooting script and dialogue script of *Chimes*),[23] Welles uses material from four different scenes and two plays. Welles's very short second court scene (his scene 9) contains lines from *Richard II* and both parts of *Henry IV.* Even when he uses extended bits from the same scene, he breaks them up, so that inverted and transmogrified sections of *1 Henry IV* 1.2 appear in Welles's scenes 5, 5A, and 5B ("WSS," 13–21, and "WDRS," 6–11). W. H. Auden said of Falstaff that "Half his lines could be moved from one speech to another without our noticing."[24] Orson Welles's film is a validation of that statement, not only for Falstaff but for many of the other characters.

Welles's lifelong familiarity with his material and his multiple experiences in cutting and performing it resulted in the most powerful of all his Shakespearean adaptations and one of his best films. Gordon Gow says, "I feel bound to call his *Chimes at Midnight* the most mature of his Shakespearean excursions."[25] For Charlton Heston too, "Orson's CHIMES AT MIDNIGHT is remarkable . . .

perhaps his best since KANE."[26] David Bevington, in his introduction to the Oxford *Henry IV, Part I,* writes that because of Welles's very free cutting and rearranging of scenes "inevitably some parts of the play suffer, but in return we are given a remarkably sensitive reading."[27]

The complexity and care of Welles's readings and their adaptation to film shows an analytical responsibility to the text as film and, reciprocally, to the film as text. It is unfortunate then that much of the literature devoted to Orson Welles has eschewed that kind of analytical responsibility and is essentially impressionistic. Brian Henderson maintains that Joseph McBride, among others, has ignored "the visual-sound construction of the film," justifying such "neglect by speaking of Welles' 'breaking the bounds of his tools,' and serving his actors with the camera in contrast to *Citizen Kane*'s 'trickery' (a term used throughout as though it is self-explanatory). This is nonsense." Henderson calls *Chimes* "a visual-sound masterpiece, one of the greatest stylistic achievements as well as one of the greatest films of the sixties."[28]

One symptom of this impressionistic critical climate is that no extended study of *Chimes at Midnight* has hitherto compared the shooting script to the film itself.[29] The shooting script is particularly useful because, despite numerous changes between script and screen, it provides a reliable guide to Welles's intentions. The variations that emerge are almost always different means to the same end.

The working of the process can be seen in Falstaff's counterfeit death at the Battle of Shrewsbury. In the shooting script, Hal becomes aware of the counterfeit when "AN INVOLUNTARY HEAVE CATCHES" his attention ("WSS," 93). However, since Falstaff in armor looks rather like an early ironclad, the *Merrimac* or *Monitor,* that has swum ashore and begun to churn up the mud, it might have been difficult to notice a heave, involuntary or otherwise. The film has Hal speak the line, "I could have better spared a better man." Then, seeing the telltale mist of Falstaff's frosty breath, he says in a nicely judged mixture of relief, exasperation, and humorous threat, "Embowelled will I see thee by and by." In both cases Hal comes into possession of the same important fact at the same point, both texts indicate a particular interpretive decision by Welles, and the examination of one helps to confirm a reading of the other.

Also, the shooting script provides instructions for the actors, illuminating the signals Welles intended them to send. Thus, after Hal notices the involuntary heave, the shooting script continues,

"THE PRINCE'S EYES NARROW IN A MIXTURE OF AMUSE-MENT AND ANGRY RELIEF" (93). This instruction says much about the affectionate relationship between Falstaff and Hal. Clearly, in addition to Welles's position as auteur and his long professional and personal identification with the material, an accurate interpretation of the film must also account for the material in the shooting script.

## The Central Interpretation

The complexity and rigor of Welles's adaptation endows that word with a special seriousness and should help to make the point that films deserve to be treated as texts despite their lack of pages. Also, with an adaptation such as *Chimes,* complicated by the rearrangement of Shakespeare's material and its own wealth of visual and auditory detail, textual inattention can easily turn to interpretive misunderstanding. An additional difficulty here is that the critic's expectational text may distort his impressions.[30]

Joseph McBride, for example, compares Hal to Iago and says, "Hal schools himself in hypocrisy. . . . Welles makes clear that Hal's merry-making with Falstaff is fraudulent . . . from his first soliloquy . . . delivered with Falstaff musing vaguely in the background."[31] However, this ignores a number of distinct signals in the scene, not the least of which is the prince's boyish enjoyment. When Poins convinces him to go on the Gad's Hill expedition, Hal and Falstaff forget their small quarrel and hug each other, the prince hurling himself on the fat knight rather like a puppy at play. For the soliloquy itself, Hal and Falstaff share the screen, their two faces in close-up, with Hal nearer to the camera, his back to his friend, while Falstaff, being closer to the center, is more prominent in this two shot.

Falstaff is very much an audience for the soliloquy,[32] smiling at the small joke in "Being wanted, he may be more wondered at."[33] And Hal finishes with a wink to the fat knight (at "I'll so offend to make offence a skill") before he moves happily away, running and leaping in the air to click his heels. That Falstaff has understood the meaning of the speech can be seen in the question he asks as Hal is leaving, "I prithee, sweet wag, shall there be gallows standing in England when thou art king?" He seems only partly reassured by Hal's joking response, "No, thou shalt have the hanging of the thieves and so become a rare hangman."

Welles's treatment of this scene in his shooting script makes his intentions clear. Following the line "The unyoked humour of your idleness" is the direction "FALSTAFF RAISES HIS WINE CUP IN IRONIC SALUTATION" (20). After "he may be more wonder'd at" is "FALSTAFF WATCHES HIM WITH A GRIN, BUT BEHIND THE TWINKLE IN THE OLD MAN'S EYE THERE IS A FAINT SHADOW OF FOREKNOWLEDGE" (21). Welles also moved the material concerning thieves and hanging from immediately before the soliloquy, where it might have been taken as the cue for Hal's speculation, to immediately afterward, where, in the light of Hal's threatened reformation, it seems a logical question for Falstaff to ask.

Welles says that the relationship between Falstaff and Hal is not comic or simple "but always a preparation for the end. And as you see, the farewell is performed about four times during the movie, foreshadowed four times."[34] Hal's only "soliloquy" has become one of those foreshadowings, a future unpleasantness that both characters foresee.

As might be expected, Welles has reinforced the visual and textual message by his use of sound. There is a reassurance not only in Hal's exuberance as he moves away but also in his voice, which remains cheerfully close even when he is halfway across a field. We have already heard the obverse of this technique when in scene 3 ("WSS," 7–9, and "WDRS," 2–3), Henry IV says, "Worcester, get thee gone." The sound itself seems to pull back in disapproval. There are, however, also ominous sounds and signals in Hal's scene with Falstaff. The tolling of bells and slow organ music pre-echoes the bells and solemn horns at Hal's coronation and Falstaff's rejection. In addition, as the prince moves out into the sunlight, we see the frost of his breath and are reminded of Henry IV in his palace in the sunlight speaking cold puffs to the Percys.

Welles's use of his medium in the service of Shakespeare is both varied and subtle. Brian Henderson finds that "because of the formal diversity of its sequences" *Chimes* creates a new type of filmic expression, intersequence cuts. Such cuts, used with extremely effective sound editing, "as in the cuts from raucous tavern (dark on light) to somber castle (light on dark) . . . provide . . . overwhelming changes of mood, tempo, and tone as well as high dramatic contrast."[35]

There are many such connections and contrasts, large and small, in the film. Hal's "I know you all" speech, where he stands in front with Falstaff behind, becomes the pattern for Falstaff's soliloquy on honor and also his praise of wine. In the first of these,

Hal stays relatively close, and the two of them are essentially alone. In the second, Falstaff is also addressing a larger audience (as he does in the tavern scene), and there are more cuts than in the earlier scenes to break up the comfortable two shots, cuts from Hal to Falstaff and from Falstaff to the audience. At the end Hal walks slowly away, dropping his wine cup. It is a dispirited re-enactment of the conclusion of his own soliloquy, with a reminder that the future slides into the present and holidays—like lives— must have a stop. In their last encounter, Hal stands with his back to Falstaff as he says, "I know thee not, old man." This time, however, the physical and emotional distance between them has greatly increased.

Another, smaller, but also important example in the early scenes is the linking of Hal and Hotspur. Hotspur insults Hal, saying, "But that I think his father loves him not. . . . I would have him poisoned with a pot of ale!" This is all the introduction Hal gets; there is an immediate cut to a shot of him drinking from a mug and wiping his mouth. Nevertheless, it makes a direct and forceful link between the two rivals, and it sets up one of the more interesting changes Welles made in Shakespere's material. The first tavern scenes (5, 5A, and 5B) are surrounded by Hotspur: he has introduced Hal in scene 4, while his castle is the setting for scene 6. Welles very probably expected those members of his audience who had noticed the chill breath of Henry and Hal to be delighted by the image of Hotspur in the bath with steam rising around him. And when Hotspur himself rises from his tub shortly after and shouts down from a window to his Uncle Worcester, we are reminded of cold Bolingbroke and his frosty son and also of the line "But that I think his father loves him not," for we hear Hotspur, speaking of his own father, say, "now in very sincerity of fear and cold heart, will he to the king and lay open all our proceedings."

In Shakespeare, of course, these lines apply to the "Lord Fool," whose letter Hotspur is reading (*1H4* 2.3.29–31). Interestingly, Orson Welles followed Shakespeare in his shooting script (23) and made this rather startling change only when he came to film. The result is to associate Hal and Hotspur as rebels against their fathers and to suggest that both fathers mistrust their sons. Welles has managed at the same time to range Hal with and against his father, to suggest that Hal and Hotspur share qualities and yet are polarized by antipathies. This is perhaps the largest interpretive change Welles made between the shooting script and the screen, but it is in keeping with his other points about Hal and Hotspur, and it brings into sharper focus yet another of the mentor-pro-tégé relationships, which are the heart of the film.

Certainly, it is dangerous to miss even the smallest of Welles's signals to the complex of relationships around which he has built his film. *Chimes* is often taken to be a simple glorification of Falstaff and a lament for his passing, an attitude that has been encouraged by the frequent quotation of one of Welles's own remarks, "What is difficult about Falstaff, I believe, is that he is the greatest conception of a good man . . . in all drama." However, immediately before this he had said, "Falstaff is a man defending a force—the old England—which is going down." He went on to say, "The film was not intended as a lament for Falstaff, but for the death of Merrie England."[36]

There is a difficulty in identifying Falstaff too closely with Welles. Welles the actor may have seemed destined for the part and was certainly enthusiastic about it; "I've always wanted to play him, which is unusual, as there are very few characters who really tempt me."[37] Nevertheless, it is excessive to link them as Jack Jorgens does when he speculates that Welles might have identified too closely with Falstaff: "To a man who directed and starred in a masterpiece and has since staggered through three decades of underfinanced, hurried, flawed films . . . the story of a fat, aging jester exiled from his audience . . . might well seem tragic."[38]

This traditional version of Welles's personality and career may be traced to Charles Higham, who says of Welles, "He has dis-played a manic excess and self-destructiveness."[39] It has been strongly challenged by Barbara Leaming in her biography, which was partly based on extensive interviews with Welles himself.[40]

Leaming argues that Welles had strong reasons for identifying with Hal in *Chimes at Midnight* and that the intensely personal quality of the film is a result of Welles's feeling of reenacting one of his own earlier choices. Orson Welles's father, Dick Welles, was an alcoholic, and when Orson was fifteen, he had, on the advice of one of his mentors, Roger E. ("Skipper") Hill, refused to see his father again until he stopped drinking. Dick Welles died soon after. " 'I've always *thought* I killed him,' says Orson about a life-time of despair at having betrayed Dick."[41]

Nor was that the end of choosing between mentors. Dick Welles's will provided that Orson was to select his own guardian, which meant a choice between Roger ("Skipper") Hill and Maurice ("Dadda") Bernstein. However, "when Orson asked Skipper to become his legal guardian, Skipper" refused, since "this was sure to break Dadda's heart."[42] Interestingly, this is the period of

Orson Welles's first production of the material that was to become *Five Kings* and then *Chimes*.[43]

Leaming finds elements of both Dick Welles and Skipper Hill in Orson Welles's portrayal of Falstaff, arguing that by, in a sense, combining the two "he allowed himself to repeat the scene of rejection while changing the outcome, so that, in the film. . . . The drunkard is spurned . . . but *not* the father."[44]

While this sort of motivation obviously made the film a very personal one for Orson Welles, the multiple versions of himself (and the amalgamation of his father and mentor) gave him the kind of distance (or divided interest) that a director must have. In fact, there are many more mirrors for Welles in the film. Orson's daughter Beatrice, who looks very much like early pictures of her father, was cast as Falstaff's page. Leaming finds Hal (one version of Welles) causes the death of the drunkard, while the page boy (another mirror) laments that death: "Hal has 'killed his heart' " which, in a realized metaphor, Orson remorsefully shows himself to have done by playing . . . the one who is killed."[45]

Though this is not part of Leaming's thesis, it seems to me that Hotspur must be another of these mirrors. I have already indicated that Hotspur is a rebel against Hal's father and (inadvertently) his own. However, by his manipulation of Shakespeare's material, Welles has also placed Hotspur in the position of siding with his uncle against his father. Like Hal (and Welles), Hotspur has had to choose one guide and give up another. Hotspur has an additional link with Welles in the bathtub scene. John Houseman describes one of his early meetings with Welles, who was still in his bath, "a monstrous, medieval iron cistern which, when it was covered . . . served . . . as a marriage bed. . . . He got up . . . with a great splashing and cascading of water."[46] Welles's ambiguous relationship with Houseman may have been the psychological starting point for Hotspur's scene, since Houseman was a mentor whom Welles saw as having betrayed him.[47] Hotspur is placed between a father who betrays by telling the truth to the king and an uncle who betrays by hiding the truth from Hotspur. The similarities in the situation plus Hotspur's resemblance to the "uncontrolled" persona that Welles sometimes adopted suggest that Hotspur too is a portrait of the auteur as a young man. Another level of irony is added by Welles, as Frank Brady notes, supplying the voice of Worcester.[48]

Even this is not the end of the selves of Orson Welles who can be traced in *Chimes*. Richard T. Jameson (in an essay appropriately titled "An Infinity of Mirrors") points out that in the encounter between Falstaff and Bullcalf "Falstaff challenges the recruit, who replies, 'Oh sir, I am a diseased man!' Out of him comes the voice—*a* voice—of Orson Welles. Orson Welles spends a delightful moment conversing with himself on the soundtrack."[49] There is also an additional auditory identification. Welles "selected the Italian comedian Walter Chiari for the role of Silence, equipping him with a stammer identical to that of Welles's brother, Richard."[50]

I do not mean to suggest by all of this that Falstaff is not or was not meant to be the center of the film. Welles himself said, "I wouldn't act a role if it was not felt as dominating the whole story."[51] Indeed, it seems clear that Welles had both thematic and personal interest in many of the characters, that in fact the relationships and the choices within them were what motivated his making of the film, and there is much critical support for Welles's contention that his role of actor did not prejudice his performance as director.

One of the best indications of this is the balance he has achieved in the presentation of Hal, a balance greatly aided by the appealing and multifaceted performance of Keith Baxter that emerges on film. There is a long tradition among the worshipers of Falstaff of darkening and diminishing Hal in order to brighten and enlarge (if such a thing can be contemplated, let alone carried out) the fat knight. Bradley, for instance, condemns the prince's rejection of Falstaff as "ungenerous" and "dishonest . . . disagreeably like an attempt to buy the praise of the respectable at the cost of honour and truth."[52] And it is certainly possible to direct Shakespeare's material in such a way as to create the prince whom Bradley describes.

Orson Welles *has* built a strong Falstaff; however, as William Johnson says, "he does not do this at Hal's expense." Johnson concludes, "Welles makes it as difficult as he can for the audience to take sides between Hal and Falstaff—or rather, to take one side and stick to it throughout."[53] David Bordwell finds that Welles (and Shakespeare) has made a world where "Prince Hal must choose among three ways of life—that of king, warrior, and roisterer . . . [but] each way of life has become sterile."[54] As Renaissance prince, "Hal becomes their synthesis. Like the sun he compares himself to, he is a source of power that will revivify England."[55] Though he talks of only two worlds—court and tavern, or everyday and holiday—Lorne Michael Buchman also believes that Welles's "Hal emerges as the one who must reintegrate a country of isolated parts."[56] These interpretations give Hal a centrality and vitality he usually achieves only in productions of the complete tetralogy or isolated versions of *Henry V* like Olivier's and Branagh's. There is a suggestion here that Welles's lifetime of studying and directing Shakespeare's histories had allowed him to compress the material without suppressing its complexities.

In collapsing the two parts of *Henry IV* and borrowing from other plays, Welles had the opportunity to eliminate much of Falstaff's bad behavior; he did not do so. In *2 Henry IV* 3.2, for example, we see Falstaff taking bribes from the poor while drafting the destitute. Welles includes the scene, placing it before the Battle of Shrewsbury. "By doing so, he strikes a bold contrast between the lovable Falstaff of the Boar's Head and the repellent one of the war."[57]

The film achieves an interesting irony with the addition of a scene (rather like Olivier's) of the knights being hauled into the air on ropes as a prelude to lowering them onto their horses. Hotspur (who is standing safely on the ground at the time) speaks the lines "Harry to Harry shall, hot horse to horse, / Meet and ne'er part till one drop down a corse." Shortly after this we see an enormous knight being hauled into the air and (as everyone expects) dropped. Thus, we have the words of Harry Percy and the accident to John Falstaff, both of whom will drop down as corpses in the coming battle. Ironically, Falstaff's accident preserves him to run and hide, pointing the way to slaughter for other men and even indicating Hal to Hotspur (to avoid any possibility that the fat knight might be taken for the lean prince). Since the film omits Henry IV's counterfeits, Falstaff ends up carrying (along with the dead Hotspur) a larger than usual share of the blame for the death of honor.

Welles has actually done more to tarnish Falstaff's reputation than Shakespeare did because in *Chimes,* the old knight's dishonestly chosen men are visible and individual to us (as they are not in *1 Henry IV*) and because his cowardice is set alongside the naturalistic horrors of the battle that follows and in which Falstaff's men are killed. It is a spectacular affair that begins with a strong sound of wind. The combatants (most of whom look as though they were chosen by recruiting sergeants of Falstaff's stamp) are viewed against an enormous, cloud-filled sky and an equally large barrenness of land, which dwarf them. This clash has all the cinematic style but none of the pageantry or prettiness of Olivier's battle in *Henry V.* It rapidly becomes an affair of mud, blood, and indiscriminate bashing, where men are beaten to death with clubs and their bodies are heaped up like cordwood. Falstaff does not stab Hotspur in the thigh, but the very conjunction of what Auden called his *"opera buffa* world"[58] and this open-air dying space is enough to make us see him differently.

At the same time, in the process of exploring the relationship between Hal and his two fathers, Welles has actually answered one of the structural questions about the tetralogy at Falstaff's expense. For some critics, there are more reconciliations between the king and his son than are consistent with Henry IV's renewed distrust in *2 Henry IV*. In Shakespeare's text Hal and his father are reconciled before the battle when the prince promises to kill Hotspur. There is a repetition of this during the Battle of Shrewsbury when Hal saves his father's life, and presumably this amity is trebly confirmed when the king learns that his heir has been as good as his word and disposed of Harry Percy.

Orson Welles has omitted the battlefield rescue (along with any actual fighting by Henry IV), but he begins his rewriting of reconciliations even earlier. The shooting script follows Hal's words, "Then I shall make this northern youth exchange / His glorious deeds for my indignities!" with the instruction "THE KING MOVES FORWARD" (62). The prince continues, "This, in the name of God, I promise here!" The king still does not respond; the direction says, "THE KING STANDS IN FRONT OF HIM SEARCHING HIS SON'S FACE. . . . AFTER A MOMENT HE MOVES PAST HIM TO THE DOOR" (62.). Hal goes on, "And I will die a hundred thousand deaths / Ere break the smallest particle of this vow!" But even this is not enough, "THE KING STOPS, AND LOOKS BACK AT HIM, STILL BLEAKLY UN-CONVINCED" (62).

Welles tightened the scene but did not change its message when he shot it. On Hal's words, "This in the name of God," the king turned away. The prince's lines are cut after "I promise here!" Henry does not look back, walking away into shadow as he gives his rigid instructions: "The Earl of Westmoreland sets forth today, / On Wednesday next, Harry you shall set forward, / Our hands are full of business, let's away."

Welles heightened the impact of this scene by changing Henry IV's reaction when Hal offers to fight Hotspur (*1H4* 5.1). The shooting script duplicates Shakespeare's text: "And Prince of Wales, so dare we venture thee, / Albeit, considerations infinite / Do make against it" (87). But the film omits those lines; Gielgud contemptuously ignores Hal's challenge as he has previously ignored his promise.

This, then, is the charged atmosphere that exists between Hal and his father as the battle groans to its conclusion. Welles increases the tension and foregrounds the choice the prince must make by introducing Henry IV into the scene between Hal and the resurrected Falstaff. Hal has knelt to turn Hotspur's corpse (flung down in the mud by the fat knight) over onto its back. Falstaff ends his justification with the words "I grant you I was down and out of breath; and so was he; but we rose both at an instant and fought a long hour by Shrewsbury clock!" Now, from Hal's point of view, we see the hem of the king's cloak, and then, as Hal rises, the camera rises with him until father and son are looking directly at each other. Then Falstaff repeats an earlier line, "I look to be either Earl or Duke, I assure you." This is a change from the shooting script, where Falstaff remains quiet (96). We cut to him, back to Hal, to the king, and so on through a long silence during which the prince gets the attention his father had earlier denied him. As the shooting script puts it, "HAL MEETS HIS FATHER'S EYE, BUT MAKES NO REPLY TO THE UNSPOKEN QUESTION, STUBBORNLY REFUSING TO SPOIL FALSTAFF'S JOKE" (96). Perhaps too he sees that he is no more likely to be believed this time than he was before. The shooting script continues, "THEN SUDDENLY THE WEARY DISAPPOINTMENT IN THE KING'S FACE TOUCHES HIM. . . . BUT IT'S TOO LATE: THE KING HAS TURNED AWAY" (96).

The king moves off to his horse to the accompaniment of the solemn horn music that will be heard again at Hal's coronation. The music stops when Henry IV in a fit of weakness almost falls from the saddle he has so recently mounted. Far from being the one good man who is abandoned by a loved foster son, Falstaff emerges in Welles's restructuring as a corrupter of words and deeds (if not of youth) who has hurt his "good angel" without helping himself. This is another of those preparations for the farewell, but here it is the king who retreats and is weakened by his son.

However, it is misleading to focus entirely on single characters or even on the complex relationship that the three principals share. *Chimes at Midnight* has too often been treated in this way, not as an artistic whole but as certain broad comic and pathetic effects that emerge from a background that can safely be ignored. Jack Jorgens says, for example, "The most important reason for the film's inaccessibility, however, is its incredible unevenness. Between scenes of true genius . . . are sketchy, rushed through and patched together scenes that bewilder and bore."[59] Such an approach almost guarantees that the critic will come away with the traditional "good Falstaff, bad Hal" version of the film. And though Jack Jorgens is too skillful to get more than one foot tangled in the snare, Roger Manvell, his most illustrious predecessor in the field of Shakespeare on film, is well and truly caught.

Manvell sees *Chimes* as "a deeply moving film, in which Falstaff, the central figure, has an essential goodness, even a greatness about him, which Prince Hal . . . can no longer permit himself to recognize or even tolerate." He misses the existence of and the reason for the shared soliloquies. His memory and his point of view deceive him into saying, "Falstaff, covered in shabby unpolished armour, speaks his fatalistic speech on honour while the armoured knights are lowered onto their horses by ropes thrown over the branches of trees."[60]

As I said earlier, Falstaff speaks the speech on honor to Hal, and it is part of a pattern the two of them share. The lowering of the knights onto their horses (which comes immediately before Falstaff's speech) also forms a pattern. The rebels are placed on their horses precisely as Manvell says they are, "by ropes thrown over the branches of trees." But on Henry IV's side, the ropes are thrown over scaffolds that are uncomfortably reminiscent of the gallows hung with dead bodies at the beginning of the movie. I have previously alluded to the extra layer of irony it adds to Hotspur's "till one drop down a corse." It is also an enactment of the jokes about the hanging of Falstaff. There will be actual corpses dangling during the brief narration that marks the transition between the end of the battle and the king's return to court.

Jack Jorgens, commenting on the film's visual style, says, "the tavern stresses horizontals and diagonals. . . . The court stresses verticals."[61] Welles has here provided just such a contrast between the essentially vertical scaffolds for the king's men and the verdant horizontals of the trees for the rebels. It is no wonder that Falstaff falls from this uncharacteristically upright height. The fat knight is a rebel against law, even though for the moment he's paid to fight on the king's side, and he spends most of the battle hiding behind various trees and bushes.

By killing Hotspur, Hal seems to have joined his father's world of stark verticals, the leafless, lifeless forests of lances that appear to grow about the king and do, in fact, spring up around Hal during his coronation, almost barring Falstaff's desperate approach. There is even a shot of the dying Hotspur framed against trees and then one of Hal bleakly outlined against the sky, with the trees masked by mist.[62] But Welles's filming is not so schematic and his characterization is not so simple.

In Buchman's words, "the composition of the shots informs the moment: Hal stands beside a majestic tree and, as he speaks the soliloquy, he nervously thumbs a twig. He is the young boy on the threshold of majesty."[63] This is another way of saying that Hal is a potentially unifying and revivifying force and, even, of indicating that the rebels themselves, inhabitants of a "green world," may possess a wholeness denied to the "legitimate" Henry IV. After all, like Hotspur and Falstaff, Hal is a kind of rebel, but paradoxically all of them are rebels against a usurping king. And all of them are part of a dying world.

It is a critical commonplace that *Chimes* is a film about endings. Welles himself said, "It is more than Falstaff who is dying. It's the old England, dying and betrayed."[64] After comparing *Chimes* to *The Magnificent Ambersons*, another of his films about the ending of an era, he went on to say, "Almost all serious stories in the world are stories of a failure with a death in it. . . . But there is more lost paradise in them than defeat. To me that's the central theme in Western culture: the lost paradise."[65]

Welles removed the shots of Falstaff and Shallow walking in the snow because he thought they "would have hurt the real, internal rhythm of the picture."[66] However, in using them before the titles, he clearly signaled (especially to members of his audience who had studied his earlier films) that *Chimes at Midnight* was about the whiteness of death and the pure image of the lost paradise.[67]

In a similar way, "*Kane* begins with the end—the death of the protagonist. . . . In his final moments of life, the old man holds a small crystal ball containing a miniature scene that flurries with artificial snow."[68] In both *Kane* and *Ambersons* the white of snow or of fabric becomes a multiple symbol—for death, for the lost paradise, or for what William Johnson identifies as a theme that "can be summed up as loss of innocence."[69]

Thus, Kane dies holding a paperweight that "is not merely an artificial snow scene recalling a real one but a snow scene encapsulated and unattainable";[70] Bernstein remembers a girl in a white dress he had seen "only for a second"; and *Ambersons* contains "the hilarious, breathtaking scene of the automobile ride in the snow,"[71] the juxtaposition of a world of leisure with the twentieth-century artifact that will destroy it.

If, as seems clear, such dark films as *Citizen Kane* and *The*

*Magnificent Ambersons* can be viewed as Wellesian excursions into the realm of the lost paradise, it is safe to assume that Welles is not a presenter of paradises; he is far more likely to suggest the loss, to offer the symbol of the unattainable, the unimaginable happiness that is never written on his painfully white page. This was Welles's vision for almost all of his life. Barbara Leaming describes him at the age of eleven as "straining frantically beyond his meager years, all the while glancing fondly, sentimentally backward at a fabled childhood from which, paradoxically, he had ever been in flight."[72]

That this sentimentality was not allowed to pervade his films is clear from the people in them—Charles Foster Kane and George Minafer—who look unsuccessfully for paradise. Falstaff is immediately placed in this company by the simple beauty of the snow scene, the clear association of age and whiteness with death, the nostalgic message of the scene itself, and its encapsulation before the credits so that it seems a lost moment of peaceful reverie, symbolic of all those other bits of still beauty time has flicked away.

But there is an additional factor in this scene before the credits, and that is Justice Shallow. An English don in a Reginald Hill novel suggests that "in every Toby Belch there's an Andrew Aguecheek trying to get out."[73] And in Falstaff, shielded by the flesh, the flashes of wit, and the wicked smile, there is a skinny Justice Shallow, given to lying, who would be equally pathetic in his deceptions if his sighing and grief had not blown him up into a humor.

In all his cutting, Welles has kept and emphasized the connection between the two old men; indeed, he has almost suggested that the film itself is their shared recollections, "since the main action of the film is appended to the prologue like a huge flashback."[74] Charles Higham says that both Falstaff and Mr. Justice Shallow are "crumbling ruins, symbols of an England of carefree jollity and wassail doomed shortly to be destroyed."[75] For Anthony Davies, "Shallow's fondness for reminiscence suggests that . . . he has like Falstaff tasted the sweetness of the lost Paradise."[76]

Like so much else, Shallow is a reminder both to Falstaff and the audience of the fat knight's mortality, his smallness. As David Bordwell puts it, "When, at Justice Shallow's house, Falstaff has been meditating on his death, a deep shot shows Falstaff sitting stonily in the distance, for once positively minuscule."[77] There are similar shots in the film's scene 25 ("WSS"; 24 "WDRS"). Welles has reversed his technique of magnifying Falstaff by shooting him from below; now that angle is reserved for Henry V, and the fat knight shrinks as he is forced to look up.[78] At last, left with Shallow, his face shriveled by grimaces, Falstaff drifts into the distance, a small old man against the masses of vertical masonry.

Shallow serves yet another function in the film. As he reminds us when his office has passed away, he is a representative of Henry IV. This tired old man is never far from anyone's thoughts; he is a kind of chill center around which all revolve. His voice is imitated by Hotspur, Falstaff, and even by Hal. He is the father against whom Harry Monmouth and Harry Percy rebel, just as he is the successful rebel whose authority Worcester and Falstaff would like to seize and wield. Admittedly, Falstaff's ambitions are more personal: he is interested in playing the role of father to Hal and therefore, in a sense, supplanter of the king.

Falstaff and Henry IV have long been seen as parallel figures. In his excellent and extended discussion of the connections, James Winny says, "The general parallel between Falstaff and Bolingbroke as diseased and aging men, and between the King and his unhealthy realm, is too plain to be overlooked."[79] And though Welles has removed the double counterfeiting from the battle, the similarities between the two men are still plainly perceptible. As Jack Jorgens says, "The robbery at Gadshill in holy robes is a parody of the battle at Shrewsbury in chivalric armor. . . . Both King-fathers die false deaths and are 'reborn'— Falstaff on the battlefield and Henry in bed."[80]

However, the point that Welles is making is more subtle than Jack Jorgens's recounting of it. *Chimes at Midnight* makes it clear that the deaths of the king-fathers are real; it is, instead, their recoveries that are false. James Winny points out that Falstaff and Henry IV are so closely linked that "every reference to Falstaff's increasing age and ill-health takes on an ambiguous significance . . . impelling attention towards a second figure."[81]

Orson Welles has intensifed this sense of the king's illness by attaching it not only to Falstaff but also to the failed rebel cause and the dead rebels who hang from gibbets. The king's swaying in the saddle comes in conjunction with his words "Rebellion in this land shall lose his sway / Meeting the check of such another day!" Welles also added a transition (which was not in the shooting script) between the last shot of the battlefield and the move to the king's bedchamber. The words come from Holinshed, and Welles uses the dissolve, an uncommon transitional device for him in this film: "From the first, King Henry's reign was troubled with rebellion." (A dissolve to a scene of corpses hanging on gibbets begins.) "But in the year of our Lord 1408, the last of his enemies had been vanquished." (A dissolve to the scene of the palace begins.) "The King held his Christmas this year at London, being sore vexed with sickness." It is almost as though the king has been infected by those corpses.

If Falstaff's sicknesses seem also to be attached to that shadowy second figure whom he parodies, so too do the farewells that the director-auteur has made so prominent a part of the film. Because it comes after the poignant scene of the two old men in the snow, it is possible to see more clearly in Hal's soliloquy something that has always been there but that is usually obscured—a realization of the brevity of life. The lines "If all the year were playing holidays, / To sport would be as tedious as to work; / But when they seldom come, they wish'd for come" can easily be taken as Hal's expression of weariness with his unending holiday. But in *Chimes at Midnight,* this interpretation is emphatically contradicted by Keith Baxter's energetic enjoyment of what he is doing. Instead, it fits in with the many farewells, becoming Hal's recognition that this small holiday of youth will soon be ended and all the aches of kingship will descend.

The farewell to Falstaff is also a farewell to Hal's youth and to that father ruffian, that reverend vice, that king-rebel, Henry IV. In this film (and—Welles makes us think—very probably in Shakespeare's play as well), Falstaff's words are a death knell for Hotspur (in whom the king sees himself—"And even as I was then is Percy now!"), for Hal's holiday (as some part of Hal dies with Hotspur, his namesake and "factor"), and for Hal's two fathers, who must give up their places to the new man. Ironically, Welles's Falstaff shouts the words with all the vicarious relish of one who has the excitement of a fight without being in it, "Here's no boy's play, I warrant you!"

The fat knight's counterfeit death comes during the fight. Either from too energetic watching or from backing away too quickly when the violence approaches him, Falstaff overbalances and falls backward. Dozens of critics have commented on the parallels between the dead Hotspur and the "dead" Falstaff. As David Bevington phrases one of the more common versions, "We see the protagonist standing over two seemingly dead bodies. . . . Excessive devotion to chivalric honour and irresponsible pursuit of pleasure both appear to have been defeated, with Hal as the intelligent survivor."[82] Or in Robert Speaight's words, "Falstaff's observation 'I live out of all order, out of all compass' applies to Hotspur as well as to himself."[83] It applies to all three rebellious "youths" (especially to that goodly corpulent rebel against age itself) and to Henry IV's England, which in Welles's vision, Falstaff personifies. In the frozen life's breath that steams up through Falstaff's visor, Welles found a neat symbol for the fat knight's perilous position, closer to what he counterfeits than he would like to admit. For Hal too something has ended, and his own breath (which was clear during the battle with Hotspur) has turned white.

The boy's play ended at Gad's Hill in one of those marvelously evocative Wellesian scenes that suggest paradise though they do not present it. Like the snowbound worlds of the young Charles Foster Kane and the Ambersons, this is a garden where the leaves have already fallen, a premature autumn (if the trees at the Battle of Shrewsbury are anything to go by)[84] that prefigures other endings. Again Welles has used white as a symbolic color; this time it is the "warm" white of the monks' robes in which the thieves diguise themselves. Jack Jorgens says, "the most striking quality of this film is its simplicity," and the first example he gives is "Hal's symbolic gesture of throwing autumn leaves on Falstaff before the robbery."[85] I would add to that Hal's throwing himself onto the ground and hence into the leaves and then effortlessly leaping up again, all of this coupled with Falstaff's expressed need for levers to execute the same feat (and indeed it takes both Nym and Bardolph to resurrect him in his armor at Shrewsbury). I would also add one of the great visual delights of the film, Falstaff and the thieves running nimbly in and out among the skinny trees, while the black, deathlike figures of Hal and Poins pursue them.

From these simplicities, however, Welles has made a net of connections. The three worlds of Gad's Hill, tavern, and the battle are inextricably linked. All three feature rapid running among obstacles—Falstaff moves through the trees similarly at Gad's Hill and Shrewsbury, while the coming of the officers to the inn precipitates an amazing turmoil of dashing figures. All three contain a dethronement of the fat knight by his princely foster son—Hal forces Falstaff to rise and flee at Gad's Hill, restealing the stolen money, deposes him in the tavern, snatching his cooking pot crown (Falstaff in his turn snatches his page's cap to play the part of the young prince), and abandons the King of Sack after the battle, dropping the symbol of Falstaff's royalty as he goes. In all three Falstaff undergoes a mock death—with the "burial" in autumn leaves and the pursuit of the black figures, with his descent into the space below the floor of the tavern (the Elizabethan stage hell and natural home for such vices as Falstaff),[86] and with his counterfeiting during the battle. As Hal rides away from the tavern shouting, "Farewell, blown Jack! Farewell, all-Hallown summer!" the very last warm breath of that long-lingering autumn goes with him.

Welles's restructuring of Shakespeare's material raises some interesting critical questions. The careful links he builds suggest that the counterfeit deaths of both Falstaff and Henry IV are symbolically real. In Henry IV's case, the interval between his two deaths is exceedingly brief, but since Welles has moved the king's weakness back to the battle of Shrewsbury, he has, in effect, made most of the material in *2 Henry IV* a deathwatch. His film also suggests that it is not merely Falstaff and the king who are old and loaded with diseases but the world they inhabit as well.

This is a critical commonplace, of course, but Welles has gone beyond the simple expression of a diseased land to the vision of a complex world with room for Hal and Hotspur, Worcester and Shallow, kings and highwaymen. Neither Shakespeare nor Welles has tried to paint the place as a paradise, but as Maynard Mack says about kingship, "Like the Golden Age it seems most visible when it is moving away, into the past."[87] It is a curiously disorderly world, with a usurper king and a truant prince; nevertheless, this is the world Orson Welles describes as "Merrie England," and the fighting, roistering figures within it sustain themselves and each other. Thus, in a curious way, Henry IV's ending of rebellion is also the ending of his own reign. And by the same reasoning, the crowning of Hal and the rejection of Falstaff are a result of that earlier world's collapse. The final farewell, so long foreseen and so often rehearsed, has arrived.

As they slip into the past, Falstaff and his age acquire a great poignancy, a feeling (unjustified but there nevertheless) of a paradise vanishing. This is partly because they serve as reminders of many other things that have similarly vanished. It is also partly because Falstaff and his world have briefly seemed to be outside time. As A. D. Nuttall notes, "He is an old man but he is also a sort of timeless baby."[88]

From *Citizen Kane* on, Welles used images to slow and trap time. As Charles Affron says about *Kane*, "Its deepest images tug against the narrative's rapid pace, prefiguring their function in the elegiac *The Magnificent Ambersons*"[89] and, as he might have added, prefiguring their function in *Chimes*.

The film is seemingly a reminiscence that grows from the encapsulated scene between Falstaff and Shallow. As a result, Falstaff appears to be remembering all of his life—including his own death, one scene inside another in the same way that the Falstaff and Shallow snow scene is repeated later in the film. In a typically Wellesian paradox, Falstaff becomes a symbol for the lost paradise (in fact, for the paradise that has never been found) and also one of the many people who suffers because it is lost.

At the same time, Welles makes it clear that no image is permanent (indeed no image can be permanent in a film), and therefore it is not within the new king's power to keep Falstaff from being wheeled away in that enormous black coffin any more than it was possible for him to lengthen his father's life or extend his own boyhood. One of *Chimes at Midnight*'s most important achievements is that it puts the rejection of Falstaff in context; like so many of Shallow's friends, he must needs be old and then—to almost everyone's great regret—dead. The flow of time cannot be stopped, even by so large an obstacle. Falstaff's Merrie England—or what passed for it—is gone, and he must go with it. Welles's film makes him a sprawling, charming symbol for his age and, in the process, absolves Hal of the crime of killing the heart of either the world or the man.

Both Joseph McBride[90] and Jack Jorgens, who quotes him,[91] see Falstaff as Hal's victim and the concluding narration from Holinshed, which says of Henry V that he was "so humane withal, he left no offence unpunished nor friendship unrewarded" is taken as simple irony, flatly contradicted by the events of the film. However, McBride's argument has a number of problems and misinterpretations. He reports that "after my book was published, Mr. Welles suggested that my analysis of Hal's conduct here [the reason for Hal's decision to wage war] was mistaken."[92] But this was added as a footnote, not made part of a reworking of the general argument.

McBride also casually mentions "the historical Henry V, who had Sir John Oldcastle, Falstaff's prototype, executed for treason,"[93] as though the situations are essentially parallel. Leaving aside the vexed issue of just how much of John Oldcastle was used to stuff out Jack Falstaff, the historical Henry V's treatment of the Lollard rebel is certainly not a good example of ruthlessness. Oldcastle's conviction for heresy came in 1413, but "execution was stayed at the behest of the king, who endeavored personally to reconvert his friend to orthodoxy."[94] Oldcastle next escaped from the Tower. The "escape may have been arranged with the connivance of the king."[95] If it was so, Henry was not well rewarded for his action. The determined Sir John then organized a revolt and conspiracy whose goal (in addition to wholesale religious and social changes) was the murder (or at least the seizure) of King Henry and his brothers.[96] The revolt was efficiently foiled, but Oldcastle escaped, "and though pardons were afterwards offered . . . yet he would not come in to claim them."[97] In 1417, while Henry was in France, the thirty-nine-year-old knight[98] was taken and "roasted alive as he swung in chains from a gibbet."[99]

In "The Fortunes of Oldcastle," Gary Taylor goes so far as to argue that "when he wrote Part 1, Shakespeare was anticipating a sequel . . . in which Henry's rejection of his old friend might have easily been based . . . on that friend's own treachery (like Scrope's)."[100] Oldcastle was actually implicated in Scrope's plot, and there is a certain logic in Olivier's replacing the traitors with a coconspirator. Is it entirely coincidental that Welles has also rearranged and rewritten in order to connect Falstaff's fate with Vernon and Grey? The shooting script makes Welles's original intention clear; "THE KING SMILES GENTLY AT HIM . . . (GREY AND VERNON ARE FORMER REBELS WHOM THE KING HAS PARDONED)" (170). They are, then, another example of Hal's mercy, a mercy imposed in this case by Orson Welles in direct opposition to Shakespeare's text. But the juxtaposition enhances Hal and links Falstaff with traitors.

I do not mean to suggest by this that Welles (or Olivier either) is doing anything more than blackening Falstaff with a touch of pitch. However, it is, I think, misguided to see the fat knight as a moral as well as comical exemplar.[101] Joseph McBride says, for instance, that Hal's "last words in the film show how much he has deluded himself: 'We consider it was excess of wine that set him on.'"[102] The assumption here is, I suppose, that what set Falstaff on to his foolishly public confrontation with its inevitable ending was excess of love.

This ignores the drunken revelry in which we have seen Falstaff, Shallow, and Silence indulging. Welles highlights the contrast by cutting directly from Hal's "Now call we our high parliament" to Shallow and Silence swinging round and round, arm in arm, while singing silly songs. As the shooting script puts it early in the scene, "THEY HAVE BEEN DRINKING ALL DAY" (150).

Nor is drinking the only vice associated with Falstaff and his cronies. Peter Cowie says that "Poins appears in *Chimes at Midnight* with the status almost of a lover [Hal's], whose ambivalent lines . . . bring a sinister note to the film."[103] That same note is struck in Shallow's house by the effeminate, almost girlish Davy, who knows very quickly about the foul linen of Sir John's men. Indeed, the shooting script, which devotes considerably more time to Shallow's entourage, makes the matter much plainer:

> *Falstaff. (To Shallow.)* This Davy serves you for good uses; he is your
> serving man and your husband . . .
> *Silence. (Continuing his song.)*
> "When flesh is cheap and females dear,
>   And lusty lads roam here and there
>     So merrily,
>   And ever among so merrily!"
> *Falstaff.* I did not think Master Silence had been a man of this mettle.
> *(He gives him a look.)*
>
> ("WSS," 155)

While there are almost certainly homosexual overtones in the original Shakespeare text (*2H4* 5.3),[104] Welles's rearrangement and the casting of Davy suggest he meant to emphasize those overtones.[105] The change from shooting script to film is very probably a matter of shortening the entire work. The audience is left nevertheless with an unsavory portrait of Falstaff's old friend, and the lucent scene of the two men walking in the snow is to some extent darkened, their shared memories—that encapsulated paradise—are seen to contain unsuspected ambiguities.

It is in this atmosphere, after more drinking and drunken singing, that Shallow says, "Peradventure I will with ye to the court." And Falstaff, who apparently still has at least some of his wits about him at this point, is described as "pained at the very notion, but manfully conceals this" ("WSS," 156). When the two of them do come to court, the fat knight's remarks smack more of a boasting tongue than a bursting heart: "Stand there by me, Master Robert Shallow! I will make the king do you grace." Hal's willingness to believe that it was excess of wine is more merciful than some other assumptions he could have made. It is also more in keeping with a reenactment of the life of Orson Welles: the drunkard is rejected but the father—who is Falstaff as well as Henry IV—is loved.

McBride believes that Hal's "fun takes odd and vicious forms. . . . He wants to see Falstaff 'sweat to death' running from the Gad's Hill robbery, wants to expose him as a monstrous liar, wants to 'beat him before his whore.'"[106] The line "Let's beat him before his whore" (*2H4* 2.4.264) belongs, of course, to Poins, not Hal, but none of the viciousness McBride sees is a part of *Chimes*, as the shooting script and the film itself demonstrate. I have previously commented on the warmth of the relationship between the fat knight and the lean prince. Indeed, the tavern scene that McBride cites as an example of Hal's cruelty to Falstaff is instead one in a series of affectionate games that the two of them play.

The shooting script makes Welles's intentions obvious. Hal and Poins are disguised as servants:

> *Doll.* Sirrah . . . what humour's the prince made of?
> *Falstaff. (Calling.)* Francis!
> *Prince Hal. (In a broad Cockney accent.)* Anon, anon—
> FALSTAFF HAS RECOGNIZED HAL, BUT PRETENDS NOT TO. . .
> *Falstaff. (Calls after him.)* Francis—
> *Prince Hal.* Aye, sir
> *Falstaff. (Calls after him.)* Take away these chalices; go brew me a pottle of sack.
> *Prince Hal.* With eggs, sir?
> *Falstaff.* Simple of itself; I'll have no pullet-sperm in my brewage. . . (*To Doll.*) The Prince?
> HAL STOPS AT THE DOOR NOT WANTING TO MISS THIS. . .
>> The prince? Mmmm . . . a good shallow young fellow: a'would have made a good pantler, a would ha' chipped bread well.
>
> ("WSS," 126)

Hal and Poins threaten Falstaff in asides, but in this atmosphere they are not to be taken seriously. The game ends in general mirth:

> HAL SITS DOWN NEXT TO FALSTAFF WHO FINDS HIMSELF STARING INTO THE PRINCE'S GRINNING FACE. . .
> *Prince Hal.* Is it not strange that desire should so many years outlive performance?
> *Falstaff. (Feigning great astonishment.)* Ha!—a bastard son of the king?
> (HAL COLLAPSES WITH LAUGHTER . . . ALL THE OTHERS TAKE THEIR CUE FROM THE PRINCE—EXCEPT FALSTAFF, WHO PLAYS IT DEAD-PAN. . .
>
> ("WSS," 127–28)

Welles made a number of changes when he came to film this scene, including putting Falstaff and Doll Tearsheet on a bed and hiding Hal and Poins in a loft above them. Nevertheless, Falstaff is still in on the secret, and his conversation with Doll remains one of his games with Hal. On Falstaff's line "Let 'em play," there is a cut to Hal and Poins as the prince hits his head and makes a noise. Falstaff seems to be delivering the line "Thou wilt forget me when I'm gone" as much as to Hal as to Doll because he looks away from her and up to where the camera (shooting from Falstaff's view-point) has just caught Hal and Poins replacing the boards they had moved in order to watch.

Throughout the scene, Hal and Poins shuffle about, move boards, and lean out over the edge of the loft. Falstaff looks up after his line "Thou dost give me flattering busses" and again just before Doll's question, "What humour's the Prince made of?" Hal laughs delightedly at Falstaff's "A bastard son of the king" and the fat knight accompanies the words "Why, Hal, I did not think thou wast within hearing" with a quick wink. As Welles himself says, "What is fine, in the character of the prince, is that he is always Falstaff's friend."[107]

In his refutation of McBride, David Bordwell convincingly argues that to see Falstaff as Hal's victim "underestimates Welles' irony." Hal is himself a victim of political circumstance who struggles to aid his friend in private even though he must humiliate him in public. "Even after the rebuff at the coronation, Hal privately (in an inserted text from *Henry V* that originally did not refer to Falstaff (orders his counsellors to 'enlarge' (!) Falstaff."[108]

Welles's filming of the rejection scene fully supports this view and flatly contradicts McBride's idea that Hal's "fun takes odd and vicious forms"[109] and Jorgens's similar point that "finally, it seems, Falstaff is cornered and the triumph will be Hal's."[110] There are grief and fondness here but not triumph.

Hal begins with his back to Falstaff. Even after he turns, he manages to keep his voice harsh and his face stiff until he reaches the words "know the grave doth gape / For thee thrice wider than for other men." Here by force of affection and habit, he smiles at one more shared joke, and Falstaff rises to speak, with, as the shooting script puts it, "THE BEGINNINGS OF A NERVOUS LAUGH" (164). There is a flicker of time when the old man hopes that the game can continue as it always has. Hal has to catch himself and stop Falstaff and go on. The young king keeps his countenance until after the line "Not to come near our person by ten mile." The direction that follows this in the shooting script is, "DEATH IS IN FALSTAFF'S FACE. . . . THE YOUNG KING SEES THIS, AND SPEAKS MORE GENTLY" (164). In fact, Keith Baxter's voice drops into huskiness and almost breaks on the line "For competence of life I will allow you." It is a confession of love and a recognition of the inevitable that Falstaff's smile says he shares. As David Bordwell summarizes, Holinshed's words at the end of the film "constitute not a sarcastic dig but a sublime irony, . . . the richest and most basic one of man's experience, so vast that we usually split it into tragedy and comedy."[111]

It is an inevitable ending, of a world becoming something else, of the past slipping backward and away and glowing briefly as it goes, of a paradise that is an imperfect memory of a place that did not exist and an innocence that cannot be reached except to be destroyed like the encapsulated snow scene in *Citizen Kane* or the apple Poins eats as he walks past Falstaff's coffin.[112] But it is not, ultimately, a simple matter of betrayal, of one good man and one bad one, or of one choice that could have stopped the tide's flow. As William Johnson says, "in *Falstaff*, as in *Ambersons*, the loss of innocence lies in the transition between two historical ages."[113] The film itself has said this again and again in its many farewells and poignancies, from the first grieving for a past age to "the concluding panoramic sweep of the countryside with the fortress in the background [which] shows the fluidity of the passage of time and historical perspective."[114]

It is a part of the large achievement of the film and of Welles as director that he has not allowed his lament for the passing of Falstaff's age to become a condemnation of the one that follows it. Like the Shakesepearean texts he mined for material, Welles's work is a matter of oppositions and of balances. In William Johnson's words, "The struggle between tradition and progress, old and new, order and disorder, is one of the most powerful forces behind Welles's work."[115] It is the very texture of *Chimes at Midnight*.

Certainly a film as complex as the one Orson Welles has created deserves the kind of scholarly attention that has traditionally been given to printed texts. As Joseph McBride says, "A Welles adaptation of Shakespeare is not an *ad hoc* project but the result of a lifetime of scholarship and creative experiment."[116] The videocassette has made it possible to consult such films easily and repeatedly; the rich materials they offer are now readily accessible. Many films, including those of Orson Welles, were made with the idea that they would be watched repeatedly and studied in detail, that, in fact, they could not be evaluated and appreciated until they had been subjected to scholarly process. As Welles put it, "I . . . hope that somebody will see one thing and someone else will see another. . . . I don't think a film should be entirely evident: there should always be something else to see."[117]

# 8
# Conclusion

## Reevaluating Screened Shakespeare

The videocassette makes detailed studies of films possible; in fact, it makes film, television, and video as accessible, as susceptible to the scholarly process, as are novels and poems. These performance texts can help to expand and explain the printed originals from which they are fashioned, when static texts acquire motion and flesh. New interpretations may emerge from the examination of stress and counterstress, from the weighing of gestures and other small signs lost on the immobile inadequacy of the page. Such interpretations may serve as confirmations of or contradictions for other kinds of criticism, a crucible of practice where theories interact and are tested. They form a significant body of criticism, hitherto imperfectly available to scholarly inquiry and serious debate. And these theatrical and filmic touchstones may prove especially valuable indicators in a time when some Shakespeare scholars maintain, as David Norbrook laments, that "there is no objective criterion for the truth of an interpretation," that "the only real arbitration can come from fashion, and from the marketplace."[1]

The four plays and six films examined in the preceding chapters indicate the value of film and the videocassette to the study of Shakespeare. Even the BBC productions, which have generally been regarded as less important, contain critically valuable interpretations that emerge from the dialectic of discovery among producer, director, and actors as central to the films they inform.

Using a modern reading of Richard's time and concentrating on realism and historical accuracy, the BBC *Richard II* challenged the Tillyardian world picture and created a consistently tyrannical but subtly sympathetic Richard, validating much of Shakespeare's history in the process. The BBC *1 and 2 Henry IV* and *Henry V*, benefiting from the chance to do the three plays as a unity, were able to explore the tensions between Hal and Falstaff, the darkness in the fat knight and the purpose in the prince, within the structure of a Henriad, as Hal grows into kingship.

Olivier's *Henry V*, long undervalued as a propaganda piece that emphasizes Henry as warrior, is, in fact, an exploration of the play's metatheatrical (and by extension the film's metacinematic) themes. An examination of the two surviving shooting scripts using the videocassette to make a detailed comparison with the film itself reveals Olivier functioning as an auteur who intentionally deemphasized the violence and foregrounded those elements he saw as central to Shakespeare's meaning.

Writing immediately after Laurence Olivier's death, Brad Darrach called *Henry V* "the first and finest of four movies he adapted from Shakespearean dramas."[2] It is a carefully crafted film that suggests that the play behind it is more complex than some critics have been willing to admit. It is also an innovative film in its own right. In commenting on "the return of the dramatic action to the Globe . . . through non-defined distinctions between medieval France and Elizabethan England on the one hand, and between theatre and cinema on the other," Anthony Davies says that though most critics have failed to notice what the film achieved, and "Jean-Luc Godard is more often credited with being the pioneer in the manipulation of diegetic space in the cinema, . . . Olivier, with *Henry V*, had broken away from single diegesis more than twenty years before."[3]

Orson Welles's *Chimes at Midnight*, a more daring manipulation and compression of Shakepeare's text, was equally carefully constructed. Welles, who described himself as an auteur and functioned as scriptwriter, star, and director, spent, for example, almost three weeks working from "eight thirty in the morning until seven in the evening," editing the battle sequence.[4] As Stanley S. Rubin puts it, "the director must have been imaginatively in possession of Falstaff, as his own creation, prior to beginning work on the film."[5] It was, in Daniel Seltzer's words, "a *reimaging* of the texts. . . . The director's rearrangement . . . emphasizes an underlying statement in Shakespeare's text itself: the *effect*, theatrically, may be supposed to be close to the one intended."[6] The effect is an extremely skillful exploration of the complexities in the Hal/Falstaff/Henry relationship, which energizes the film and explicates the play.

Clearly, there is much to be gained from a detailed examination of Shakespearean filmtexts. Now that technology has made such examinations not only feasible but easy, the primary barrier to future studies is the unexamined prejudices of critics, the expectational texts that should be, but have not yet been, rewritten.

## Revising Expectational Texts

There has been much resistance to filmed Shakespeare and even more resistance to the televised variety. Too often the critic's expectations delimit his perceptions, direct his explorations, and dictate his conclusions. This is especially true for film in its various forms, since both message and medium may be misinterpreted as the result of long-held but seldom-examined notions. Such notions may have been originally naive and therefore invalid or may have been rendered obsolete by technological change. In either case, critical judgments fail.

Sheldon Zitner, for example, sees a danger in shifting from stage to film to television because "the audience changes from active collective to passive collective to passive individual,"[7] and Shakespeare's message may be modified, his very genre changed in the process. This assumes a continuity in theatrical experience between Shakespeare's time and our own, which would be difficult to demonstrate. It also idealizes modern theatergoers as active, when their primary activity may be shuffling their programs and their sole interaction with the stage may be the round of applause they supply at the end of a performance. I have discussed earlier the similarities between the Shakespearean stage and the fluidity of film and television and pointed to the opinions of both Laurence Olivier and John Wilders that Shakespeare was a screenwriter ahead of his time.

Zitner, however, dismisses film and television audiences as "passive." As Roger Ebert describes the filmviewing experience, "the movie image appears—enormous and overwhelming. If the movie is a good one, you allow yourself to be absorbed in its fantasy, and its dreams become part of your memories."[8] If to be unable to influence the performance is to be passive, then this may be so defined, but it seems to me that acquiring and internalizing an experience, whether from a stage, screen, or page, is a sign of active participation, not passive acceptance.

Nevertheless, Roger Ebert himself would call television viewing passive because of the small size of the screen and his inability to lose himself in a television image.[9] Here, technology has clearly changed (and is continuing to change) the circumstances so radically that old definitions and attitudes must be abandoned. The simple watching of television may be a kind of inaction, but the use of a videocassette to fast forward, to repeat, to stop the frame creates an active audience, an audience in control of a medium in a way that is analogous to the active control a reader exercises over a book. In fact, the two processes are being blended so that new computer software systems, called hypertext, "with links to video and audio could make Laurence Olivier's production of *Hamlet* an integral part of reading the play."[10]

Sheldon Zitner admits that "The videotape of *As You Like It* is . . . remarkably better when seen on a four-foot screen in the company of thirty than when watched at home with a cat."[11] This is in part Zitner's prejudice about the nature of audiences, yet it points to the increasing interchangeability of film media, as big-screen television comes closer to merging with the movie experience. Even those critics who deny that there has been any real change will eventually have to face the new technological facts. Roger Ebert, for example, says, "The TV signal has only 625 lines[12] to obtain its information no matter *how* large the screen is, and so a larger screen means a faded picture."[13] But improved-definition large-screen televisions, which solve the problem by getting rid of scanning lines and digitally taking "the median of a million or so individual comparisons,"[14] are already on the market, and true high-definition television and other, even better solutions are not far off.[15] Movies themselves will soon be recorded digitally and distributed by satellite to audiences in theaters and elsewhere, and, as a result, that cineaste's icon, the film reel, will disappear.[16] In the near future, all visual media will be translating the same digital data.

Jack Jorgens complains that television Shakespeare is a "compromise" for the sake of "convenience and cheapness" and that we have traded film's "clarity, subtle colors, and carefully controlled light values" for "nervous, ill-defined images, comic book colors, and blurred night scenes." We have, he says, given up "fine . . . sound making" for "crude music and sound effects." Here again the argument has been and is being invalidated by changing technology. The fine sound of movies can be duplicated on videodisc, videocassette, and even on television. But Jack Jorgens is actually doing what many critics do, condemning the medium of television on the basis of a particular message, in this case the BBC Shakespeares. He says, "Even the best of the BBC's TV series lacks the beauty and power of the film adaptations of Olivier, Welles, Kurosawa, Kozintsev, Brook, and Zeffirelli."[17] He is also condemning underfunded television Shakespeare for being under-funded.

However, lack of funds has long been a problem in filmed as well as televised Shakespere. Orson Welles's project to film *Macbeth* was sold to Republic Studios in 1947 at $700,000.[18] More recently, Charlton Heston struggled desperately to raise the "million and a half dollars"[19] he needed for his 1972 version of *Antony and Cleopatra,* and when he finally came to assemble the film, he was forced to use such expedients as buying outtakes from the galley footage of *Ben Hur.*[20] Polanski's 1971 *Macbeth* cost $3.5 million, and he describes the picture as "ludicrously cheap to make," while pointing out that "Playboy's losses were never recouped."[21] Olivier's situation was even worse. He says of his *Richard III* that "the film's initial flop made it impossible for me to get the money to make *Macbeth*."[22]

This too is a problem that altered circumstances may help to solve. The interchangeability of film media, the ubiquitousness of a particular filmic message, has changed the nature of financing and broadened the possibility for profit as it has increased the diversity of the audience. I have discussed the monetary role of the videocassette in the creation of the BBC Shakespeares. But the role of the videocassette in funding film has expanded enormously since 1978, and "1986 was the year that VCR's surpassed theater box office in revenues for movies."[23] Films, such as Paul Mazurski's adaptation of *The Tempest,* which lost money in theaters, have "been rescued by their appearance on videocassette."[24] Other films, like *Wired,* which reportedly sold its videocassette rights in advance of production for $5 million, have reached the big screen only because of funds from the small one.[25]

In addition to the videocassette, other markets have grown in size and therefore in cultural and economic importance. Satellite and cable television now offer a variety of programming that was previously unthinkable to an audience of whom many were formerly unreachable. For instance, the asking price for Olivier's *Lear,* which aired first in the United States on pay cable, was "more than $1 million."[26] Starting in 1983, first Home Box Office Television and then its competitors, including Showtime and Disney and even Turner Network Television and USA Network, began airing original movies. While such films have budgets that are "usually less than $3 million,"[27] they represent a significant new market for classics, such as TNT's *A Man for All Seasons,* directed by and starring Charlton Heston, as well as for more ephemeral fare.

Energized by these new markets and the demand for film and

video of all kinds, television vaults have op'd and let forth a variety of sleepers, such as a 1954 "live" *Macbeth* with Maurice Evans; George Schaefer's 1960 *Tempest,* where Richard Burton plays Caliban; and a 1968 BBC *Midsummer,* featuring Benny Hill as Bottom. Nor is the activity confined to television studios. Most of the existing Shakespeare films—from Czinner's *As You Like It* and Reinhardt's *Midsummer* to Olivier's *Othello* and Trevor Nunn's *Macbeth*—have been broadcast, videotaped, or both. Full-scale versions of performances (including the audience) have been created at Lincoln Center and at Stratford, Ontario. Bard Productions, a California parallel to the BBC Shakespeare, began filming on a replica of the Globe Theatre (sans audience) in 1981, bypassing television and selling its material exclusively on videocassette. And Shakespeare has returned to the big screen in the form of Kenneth Branagh's multimillion-dollar *Henry V.* Its cast includes Derek Jacobi and Paul Scofield, and Branagh said before the film's release that it was designed to "satisfy the Shakespearean scholar and the punter who likes 'Crocodile Dundee.'"[28]

It may be, then, that innovations in technology and consequent shifts in marketing strategy will make new Shakespeare films financially feasible as they have made previous ones widely available. However, ultimately, filmed and televised Shakespeare will succeed in doing what they are expected, permitted, and funded to do. For instance, filmed Shakespeare is often criticized for its linear nature, for the director's control of what the spectator sees, so that the full-stage picture is cropped by the camera. However, as the deep focus in Joseph Mankiewicz's 1953 *Julius Caesar* and in the films of Orson Welles demonstrates, the full-stage picture can also be filmed. Television is often thought of as a medium that naturally requires realism and revels in close-ups, but some of the BBC's most successful Shakespeares were—as in the case of *The Winter's Tale* and *Henry V*—highly stylized. Even though the BBC project was hampered by lack of funds, what the BBC Shakespeares could afford to do was less important than what the producers and directors thought television Shakespeare was capable of doing and what the "sponsors" thought it should be allowed to do.

A similar set of problems afflicted Olivier's *King Lear.* R. Alan Kimbrough, for instance, recommends that we "resist any rapid conclusions about the differences between film and television as media for dramatic productions, especially of Shakespeare that would result from inferences based on" comparing Olivier's production "with the notable film versions." Kimbrough calls it a "slavishly faithfull [*sic*] performance of Shakespeare's text for a popular television audience . . . presumed interested in or capable of grasping only the most literal visualization of that text."[29] After giving examples of the problems and lack of imagination in the production, Kimbrough sums up: "Sadly, Olivier's *Lear* is simply dated." He offers "by way of contrast . . . David Giles's imaginative use of the medium in the opening of 5.5 for the *Richard II* he directed for the BBC."[30] A major (but not unexpected) irony here is that the scene Kimbrough cites is the bit of nearly "arty-crafty" shooting that made Messina uneasy and that went against the BBC's unacknowledged but largely inescapable "house style."

One additional problem faced by filmed Shakespeare has been an economy and therefore a psychology of scarcity. For years it was assumed that a single filmed version of a Shakespeare play saturated and therefore preempted the market, acquiring status not because it was necessarily "definitive" but because, if nothing else, it was repetitive, the one incarnation of the play most people would see. As a result, critics tended to distrust these solitary beacons, not only because their messages were (before the videocassette) approximately as difficult to study as pulsing signal lights but also because the flickering beams from such isolated sources often did not successfully illuminate the plays.

Paradoxically, then, as Shakespearean films become more common and therefore less important individually, they should be more readily accepted as a vital source of critical interpretations. With five *Midsummer*s and six *Macbeth*s readily available, with *The Tempest* coming to life in three straightforward productions and three adaptations, there should be no danger of a student (or any other audience member) mistaking the film for the text, the incarnation for the original message. Further, with such a range of examples before them, Shakespearean critics should be more willing to examine each film in terms of its own assumptions. It will be one in a series, yet another taped essay on and journey into the play, not a unique challenge to their most cherished assumptions and expectations.

Kenneth Branagh said of his *Henry V*, "I'm not making this film to see if I can score a draw with Olivier, but because I passionately believe that all of Shakespeare's plays need to be constantly reinterpreted."[31] In fact, the value of Branagh's film is greater because Olivier's version exists; Branagh is freer to pursue his own separate interpretation, because while Olivier has not preempted the play, he has traversed the paths to Agincourt and provided a battlefield map. Not surprisingly, some of Branagh's statements, such as "I feel it has been unjustly treated as a jingoistic hymn to England" and "I feel the play is about a journey toward maturity,"[32] have been previously validated onscreen by Olivier and by David Giles and the BBC.

The worst danger to the future of filmed Shakespeare is not insufficient funds but inefficient imaginations. The expectational text can not only hinder the viewer from correctly interpreting the medium, it can also deter the auteur from imaginatively exploring it. However, each new example of filmed, televized, or videotaped Shakespeare helps to rewrite expectational texts, helps to suggest more fully the contours of the play it presents and the medium it represents. The film library that Garrett, Hardison, and Gelfman futilely wished for in 1971 is here, and it is growing daily more technologically sophisticated, more easily controllable, and more firmly linked to other forms of performance and scholarship. If the screen is not *the* means to understanding Shakespeare in the twentieth century, it is certainly becoming one of the most important.

# Notes

## Chapter 1.

## Introduction

1. George P. Garrett, O. B. Hardison, Jr., and Jane R. Gelfman, eds., introduction to *Film Scripts One* (New York: Appleton-Century-Crofts Educational Division, Meredith Corporation, 1971), 7.

2. Ibid., 11.

3. Ibid., 12.

4. Jack Jorgens, *Shakespeare on Film* (Bloomington: Indiana University Press, 1979), 190.

5. Charles W. Eckert, ed., *Focus on Shakespearean Films* (Englewood Cliffs, N.J.: Prentice Hall, 1972), 4.

6. Philip Gaskell's chapter on Stoppard's *Travesties* in *From Writer to Reader: Studies in Editorial Method* discusses the complexities of play texts in detail ([Oxford: Clarendon Press, 1978], 245–62). D. F. McKenzie deals with film as text in *The Panizzi Lectures, 1985: Bibliography and the Sociology of Texts* (London: British Library, 1986), 53–60.

7. Jeremy Treglown, Preface to *"Richard III" by William Shakespeare,* ed. Julie Hankey (London: Junction, 1981), v.

8. Gaskell, *Writer to Reader,* 245.

9. See, for example, Sidney Homan's "A Cinema for Shakespeare," *Literature/Film Quarterly* 4 (1976): 176–86.

10. Cited in Michael Jamieson, "Shakespeare in the Theatre," in *Shakespeare: Select Bibliographical Guides,* ed. Stanley Wells (Oxford: Oxford University Press, 1973), 34.

11. Peter Hall, introduction, in *The Wars of the Roses: Adapted for the Royal Shakespeare Company from William Shakespeare's "Henry VI," Parts I, II, and III and "Richard III,"* by John Barton, in collaboration with Peter Hall (London: British Broadcasting Corporation, 1970), viii.

12. J. Dudley Andrew, *Concepts in Film Theory* (Oxford: Oxford University Press, 1984), 97.

13. Bernice W. Kliman and Kenneth S. Rothwell, "A Tenth Anniversary Editorial," *Shakespeare on Film Newsletter* 11, no. 1 (1986): 6.

14. Susan Sontag, "Film and Theatre," in *Film Theory and Criticism: Introductory Readings,* ed. Gerald Mast and Marshall Cohen, 3d ed. (Oxford: Oxford University Press, 1985), 341; Jorgens, *Shakespeare on Film,* 7; and Donald S. Skoller, "Problems of Transformation in the Adaptation of Shakespeare's Tragedies from Play-Script to Cinema" (Ph.D. diss., New York University, 1968), 570.

15. Jan Kott, *Shakespeare Our Contemporary* (New York: W. W. Norton, 1974), 347.

16. Skoller, "Problems of Transformation," 84.

17. Sontag, "Film and Theatre," 341.

18. Andrew, *The Major Film Theories: An Introduction* (Oxford: Oxford University Press, 1976), 218.

19. John Wilders, "Shakespeare on the Small Screen," *Deutsche Shakespeare-Gesselschaft West Jahrbuch* 1982: 61.

20. John Wilders, "Shakespeare and Television: A Marriage of True Minds?" De Quincy Society Lecture, Worcester College, Oxford, 3 November 1986.

21. Roger Manvell, *Shakespeare and the Film* (New York: A. S. Barnes, 1979), 120.

22. Robert Darrell Jackson, *"Romeo and Juliet* on Film: A Comparative Analysis of Three Major Film Versions of Shakespeare's Play" (Ph.D. diss., Wayne State University, 1978), 118.

23. Peter Davison, *"Hamlet": Text and Performance* (London: Macmillan, 1983), 54.

24. Garrett, Hardison, and Gelfman, *Film Scripts One,* 11.

25. Ibid.

26. Skoller, "Problems of Transformation," 17–18.

27. Ibid., 18.

28. David Bordwell, *"Citizen Kane," Film Comment* 7, no. 2 (1971): 47; and Jorgens, *Shakespeare on Film,* 121.

29. All references to act, scene, and line numbers of Shakespeare's plays are to *The Complete Signet Classic Shakespeare,* ed. Sylvan Barnet (New York: Harcourt, 1972).

30. Orson Welles, "Falstaff (Chimes at Midnight): Un film d'ORSON WELLES, d'apres SHAKESPEARE, LISTE DE DIALOGUES ANGLAIS," Dialogue release script, The Shakespeare Institute, University of Birmingham, 96.

31. Orson Welles, "Chimes at Midnight," Shooting script, Northwestern University Library, Special Collections Department, 168.

32. Lorne Michael Buchman, "From the Globe to the Screen: An Interpretive Study of Shakespeare Through Film (Welles, Kozintsev)" (Ph.D. diss., Stanford University, 1984), 136 n. 4.

33. This is scene 21 in the dialogue script (68); it is scene 22 in the shooting script (115).

34. Charles Higham, *Orson Welles: The Rise and Fall of an American Genius* (London: New English Library, 1986), 308.

35. Charles Higham, *The Films of Orson Welles* (Berkeley: University of California Press, 1970), 172.

36. Barbara Hodgdon, "Two *King Lears:* Discovering the Film Text," *Literature/Film Quarterly* 11 (1983): 143.

37. Jorgens, *Shakespeare on Film,* 121.

38. Buchman, "From Globe to Screen," 132.

39. Jackson, *"Romeo and Juliet* on Film," 128–129.

40. Charlton Heston, *The Actor's Life: Journals, 1956–76,* ed. Hollis Alpert (New York: Dutton, 1978), 208.

41. Leslie Halliwell, *Halliwell's Filmgoer's Companion* (London: Granada, 1984), 112.

42. S. F. Bathrick, "Independent Woman, Doomed Sister," in *The Modern American Novel and the Movies,* ed. Gerald Peary and Roger Shatzkin (New York: Frederick Ungar, 1978), 147, 149.

43. Ingrid Bergman and Alan Burgess, *Ingrid Bergman: My Story* (London: Michael Joseph, 1980), 118.

44. Ibid., 119.

45. Heston, *Actor's Life*, 141.

46. Laurence Leamer, *As Time Goes By: The Life of Ingrid Bergman* (New York: Harper, 1986), 90.

47. Umberto Eco, "*Casablanca:* Cult Movies and Intertextual Collage," in *Travels in Hyperreality: Essays*, trans. William Weaver (London: Picador, 1987), 198.

48. There are two extant shooting scripts for Olivier's *Henry V,* a final shooting script and an earlier version of the shooting script. The only reference to the final shooting script I have found is in Sandra Sugarman Singer's "Laurence Olivier Directs Shakespeare: A Study in Film Authorship" (Ph.D. diss., Northwestern University, 1979). She cites it twice in footnotes but does not make use of it in her main text. The earlier version of the shooting script is held by the Birmingham Public Library and has not to my knowledge been used before in any study of the film. There are three extant scripts for *Chimes at Midnight*, a final shooting script, a dialogue release script, and a continuity script. Anthony Davies includes the dialogue release script in the bibliography of his doctoral dissertation but does not cite it in the chapter he devotes to *Chimes*. The final shooting script has hitherto been used only by Robert Hapgood in his 1986 *Shakespeare Survey* (39 [1986]: 39–52) article, "*Chimes at Midnight* from Stage to Screen." Even Bridget Gellert Lyons's continuity script (*"Chimes at Midnight"/Orson Welles, Director* [New Brunswick, N.J.: Rutgers University Press, 1988]) does not seem to have employed the shooting script (she makes no attempt to correlate her shot numbers with Welles's scene numbers), and as a result, many important actions and reactions go unreported. But this is a common problem for release and continuity scripts as future chapters indicate.

## Chapter 2. The BBC Shakespeare Series

1. Russell Miller, "And Now, the BBC's Schoolgirl Juliet," *The Sunday Times,* 29 January 1978, 32.

2. John Wilders, Personal interview, 15 June 1987.

3. Harry M. Geduld, *Filmguide to "Henry V"* (Bloomington: Indiana University Press, 1973), 48.

4. Henry Fenwick, "The Production," in *The BBC TV Shakespeare: "Richard II"* (London: The British Broadcasting Corporation 1978), 19.

5. Kenneth S. Rothwell, "'The Shakespeare Plays': *Hamlet* and the Five Plays of Season Three," *Shakespeare Quarterly* 32 (1981): 395.

6. Stanley Wells, "Television Shakespeare," *Shakespeare Quarterly* 33 (1982): 265.

7. James C. Bulman, "The BBC Shakespeare and 'House Style,'" *Shakespeare Quarterly* 35 (1984): 572. Robin Stringer quotes him as saying, "There's a temptation to think you are setting up a definitive canon. . . . But that's impossible" ("Miller's Spartan TV Bard," *Daily Telegraph*, 22 June 1979, 19).

8. Wells, "Television Shakespeare," 265.

9. Cedric Messina, "Interview: Cedric Messina Discusses *The Shakespeare Plays*," with John F. Andrews, *Shakespeare Quarterly* 30 (1979): 134.

10. Cedric Messina, Preface, in *The BBC TV Shakespeare: "Richard II"* (London: British Broadcasting Corporation, 1978), 7.

11. Cited in Michael Mullin, "Shakespeare USA: The BBC Plays and American Education," *Shakespeare Quarterly* 35 (1984): 582.

12. Messina, *R2*, 8.

13. Bulman, "*BBC* Shakespeare and 'House Style,'" 572.

14. Mullin, "Shakespeare USA," 584.

15. Cited in Martin Banham, "BBC Television's Dull Shakespeares," in *Shakespeare's Wide and Universal Stage*, ed. C. B. Cox and D. J. Palmer (Manchester: Manchester University Press, 1984), 50; italics mine.

16. Bulman, "BBC Shakespeare and 'House Style,'" 572.

17. Graham Holderness, "Radical Potentiality and Institutional Closure," in *Political Shakespeare: New Essays in Cultural Materialism*, ed. Jonathan Dollimore and Alan Sinfield (Manchester: Manchester University Press, 1985), 194.

18. Richard Last, "'Shakespeare' Creates Boxed-In Feeling," *Daily Telegraph*, 11 December 1978, 11.

19. Wells, "Television Shakespeare," 267.

20. Stringer, "Miller's Spartan TV Bard," 19.

21. Rothwell, "'Shakespeare Plays,'" 395.

22. Mullin, "Shakespeare USA," 588.

23. *Shakespeare on Film Newsletter* for April 1984 in "Shakespeare on Video: Good News for Teachers" (8.2 [1984]: 9) lists the price of Olivier's *H5* on VHS or Beta as $69; Zeffirelli's *Rom.* is $66.95; and Welles's *Mac.* is $59 in the same formats.

24. Wilders, "Shakespeare on the Small Screen," 57.

25. Ibid.

26. Ibid.

27. Russell Miller, "BBC's Schoolgirl Juliet," 32.

28. Bulman, "BBC Shakespeare and 'House Style,'" 573.

29. Wells, "Television Shakespeare," 268–69. Miller had originally hoped to work with Peter Brook and Ingmar Bergman (Stringer, "Miller's Spartan TV Bard," 19).

30. Messina, "Interview," 137.

31. Bulman, "BBC Shakespeare and 'House Style,'" 573. Because the BBC did not have the option of developing its own acting company, it was more likely to choose actors who had already succeeded in the roles under consideration. Sean Day-Lewis asks, "Would the BBC not have done better to assemble its own Shakespeare company for the sake of necessary stylistic unity and ensemble acting? There can be little doubt about this, but when the idea was put to Equity the union turned it down flat" ("Giving Shakespeare the Works," *Daily Telegraph*, 11 December 1978, 10).

32. Messina, *R2*, 8.

33. Cited in Virginia M. Carr, review of *Measure for Measure*, by William Shakespeare, BBC-TV/Time-Life Inc. Production, PBS Stations, 11 April 1979, "The Shakespeare Plays on TV: Season One," *Shakespeare on Film Newsletter* 4, no. 1 (1979): 5.

34. Messina, *R2*, 6.

35. Wilders, "Shakespeare and Television." (Taped lecture.)

36. The actual order of shooting for the first season was *Much Ado About Nothing, Romeo and Juliet, Richard II, As You Like It, Julius Caesar,* and *Henry VIII* (Messina, "Interview," 136).

37. Jack Jorgens, "The BBC-TV Shakespeare Series," *Shakespeare Quarterly* 30 (1979): 411.

38. Wells, "Television Shakespeare," 263.

39. Wilders, Personal interview.

40. Philip Purser, "Going Round Again," *The Sunday Telegraph*, 18 February

1979, 13; Sylvia Clayton, "Caesar Dominates a Cautious Production," *Daily Telegraph*, 12 February 1979, 11; Sean Day-Lewis, "Naturalism Overcomes the Bard," *Daily Telegraph*, 18 December 1978, 9; and Sylvia Clayton, "Shakespeare Played Safe Without Tears," *Daily Telegraph*, 4 December 1978, 15.

41. Sean Day-Lewis reported on 11 December 1978 that "The biggest problem for Shaun Sutton and his staff is getting plays 'serviced,' having them edited, even finding people to do make-up for actors" ("Giving Shakespeare the Works," 10).

42. Geduld, *Filmguide to "Henry V*," 22–24.

43. Ronald Gottesman, ed., *Focus on Orson Welles* (Englewood Cliffs, N.J.: Prentice Hall, 1976), 209.

44. Day-Lewis, "Giving Shakespeare the Works," 10; Mullin, "Shakespeare USA," 582.

45. That these figures are roughly accurate is confirmed by Robin Stringer, who reports, " 'Much Ado About Nothing' . . . was scrapped . . . at a cost of about £170,000" ("Miller's Spartan TV Bard," 19).

46. *Richard II* "was recorded between 12 and 17 April 1978" (BBC *R2*, 28); *Henry IV, Part I* "was recorded between 7 and 12 March 1979" (BBC *1H4*, 29); *Henry IV, Part 2* "was recorded between 11 and 16 April 1979" (BBC *2H4*, 27); and *Henry V* "was recorded between 18 and 25 June 1979" (BBC *H5*, 27).

47. Wells, "Television Shakespeare," 270.

48. Henry Fenwick, "The Production," in *The BBC TV Shakespeare: "Henry IV, Part I"* (London: British Broadcasting Corporation 1979), 25.

49. Geduld, *Filmguide to "Henry V*," 22.

50. Fenwick, *1H4*, 25.

51. Messina, "Interview," 136.

## Chapter 3. The BBC *Richard II*

1. Mary Ellen O'Brien, *Film Acting: The Techniques and History of Acting for the Camera* (New York: Arco, 1983), 100.

2. It happens, for instance, at 1.3.183, 207, 216, 242, 249, 254, 295, 303, 305, and 307.

3. Cited Carr, Review of *Measure for Measure*, 5.

4. Clive James, *The Crystal Bucket: Television Criticism from the "Observer," 1976–79* (London: Jonathan Cape, 1981), 158.

5. Jorgens, "BBC-TV Shakespeare," 414.

6. BBC *R2*, 49.

7. Michael Manheim, review of *Richard II*, by William Shakespeare, BBC-TV/Time-Life Inc. Production, PBS Stations, 28 March 1979, "The Shakespeare Plays on TV: Season One," *Shakespeare on Film Newsletter* 4, no. 1. (1979): 5.

8. Fenwick, *R2*, 19.

9. Purser, "Going Round Again," 13.

10. Fenwick, *R2*, 20.

11. Ibid.

12. Cedric Messina, "Interview," 136–37.

13. Ibid., 137.

14. In Messina's defense, I note that even some reviewers were by no means eager for the Bardathon. Philip Purser described the project as "an admirable service to Shakespeare, but not necessarily a service to television" ("In Tight

Focus," *Sunday Telegraph,* 17 December 1978, 15). And Russell Miller felt that at least some of the plays could be dispensed with. "Titus Andronicus [*sic*] is widely considered to be unwatchable and Timothy of Athenea [*sic*] is unlikely to attract a mass audience. So why include them?" ("BBC's Schoolgirl Juliet," 32).

15. Evidently one other motive here is to avoid copying the Olivier *Henry V,* which had used *The Book of Hours.*

16. Fenwick, *R2,* 20–21.

17. Ibid., 20.

18. A similar example emerges from the first season's production of *Julius Caesar.* The director, Herbert Wise, was chosen by Messina largely because of his experience with *I Claudius.* " 'If anybody knows a toga, he does,' says Messina" (Henry Fenwick, "The Production," in *The BBC TV Shakespeare: "Julius Caesar"* [London: British Broadcasting Corporation, 1979], 20). Wise rejected the idea of dressing the play in Elizabethan costume with the words, "I don't think that's right for the audience we will be getting. . . . For an audience many of whom won't have seen the play before, I believe it would only be confusing" (20).

19. Fenwick, *R2,* 21.

20. David Bevington, *The Oxford Shakespeare: "Henry IV, Part I"* (Oxford: Oxford University Press, 1987), 84–85.

21. Patrick McGilligan, *Cagney: The Actor as Auteur* (New York: Da Capo Press, 1979), 199.

22. Ibid., 202.

23. Ibid.

24. Manheim, "Shakespeare on TV," 5.

25. Fenwick, *R2,* 24.

26. Wilders, "Shakespeare on the Small Screen," 57.

27. Stanley Wells, *Royal Shakespeare: Four Major Productions at Stratford-upon-Avon* (Manchester: Manchester University Press, 1979), 68–69.

28. Fenwick, *R2,* 20.

29. Russell Miller, "BBC's Schoolgirl Juliet," 32.

30. Fenwick, *1H4,* 21.

31. Ibid., 19.

32. Ibid., 20.

33. Jonathan Miller, "Interview; Jonathan Miller on *The Shakespeare Plays,*" with Tom Hallinan, *Shakespeare Quarterly* 32 (1981): 137.

34. Malcolm Page, *"Richard II": Text and Performance* (London: Macmillan, 1987), 55. Sean Day-Lewis said, for example, "In my view the first season has contained three duds ('Romeo and Juliet,' 'As You Like It,' and 'Julius Caesar') and three successes ('Richard II,' 'Measure for Measure,' and 'Henry VIII')" ("Years of the Bard," *Daily Telegraph,* 5 March 1979, 11).

35. Sheldon P. Zitner, "Wooden O's in Plastic Boxes: Shakespeare and Television," *University of Toronto Quarterly* 51 (1981): 7.

36. Banham, "BBC Television's Dull Shakespeares," 50.

37. For discussions of this much-praised production, see Peter Thomson, "Shakespeare Straight and Crooked: A Review of the 1973 Season at Stratford," *Shakespeare Survey* 27 (1974): 151–54; Wells, *Royal Shakespeare,* 64–81; Page, *R2,* 57–68; and Richard David, *Shakespeare in the Theatre* (Cambridge: Cambridge University Press, 1978), 164–74.

38. Fenwick, *1H4,* 20.

39. Samuel Crowl, Review of *Henry IV, Part 1,* by William Shakespeare, BBC-TV/Time-Life Inc. Production, PBS Stations, 26 March 1980, "The Shakespeare Plays on TV: Season Two," *Shakespeare on Film Newsletter* 5, no. 1 (1980): 3.

40. Manheim, "Shakespeare on TV," 5.

41. Holderness, "Radical Potentiality," 197.

42. In Holderness's own words, "Messina saw the history plays conventionally as orthodox Tudor historiography, and the director employed dramatic techniques which allow that ideology a free and unhampered passage to the spectator" (Ibid., 197).

43. Ibid.

44. Fenwick, *R2*, 24.

45. In 1973, "Gloucester's widow was played as a ghost, emerging from the downstage grave-trap with a skull in her hand, and speaking with the aid of echo effects" (Thomson, "Shakespeare Straight and Crooked," 152). "This created a melodramatic impression which exemplified the dangers of stylisation, and in 1974 she simply entered from the wings and spoke quietly, though she still carried the skull" (Wells, *Royal Shakespeare*, 69).

46. Paul Johnson, *"Richard II,"* in *Shakespeare in Perspective*, ed. Roger Sales vol. 1, (London: British Broadcasting Corporation, 1982), 35.

47. Ibid., 34.

48. E. M. W. Tillyard, *Shakespeare's History Plays* (London: Chatto and Windus, 1951), 261.

49. Ian Richardson, *"Richard II,"* in *Shakespeare in Perspective*, ed. Roger Sales vol. 1, (London: British Broadcasting Corporation, 1982), 39.

50. Ibid., 41, 43.

51. Fenwick, *R2*, 22.

52. "Wilders Interview at MLA," *Shakespeare on Film Newsletter* 4.1 (1979): 3.

53. Robert Hapgood, "Shakespeare on Film and Television," in *The Cambridge Companion to Shakespeare Studies*, ed. Stanley Wells (Cambridge: Cambridge University Press, 1986), 279.

54. Holderness, "Radical potentiality," 197.

55. Peter Saccio, *Shakespeare's English Kings: History, Chronicle, and Drama* (New York: Oxford University Press, 1987), 4.

56. J. L. Kirby, *Henry IV of England* (London: Constable, 1970), 2.

57. Fenwick, *R2*, 22.

58. Richard David, for example, maintains that the issues in *Richard II* "cannot be appreciated without some identification with the Elizabethans" (*Shakespeare in the Theatre*, 45).

59. John Gielgud, "King Richard the Second," in *Shakespeare "Richard II": A Casebook*, ed. Nicholas Brooke (London: Macmillan, 1978), 77.

60. In John Neville's words, "there are two different characters. . . . We quite blatantly made no attempt to link the two; he came back from Ireland a different man" (cited in Page, *R2*, 20).

61. Fenwick, *R2*, 22.

62. John Russell Brown, "Narrative and Focus: *Richard II*," in *Shakespeare "Richard II": A Casebook*, ed. Nicholas Brooke (London: Macmillan, 1978), 84.

63. Ibid., 85.

64. Andrew Gurr, ed., *King Richard II* (Cambridge: Cambridge University Press, 1984), 22.

65. W. B. Yeats, "At Stratford-on-Avon (1901)," in *Shakespeare "Richard II": A Casebook*, ed. Nicholas Brooke (London: Macmillan, 1978), 70.

66. Gurr, *King Richard II*, 22.

67. J. L. Kirby's *Henry IV of England* (1970) and Marie Louise Bruce's *The Usurper King: Henry of Bolingbroke, 1366–99* (London: Rubicon Press, 1986)

share this vision of Richard. I am not making the claim that Kirby's book influenced the production or that the production influenced Bruce's book. I am using them only as parallel examples of a particular interpretation that can be a means of organizing both historical and theatrical materials.

68. Theodore Weiss, *The Breath of Clowns and Kings: Shakespeare's Early Comedies and Histories* (London: Chatto and Windus, 1971), 260.

69. Bruce, *Usurper King*, 69.

70. Ibid., 71.

71. Ibid., 72.

72. Ibid., 73.

73. Kirby, *Henry IV*, 25.

74. Bruce, *Usurper King*, 75–76, 80.

75. Ibid., 156.

76. Ibid., 160.

77. Kirby, *Henry IV*, 45.

78. Bruce, *Usurper King*, 164.

79. Ibid., 165.

80. Ibid., 172.

81. "So called not because it was empty of words . . . but because it gave Richard carte blanche to do more or less as he wished with the property of the unfortunate person whose name appeared on it" (ibid., 172–73).

82. Ibid., 172–73.

83. Ibid., 173.

84. Kirby, *Henry IV*, 46.

85. Ibid., 47–49. Mowbray's punishment was more severe in fact than Shakespeare shows it to be. Mowbray was allowed to live only in Prussia, Bohemia, Hungary, or among the Saracens (Bruce, *Usurper King*, 188). As Kirby rather caustically remarks, "There would soon be insufficient countries in Europe to house all the exiles whom Richard fondly hoped to keep apart" (*Henry IV*, 49).

86. Fenwick, *R2*, 22.

87. Ibid., 23.

88. Richard Last writes in his review of the BBC *Richard II*, "Apart from historical shortcomings (Shakespeare seems to have stood in the same relationship to the Tudors as Shostakovich to the Soviet tyrants)" ("'Shakespeare' Creates Boxed-In Feeling," 15).

89. F. W. Brownlow, *Two Shakespearean Sequences: "Henry VI" to "Richard II" and "Pericles" to "Timon of Athens"* (London: Macmillan, 1977), 98.

90. Saccio, *Shakespeare's English Kings*, 20.

91. Kirby, *Henry IV*, 24. Bruce says he "outspokenly criticised Richard, whom he despised as an incompetent ruler" (*Usurper King*, 62). But his criticisms could well have been the plain truth. In Kirby's words, "Richard had already shown himself completely lacking in all those qualities of tact and statesmanship that were required of a king" (*Henry IV*, 24).

92. Even that other Gloucester in *Richard III*, which is sometimes supposed to be the least historical of the history plays, has gotten support in Desmond Seward's 1983 biography, *Richard III: England's Black Legend* (London: Country Life Books, 1983). Seward says, "Shakespeare was nearer the truth than some of the King's latter-day defenders" (15).

93. Bruce, *Usurper King*, 62.

94. Saccio, *Shakespeare's English Kings*, 20.

95. Kirby, *Henry IV*, 23, and Bruce, *Usurper King*, 61.

96. Kirby, *Henry IV,* 18.

97. Bruce, *Usurper King,* 59.

98. Ibid., 96.

99. Ibid., 166.

100. Ibid., 211.

101. Manheim, "Shakespeare on TV," 5.

102. Wells, *Royal Shakespeare,* 74.

103. Aldous Huxley, *The Devils of Loudun* (London: Chatto and Windus, 1952), 324.

104. Cutting the reference to Hal is curious in a production of *Richard II* that was to be followed immediately by *1 Henry IV.* Perhaps the cut was designed (like the omission of Exeter's penitence and his praise of Richard at 5.5.113–18, and the list of executed traitors given to Henry IV at 5.6.5–18) to present Bolingbroke in a favorable light.

105. Jorgens, "The BBC-TV Shakespeare Series," 413.

106. James, *Crystal Bucket,* 158–59.

107. Manheim, "Shakespeare on TV," 5.

108. Barbara Leaming, *Polanski: The Filmmaker as Voyeur* (New York: Simon and Schuster, 1981), 121.

109. Fenwick, *1H4,* 24.

110. Ibid.

111. Leaming, *Polanski,* 121.

112. Fenwick, *1H4,* 24.

113. James, *Crystal Bucket,* 158–59.

114. Bruce, *Usurper King,* 204.

115. Roland Mushat Frye, *The Renaissance "Hamlet": Issues and Responses in 1600* (Princeton: Princeton University Press, 1984), 45.

116. Fenwick, *2H4,* 20.

117. Jorgens, "BBC-TV Shakespeare," 413.

118. James, *Crystal Bucket,* 158.

119. Ibid.

120. Fenwick, *R2,* 25. Messina says, "I wanted from the first to get Derek Jacobi," and Jacobi was, in fact, the first actor to be cast (Fenwick, *R2,* 25).

121. James, *Crystal Bucket,* 158.

122. Derek Jacobi, "Hamlet," in *Shakespeare in Perspective,* ed. Roger Sales vol. 1, (London: British Broadcasting Corporation, 1982), 186.

123. Fenwick, *R2,* 22–23.

124. Richardson, *R2,* 40.

125. Bruce, *Usurper King,* 149–50.

126. Kirby, *Henry IV,* 52.

127. Bruce, *Usurper King,* 185.

128. BBC *R2,* 43.

129. A. R. Humphreys, *Shakespeare: "Richard II"* (London: Edward Arnold, 1967), 31.

130. Frye, *Renaissance "Hamlet,"* 38–39.

131. Ibid., 40.

132. As Marie Louise Bruce puts it "to disinherit Henry was even more perilous, because the injustice of it outraged public opinion and made the king seem more than ever a tyrant" (*Usurper King,* 194). This is an unthinkable thought, to which even York has been pushed.

133. The historical Richard was, as perhaps all kings must be, an actor. But

there is evidence that hypocritical performance was part of his nature. Marie Louise Bruce refers to "yet another of the king's beloved charades. . . . With artistry he acted the part of the wronged monarch finally driven to magnanimous mercy at the pleas of his stricken subjects" (ibid., 125).

134. Gaunt himself was a "staunch believer in royal absolutism" (ibid., 153).

135. Bolingbroke is, as Shakespeare is about to demonstrate, peculiarly vulnerable to counterrevolutions. As Ruth Bird relates, "while Richard was a captive at Coventry, a deputation arrived from London to beg for the execution of Richard before he is brought any further," because they feared his retaliation if he regained power (*The Turbulent London of Richard II* [London: Longman, Green and Co., 1949], 110).

136. Fenwick, *R2,* 26.

## Chapter 4. The BBC First and Second *Henry IV*

1. Richard Last, "Masterly Falstaff from Quayle," *Daily Telegraph,* 10 December 1979, 15.

2. Bevington, *Oxford Shakespeare: 1H4,* 84.

3. Crowl, Review of *1H4,* 3.

4. Wilders, "Shakespeare and Television."

5. Fenwick, *1H4,* 20.

6. Ibid.

7. Maurice Charney, "Shakespearean Anglophilia: The BBC-TV Series and American Audiences," *Shakespeare Quarterly* 31 (1980): 288.

8. Ibid., 289.

9. Fenwick, *1H4,* 20.

10. Ibid.

11. Last, "Masterly Falstaff from Quayle," 15.

12. There are, for instance, in *1H4,* framing difficulties at 1.1.63, 86; shortly after 1.2.61; 2.3.32, 34; and 3.1.136. There are similar problems in *2H4* at 4.1.97 and 4.4.13.

13. Such shots occur at *1H4* 2.4.96 and 4.3.32, and in *2H4* at 1.2.105; 2.1.86; and 4.1.83.

14. T. F. Wharton, *"Henry the Fourth," Parts 1 & 2: Text and Performance* (London: Macmillan, 1983), 45.

15. Michael Church, "*Henry IV* BBC 2," *The Times,* 17 December 1979, 7.

16. "There is evidence that Henry was a bigot even as Prince of Wales. . . . In 1409 he personally superintended the burning of a Lollard tailor, John Badby" (Desmond Seward, *Henry V As Warlord* [London: Sidgwick and Jackson, 1987], 34).

17. Ibid., 27–28.

18. Fenwick, *2H4,* 20.

19. Seward, *Henry V As Warlord,* 22.

20. Kirby, *Henry IV,* 195.

21. Bruce, *Usurper King,* 122.

22. Banham, "BBC Television's Dull Shakespeares," 52.

23. In *Metadrama in Shakespeare's Henriad: "Richard II" to "Henry V"* (Berkeley: University of California Press, 1979), James L. Calderwood credits Alvin B. Kernan with originating the term (1). (Alvin B. Kernan, ed. "The Henriad: Shakespeare's Major History Plays," in *Modern Shakespearean Criticism: Essays on*

*Style, Dramaturgy, and the Major Plays* [Harcourt, Brace and World, Inc., 1970], 245).

24. Messina, "Interview," 137.

25. When he began the project, Messina "was described by a BBC spokesman as 'our Mr. Shakespeare'" (Russell Miller, "BBC's Schoolgirl Juliet," 32). Less than two years later, "Alasdair Milne, BBC Television's managing director, said it had never been intended that one man should supervise the entire six-year Shakespeare project" (Stringer, "Miller's Spartan TV Bard," 19).

26. BBC *2H4*, 29.

27. Wilders, Personal interview.

28. Wharton, *1 and 2H4: Text and Performance*, 54.

29. Crowl, Review *1H4*, 3.

30. Charney, "Shakespearean Anglophilia," 288.

31. Fenwick, *1H4*, 24.

32. Wharton, *1 and 2H4: Text and Performance*, 52.

33. Russell Davies, "The Nightmare Results of a Designer's Dream," *The Sunday Times*, 16 December 1979, 41.

34. Not all judgments of Finch's acting were negative. Michael Church wrote, "He delivers the great speeches with a musical strength which carries no implication of sound dominating sense" (*"Henry IV* BBC 2," 7).

35. Fenwick, *1H4*, 24.

36. Richard Last calls "Bolingbroke almost too good to ring true" (" 'Shakespeare' Creates Boxed-in Feeling," 11).

37. Crowl, *Review 1H4*, 3.

38. Ibid.

39. James Winny, *The Player King: A Theme of Shakespeare's Histories* (London: Chatto and Windus, 1968), 101.

40. C. L. Barber, *Shakespeare's Festive Comedy: A Study of Dramatic Form and its Relation to Social Custom* (Princeton: Princeton University Press, 1972), 218.

41. D. J. Palmer, "Casting off the Old Man: History and St. Paul in *Henry IV*," *Critical Quarterly* 12 (1970): 282.

42. James G. Frazer, *The Golden Bough: A Study in Magic and Religion* (London: Macmillan, 1983), 755.

43. Fenwick, *1H4*, 22–23.

44. Bruce, *Usurper King*, 248.

45. Fenwick, *1H4*, 23.

46. Wharton, *1 and 2H4: Text and Performance*, 45.

47. Ibid.

48. Ibid., 52.

49. Ibid.

50. Fenwick, *1H4*, 25.

51. Judith Cook, *Shakespeare's Players: A Look at Some of the Major Roles in Shakespeare and Those who have Played Them* (London: Harrap, 1983), 71.

52. Ibid.

53. Ibid., 73.

54. Ibid., 72.

55. David, *Shakespeare in the Theatre*, 201. Sylvan Barnet's description of Quayle's stage Falstaff makes clear a number of similarities in the performances ("Henry IV, Part One on Stage and Screen," in *The History of "Henry IV" (Part One)*, ed. Maynard Mack [New York: Signet, 1987], 276).

56. Robert Speaight, *Shakespeare: The Man and His Achievement* (London: J. M. Dent and Sons, 1977), 179.

57. Charney, "Shakespearean Anglophilia," 288.
58. Last, "Masterly Falstaff from Quayle," 15.
59. Church, *Henry IV*, BBC 2," 7.
60. Charney, "Shakespearean Anglophilia," 289.
61. Cook, *Shakespeare's Players*, 72.
62. Crowl, Review *1H4*, 3–4.
63. Wharton, *1 and 2H4: Text and Performance*, 62.
64. Ibid., 64.
65. Davies, "Nightmare Results," 41.
66. Cook, *Shakespeare's Players*, 71.
67. Charney, "Shakespearean Anglophilia," 288.
68. Fenwick, *1H4*, 23.
69. Crowl, Review *1H4*, 4.
70. Fenwick, *1H4*, 26.
71. Fenwick, *2H4*, 24.
72. Wharton, *1 and 2H4: Text and Performance*, 62–63.
73. Ibid., 63.
74. Ibid.
75. As John Wilders puts it, "In acknowledging the Lord Chief Justice as his father, as he calls him, Henry V implicitly disowns the 'father ruffian' Falstaff" ("Introduction to *Henry IV, Part 2*," in *The BBC-TV Shakespeare: "Henry IV, Part 2"* [London British Broadcasting Corporation, 1979], 16).
76. Crowl, Review *1H4*, 3.
77. Fenwick, *2H4*, 24.
78. Fenwick, *2H4*, 19.
79. Kenneth Rothwell complains that due to the camera work in the BBC *Hamlet*, "There is acting but not interacting. The loss of the facial expression of a listener concentrating on a speaker deprives the audience of an important element in the actors' craft" ("'The Shakespeare Plays,'" 396). In *2 Henry IV* David Giles has deliberately and effectively used a similar technique in the service of his interpretation.
80. David Margolies, "Shakespeare, the Telly and the Miners," *Red Letters* 17 (March 1985): 42.
81. The tears do have an effect. As Russell Davies described the shot, "Quayle produced a face so shocked that it seemed to be held together only by its tears" ("Shakespeare in Close-up," *The Sunday Times*, 23 December 1979, 43).
82. Cook, *Shakespeare's Players*, 72.
83. Frazer, *Golden Bough*, 768.
84. For James L. Calderwood, too, Falstaff "keeps asserting his 'real' identity as a performer, imposing theatricality on history" (74).
85. Barber, *Shakespeare's Festive Comedy*, 213.
86. Ibid., 214.
87. Fenwick, *2H4*, 19.
88. Ibid.
89. Cook, *Shakespeare's Players*, 72.
90. Leonard Tennenhouse, *Power on Display: The Politics of Shakespeare's Genres* (London: Methuen, 1986), 79–80. J. I. M. Stewart says, "I suggest that Hal, by a displacement common enough in the evolution of ritual, kills Falstaff instead of killing the king, his father. In a sense, Falstaff *is* his father. . . . And Falstaff, in standing for the old king, symbolizes all the accumulated sin of the reign, all the consequent sterility of the land" (*Character and Motive in Shakespeare: Some Recent Appraisals Examined* [London: Longmans, Green and Co., 1965], 138).

91. Charney, "Shakespearean Anglophilia," 289.

92. It is possible to read the soliloquy as Hal's confession that he is deceiving the people around him and see him, therefore, as similar to other characters who practice deceptions. But the situation is far more complex than Charney indicates. See, for instance, A. D. Nuttall's discussion of Hal as a "White Machiavel" (*A New Mimesis: Shakespeare and the Representation of Reality* [London: Methuen, 1983], 143–61).

93. Crowl, Review *1H4*, 3.

94. Peter Saccio, Rev. *Henry the Fourth, Part 2*, by William Shakespeare, BBC-TV/Time-Life Inc. Production, PBS Stations, 9 April 1980, "The Shakespeare Plays on TV: *Henry the Fourth, Part Two*," *Shakespeare on Film Newsletter* 6, no. 1 (1982): 2.

95. Calderwood, *Metadrama in Shakespeare's Henriad*, 68.

96. Wilders, *2H4*, 16.

97. John Wilders, *The Lost Garden: A View of Shakespeare's English and Roman History Plays* (London: Macmillan, 1982), 90.

98. Crowl, Review *1H4*, 3.

99. Wharton, *1 and 2H4: Text and Performance*, 72.

100. Though he was not commenting on the BBC Hal, A. D. Nuttall's words are interesting in this context, "Hal is inside out. Instead of concealing his human features beneath a stiff, impersonal mask, he wears the golden mask of kingship beneath an ordinary, smiling human face." (*A New Mimesis*, 150).

101. Fenwick, *2H4*, 19.

102. Saccio, "Shakespeare on TV," 2. The same sort of edgy, uncomfortable relationship is apparent in *Chimes at Midnight*.

103. Fenwick, *2H4*, 25.

104. For a discussion of mythological overtones in the relationship between Hal and Falstaff see Douglas J. Stewart's "Falstaff the Centaur," *Shakespeare Quarterly* 28 (1977): 5–21. For Falstaff as a representative of the Golden Age, see Nuttall, *A New Mimesis*, 151–53. He also compares Hal to Aeneas (160). Examinations of the stages in the journey of the hero can be found in Joseph Campbell's *The Hero with a Thousand Faces* (Princeton: Princeton University Press, 1968) and David Adams Leeming's *Mythology: The Voyage of the Hero* (New York: Lippincott, 1973).

## Chapter 5. The BBC *Henry V*

1. As Olivier puts it in a discussion of his film, "I was determined to bring in the comics, . . . for without them, it would have been two and a half hours of Henry, Henry, Henry" (*On Acting* [New York: Simon and Schuster, 1986], 271).

2. Nor is Henry the only "epic" element in *Henry V*. In Gary Taylor's words, "The critical subterfuge of elevating *Henry V* to the status of 'epic' as a prelude to damning it for being 'undramatic' justifies some scepticism about the utility of generic adjectives; but 'epic' the play self-evidently is in at least one sense: the social, national, and tonal variety of its characters. Modern discussions of the play tend to underestimate this" (*The Oxford Shakespeare: "Henry V"* [Oxford: Oxford University Press, 1984], 58).

3. Henry Fenwick, "The Production," *The BBC TV Shakespeare: "Henry V"* (London: British Broadcasting Corporation, 1979), 19.

4. Ibid.

5. Ibid., 20.

6. "The French court she [Odette Barrow, costume designer] put into blues, greens and gold; the English court in beige, brown and gold" (ibid., 21).

7. Ibid., 20.

8. Though the problem was still present, for instance, at 1.1.53, 79; 1.2.298; and 5.2.359.

9. Paul Cubeta, Review of *Henry V,* by William Shakespeare, BBC-TV/Time-Life Inc. Production, PBS Stations, 23 April 1980, "The Shakespeare Plays on TV: Season Two," *Shakespeare on Film Newsletter* 5, no. 1 (1980): 5.

10. Fenwick, *H5,* 22.

11. Ibid., 19.

12. Ibid., 23.

13. In his film, Olivier actually showed Henry cheering his troops. Branagh does the same in his film.

14. Fenwick, *H5,* 21.

15. Ibid., 22.

16. Ibid., 23.

17. Ibid., 24.

18. Ibid., 22–23.

19. Maynard Mack gives a glowing account of the transformation of Hal into Henry V as perfect king, a more institutional, less personal metamorphosis than the one the BBC chose to film (Introduction, in *The History of "Henry IV"* [*Part One*], by William Shakespeare [New York: Signet, 1987], xxxv).

20. Fenwick, *H5,* 22.

21. We are likely to remember in this production that the last time we heard "God save the King!" was as Henry V walked away from the rejection of Falstaff. Olivier and Welles also linked the traitors to the fat knight.

22. Olivier, *On Acting,* 98.

23. Ibid., 100.

24. Banham, "BBC Television's Dull Shakespeares," 49.

25. Ibid., 54.

26. Ibid., 55.

27. Ibid., 48.

28. Fenwick, *H5,* 24–25.

29. Fenwick, *2H4,* 23.

30. Olivier, *On Acting,* 283.

31. Tennenhouse, *Power on Display,* 69.

32. Fenwick, *H5,* 20.

33. Fenwick, *2H4,* 25.

34. Fenwick, *H5,* 24.

## Chapter 6. Laurence Olivier's *Henry V*

1. André Bazin writes in *What is Cinema?,* "There is more cinema, and great cinema at that in *Henry V* alone than in 90% of original scripts" (trans. Hugh Gray, 2 vols. [Berkeley: University of California Press, 1967], 116).

2. Olivier, *On Acting,* 270.

3. Ibid., 277.

4. Geduld, *Filmguide to "Henry V,"* 16.

5. William Hazlitt, *Characters of Shakespeare's Plays* (Chelsea House Publisher, 1983), 144.

6. Ralph Berry, *Changing Styles in Shakespeare* (London: George Allen and Unwin, 1981), 70.

7. Norman Rabkin, *Shakespeare and the Problem of Meaning* (Chicago: University of Chicago Press, 1981), 33–62.

8. Joanne Altieri provides a cogent criticism of Rabkin's thesis in her 1981 article "Romance in *Henry V*," *Studies in English Literature, 1500–1900* 32 [1981]: 237.

9. Berry, *Changing Styles in Shakespeare*, 81.

10. John Cottrell, *Laurence Olivier* (Weidenfeld and Nicolson, 1975), 163.

11. John Russell Taylor, *Hitch: The Life and Works of Alfred Hitchcock* (London: Sphere Books, 1981), 142.

12. Taylor, *Hitch*, 143.

13. Laurence Olivier, *Confessions of an Actor* (London: Coronet Books 1983), 123. See also Alexander Walker, *Vivien: The Life of Vivien Leigh* (New York: Weidenfeld and Nicolson, 1987), 160.

14. Cottrell, *Laurence Olivier*, 175.

15. Barry Norman, *Talking Pictures* (London: BBC Books and Hodder and Stoughton, 1987), 110.

16. Berry, *Changing Styles in Shakespeare*, 68.

17. Geduld, *Filmguide to "Henry V,"* 66. Geduld's last point is an interesting indication of the power of an expectational text.

18. Raymond Durgnat, *A Mirror for England: British Movies from Austerity to Affluence* (London: Faber, 1970), 109. As Roger Manvell puts it, "Agincourt, it is true, was scarcely a suitable parallel to the D-Day landings" (*Shakespeare and the Film* [New York: A. S. Barnes, 1979], 37).

19. Olivier, *On Acting*, 277.

20. Olivier endorsed the videocassette version of *Henry V*, saying, "It is now possible for a new generation of moviegoers, and many of those who enjoyed the earlier version of *Henry V*, to see it in a new form. I hope very much that they will enjoy the latest techniques" ("The Making of *Henry V*," in *Classic Film Scripts: "Henry V*," ed. Andrew Sinclair [London: Lorrimer, 1984], n. p.).

21. As Garrett, Hardison, and Gelfman put it, "unlike their American counterparts, it is not the custom of British production companies to preserve copies of eariler versions of scripts on file" (*Film Scripts One*, 17). I can confirm this in the case of Rank Film Distributors and *Henry V*. In a letter to me dated 23 December 1987, they said, "we do not hold a copy or even the original." Fortunately, the scripts did survive at the British Film Institute and the Birmingham Public Library.

22. There are two published versions of the release script. One was issued by Lorrimer Publishing Limited in their *Classic Film Scripts* series (1984). The other, which gives a more complete list of shots and camera angles and which seems to have been the main source for the Lorrimer version, appeared in Garrett, Hardison, and Gelfman, *Film Scripts One* (1971).

23. Laurence Olivier and Alan Dent, "*William Shakespeare's 'Henry V.':* Revised Treatment for Technicolor Film," Shooting Script, (City of Birmingham Public Library), 20. In future parenthetical references, I shall abbreviate this title as "RTTF."

24. Laurence Olivier, "'Henry The Fifth' Shooting Script" (British Film Institute), 43–44. In future parenthetical references, I shall abbreviate this title as "SS."

25. Garrett, Hardison, and Gelfman, *Film Scripts One*, 73.

26. Unfortunately, the earlier script omits most of the Agincourt battle

sequence because "Scenes 54 to 120 are Battle scenes which concern no principals" ("RTTF," 48).

27. Garrett, Hardison, and Gelfman, *Film Scripts One*, 117.

28. Ibid.

29. Olivier, *Confessions of an Actor*, 137.

30. The first Englishman to drop from a tree is shown pulling a French knight from his horse, and then with the Frenchman helpless on the ground, the Englishman raises his knife, when there is, of course, a cut away to other action.

31. Olivier, *On Acting*, 275.

32. Geduld, *Filmguide to "Henry V,"* 23.

33. Alexander Walker, *Vivien*, 130. Olivier writes that in *Fire Over England*, "I emoted too much, and in the American version they had to cut one of my scenes because the American preview audience got the giggles" (Olivier, *On Acting*, 255).

34. Alexander Walker, *Vivien*, 141. *Five Kings*, one of the stage versions of Orson Welles's *Chimes at Midnight* that preceded his film, used a revolve for similar reasons (Robert Hapgood, "*Chimes at Midnight* from Stage to Screen: The Art of Adaptation" *Shakespeare Survey* 39 [1986 (publication date 1987)]: 46).

35. Olivier, *Confessions of an Actor*, 122.

36. Foster Hirsch, *Laurence Olivier* (Boston: Twayne, 1979), 164.

37. Olivier, *On Acting*, 269.

38. Ibid. Olivier argues, "Shakespeare, in a way, 'wrote for films.' His splitting up of action into a multitude of small scenes is almost an anticipation of film technique" ("The Making of *Henry V*").

39. Olivier, *On Acting*, 270.

40. Bazin, *What is Cinema?* 88.

41. Ibid., 88–89.

42. Garrett, Hardison, and Gelfman, *Film Scripts One*, 41.

43. Sandra Sugarman Singer, "Laurence Olivier Directs Shakespeare: A Study in Film Authorship" (Ph.D. diss., Northwestern University, 1979), 47.

44. Garrett, Hardison, and Gelfman, *Film Scripts One*, 44–45.

45. Ibid., 46.

46. Singer, "Olivier Directs Shakespeare," 98.

47. Garrett, Hardison, and Gelfman, *Film Scripts One*, 67.

48. Singer, "Olivier Directs Shakespeare," 63.

49. Ian Johnson, "Merely Players," in *Focus on Shakespearean Films*, ed. Charles W. Eckert (Englewood Cliffs, N.J.: Prentice-Hall, 1972), 14.

50. Anthony Davies notes that "Olivier's HENRY V is also a cinematic treatise on the difference between cinema and theatre as media for the expression of drama" ("Shakespeare and the Eloquence of Cinematic Space: A Study of Spatial Strategy in Some Shakespearean Films" [Ph.D. diss., University of Birmingham, 1983], 72).

51. Gorman Beauchamp, "*Henry V*: Myth, Movie, Play," *College Literature* 5 (1978): 228. The implied disapproval of film as a medium in Beauchamp's statement helps to explain the less-than-careful criticism that has sometimes been directed at *Henry V*.

52. Marsha McCreadie, "*Henry V*: Onstage and On Film," *Literature/Film Quarterly* 5 (1977): 320. For an additional discussion of the impact of Olivier's *Henry V* on later stage productions see "Homage to Olivier's *Henry V*," *Shakespeare on Film Newsletter* 6, no. 1 (1982): 1 and 3 (no author given).

53. Michael Manheim, "Olivier's *Henry V* and the Elizabethan World Picture," *Literature/Film Quarterly* 11 (1983): 179.

54. Ibid., 184.

55. Graham Holderness, *Shakespeare's History* (New York: St. Martin's, 1985), 190.

56. C. Clayton Hutton, *The Making of "Henry V"* (London: Ernest J. Day, 1944), 50.

57. Geduld, *Filmguide to "Henry V,"* 48. For a scene-by-scene listing of Olivier's cuts and other alterations, see Singer, "Olivier Directs Shakespeare," 19–45.

58. Olivier, *Confessions of an Actor,* 136.

59. Beauchamp, "*H5:* Myth, Movie, Play," 228.

60. Olivier, *On Acting,* 275–76. I do not mean to suggest by this that Olivier denied the propaganda value of *Henry V,* but he was aware (as many of his critics apparently are not) that a splendid film of any Shakespeare play would have been of value to the British war effort, simply because it was paying homage to England's greatest dramatist. Also, critics tend to forget that patriotism was not Olivier's sole motive for making *Henry V.* He says, "the pull on my artistic ambitions was intoxicating" (Olivier, *Confessions of an Actor,* 131).

61. Andrew Sinclair, editor of *Classic Film Scripts: "Henry V,"* says, "The screenplay is a model of how to adapt a classic stage play to the needs of the cinema" ([London: Lorrimer, 1984], 1).

62. Geduld, *Filmguide to "Henry V,"* 28.

63. Hirsch, *Olivier,* 68.

64. Ibid., 67. In André Bazin's words, "We are not in the play, we are in an historical film . . . that is . . . we are present at a film of a kind that is widely accepted. . . . Our enjoyment of the play however . . . is in fact the pleasure to be derived from a Shakespearean performance. . . . the aesthetic strategy of Laurence Olivier was a trick to escape from . . . the usual suspension of disbelief" (88).

65. Dale Silviria, *Laurence Olivier and the Art of Film Making* (London: Associated University Presses, 1985), 84.

66. Silviria, *Olivier and the Art of Film Making,* 86.

67. The lines the BBC film omitted from act 1, scene 2 were: 1–6, 24–32, 56–90, 106–14, 117–21, 140–65, 207–10, 225–33, and 309–10 (*BBC H5,* 32–39).

68. Taylor, *Oxford Shakespeare: H5,* 38.

69. Gary Taylor, *Moment by Moment by Shakespeare* (London: Macmillan, 1985), 114.

70. David, *Shakespeare in the Theatre,* 194.

71. Silviria, *Olivier and the Art of Film Making,* 85.

72. Alan Shallcross, script editor for the BBC *Henry V* says, "As for the Salic law speech, if you keep it complete you have no choice but to play Canterbury as a fool . . . but that lands you in trouble because in the same scene he is revealed as a highly political animal" (Fenwick, *HV,* 18). Olivier kept the lines but ascribed the folly to the actor, not to Canterbury himself. The tactic is an example of the subtlety of Olivier's treatment.

73. Anthony Davies, "Shakespeare and the Eloquence of Cinematic Space," 81.

74. Silviria, *Olivier and the Art of Film Making,* 79–80.

75. Singer, "Olivier Directs Shakespeare," 69.

76. Speaight, *Shakespeare: Man and Achievement,* 184.

77. James Agee, "*Henry V,*" in *Focus on Shakespearean Films,* ed. Charles W. Eckert (Englewood Cliffs, N.J.: Prentice-Hall, 1972), 56.

78. Silviria, *Olivier and the Art of Film Making,* 80.

79. Juan Cobos and Miguel Rubio, "Welles and Falstaff: An Interview," *Sight*

*and Sound* 35 (1966): 159. Falstaff and Henry V may not be the ideal representatives of the pastoral world of Merrie England, but both Olivier and Welles seem to have viewed them in that light. A. D. Nuttall, though, offers some support for the position: "Falstaff, who cannot get on with live King Henry, is on the best of terms with dead King Arthur. If a sense of England as a ruined Arcadia or Eden survives at all in *Henry IV* it is because of Falstaff" (*A New Mimesis*, 152).

80. Singer, "Olivier Directs Shakespeare," 49.

81. Geduld, *Filmguide to "Henry V,"* 27.

82. Garrett, Hardison, and Gelfman, *Film Scripts One*, 61.

83. Geduld, *Filmguide to "Henry V,"* 32.

84. Singer, "Olivier Directs Shakespeare," 84. "The style of the painted bricks, steps, and exterior door of the Boar's Head curtain anticipate the 'actual' set for II,i. The blue-turreted palace . . . previews the more solid, but still two dimensional image we'll see repeatedly throughout the film" (ibid.). The Southampton curtain is, of course, number three. The fourth is drawn by an unseen hand at the end of the Southampton scene, and even it may be a precursor of a future set. Dale Silviria finds that "Sailing ship silhouettes are woven into the curtain" (*Olivier and the Art of Film Making*, 115), but while I am willing to concede a certain sense of shipness, I find his identification overemphatic.

85. Michael Quinn, Introduction, in *Shakespeare "Henry V": A Casebook* (London: Macmillan, 1983), 24.

86. Hirsch, *Olivier*, 71.

87. Geduld, *Filmguide to "Henry V,"* 32–33.

88. Dudley Andrew, *Film in the Aura of Art* (Princeton: Princeton University Press, 1984), 143.

89. As Olivier writes, "Bring on Falstaff . . . because he was a leader of the comics. . . . I wanted the audience . . . to have a concrete image of the dear old man" (*On Acting*, 271).

90. Singer, "Olivier Directs Shakespeare," 78–79.

91. A. R. Humphreys, Introduction, in *Henry V*, by William Shakespeare (Harmondsworth: Penguin, 1968), 45.

92. Garrett, Hardison, and Gelfman, *Film Scripts One*, 62.

93. Taylor, *Oxford Shakespeare: H5*, 44.

94. Geduld, *Filmguide to "Henry V,"* 33. Perhaps Olivier wanted this film Falstaff to suggest not only George Robey's general comic persona but also his stage Falstaff. As Peter Cotes writes in his biography of Robey, "there are many who feel that his best screen performance was his shortest: the dying Falstaff . . . in a specially written addition to the film script encouraged by Olivier's admiration for Robey's stage performance in *Henry IV*" (*George Robey: "The Darling of the Halls"* [London: Cassell], 112). I have doubts, though, about the part being a specially written addition for Robey both because Olivier does not mention such a procedure and because the earlier script already contains the Falstaff material ("RTFF," 14–15).

95. Olivier notes, " 'If you really want to shock or delight an audience, get them a little bored first,' said William Wyler. . . . I wanted the film audience to get a restless feeling . . . in the Globe's wooden O, irritated by the silly actors . . . so that when at last we leave the place . . . there's a tremendous feeling of relief and anticipation" (*On Acting*, 271). The point of transition falls just after Falstaff's death. Perhaps the death of Falstaff is also meant to suggest the abandonment of the stage.

96. Holderness, *Shakespeare's History*, 190.

97. In his introduction to the Arden *Henry V*, J. H. Walter maintains that

"The insulting reference to the Church of Rome in 'whore of Babylon' completes the last glance at the Lollard Oldcastle" (xxxix–xl). If this is correct, there is a special relevance to the substitution of Falstaff for Lord Scrope. Part of the Scrope-Cambridge conspiracy was that "Sir John Oldcastle and his Lollards would raise the Welsh border and the West Country" (Seward, *Henry V as Warlord,* 47).

98. Andrew, *Film in the Aura of Art,* 144.
99. Garrett, Hardison, and Gelfman, *Film Scripts One,* 66.
100. Ibid., 124.
101. Jorgens, *Shakespeare on Film,* 127.
102. Garrett, Hardison, and Gelfman, *Film Scripts One,* 69.
103. Silviria, *Olivier and the Art of Film Making,* 98.
104. As Olivier describes it, "I made my humble most of Orlando, but . . . [t]he director's flocks of sheep ran away with the film" (*On Acting,* 255). He screened it, along with *The Taming of the Shrew* and *Romeo and Juliet,* before filming *Henry V* (279).
105. Geduld, *Filmguide to "Henry V,"* 36.
106. Andrew, *Film in the Aura of Art,* 145.
107. Olivier, *On Acting,* 274.
108. Silviria, *Olivier and the Art of Film Making,* 139.
109. Tillyard, *Shakespeare's History Plays,* 306. Robert Egan deals interestingly with the objections of Tillyard and Mark Van Doren to the play in "A Muse of Fire: *Henry V* in the Light of *Tamburlaine*" (*Modern Language Quarterly* 29 [1968]: 17).
110. Davison, *"Hamlet": Text and Performance,* 49.
111. Emrys Jones, *Scenic Form in Shakespeare* (Oxford: Clarendon Press, 1985), 45.
112. Francois Truffaut, *Hitchcock* (London: Secker and Warburg, 1967) 108.
113. Garrett, Hardison, and Gelfman, *Film Scripts One,* 111.
114. Andrew, *Film in the Aura of Art,* 137.
115. Singer, "Olivier Directs Shakespeare," 96.
116. Talking of the horses, Olivier says, "Mine was white . . . and that of the Constable needed to be black, with no other blacks close to him ever, for the sake of identification" (*Confessions of an Actor,* 134).
117. Andrew, *Film in the Aura of Art,* 135.
118. Singer, "Olivier Directs Shakespeare," 80–81.
119. Silviria, *Olivier and the Art of Film Making,* 104.
120. Ibid.
121. Singer, "Olivier Directs Shakespeare," 97.
122. Silviria, *Olivier and the Art of Film Making,* 105.
123. This is a convincingly Shakespearean viewpoint. As John Wilders says in commenting on Burgundy's speech and Henry's victories, "The role of God in the history plays is comparable to that of the gods in *King Lear:* men hold conflicting views of Him and He remains inscrutable" (*The Lost Garden,* 63).
124. Agee, *H5,* 56.
125. Calderwood, *Metadrama in Shakespeare's Henriad,* 160.
126. Andrew, *Film in the Aura of Art,* 141.
127. Jorgens, *Shakespeare on Film,* 133.
128. Ibid.
129. Garrett, Hardison, and Gelfman, *Film Scripts One,* 80.
130. Ibid., 83.
131. Taylor, *Moment by Moment by Shakespeare,* 123.

132. Silviria, *Olivier and the Art of Film Making*, 131.
133. Ibid., 136.
134. Ibid., 132.
135. Geduld, *Filmguide to "Henry V,"* 9.
136. This is the release script's usual spelling of the name.
137. Garrett, Hardison, and Gelfman, *Film Scripts One*, 134.
138. Silviria, *Olivier and the Art of Film Making*, 138.
139. Singer, "Olivier Directs Shakespeare," 65.
140. Anthony Davies, *Filming Shakespeare's Plays*, 89.
141. For example, the shooting script has "ORLEANS . . . picks up a burning brand from a fire. . . . He then deposits his brand in the cart" ("SS," 114). For the release script, however, the actor remains unidentified. He is simply a French knight, "The Knight flinging the fire brand into the cart" (Garrett, Hardison, and Gelfman, *Film Scripts One*, 115).
142. Silviria, *Olivier and the Art of Film Making*, 139.
143. Singer, "Olivier Directs Shakespeare," 66.
144. Ibid., 65–66.
145. In his discussion of *Henry V*, Roger Manvell talks about "sequences which stay in the memory" (40).
146. Andrew, *Film in the Aura of Art*, 151.
147. Wilders, *The Lost Garden*, 143.

## Chapter 7. Orson Welles and *Chimes at Midnight*

1. Francois Truffaut, *"Citizen Kane,"* in *Focus on Citizen Kane*, ed. Ronald Gottesman (Englewood Cliffs, N.J.: Prentice-Hall, 1971), 131. Or as Peter Cowie puts it, "I am more than ever convinced of his place among the immortals" (*A Ribbon of Dreams: The Cinema of Orson Welles* [London: Tantivy Press, 1973], 13).
2. Andrew, *Film in the Aura of Art*, 152.
3. Higham, *Orson Welles*, 12. Louis Giannetti quotes Welles as saying, "A film is never really good unless the camera is an eye in the head of a poet" ("Paradise Lost: The Cinema of Orson Welles," in *Masters of the American Cinema* [Englewood Cliffs, N.J.: Prentice-Hall, 1981], 268).
4. Juan Cobos, Miguel Rubio, and J. A. Pruneda, "A Trip to Don Quixoteland: Conversations with Orson Welles," in Gottesman, *Focus on Citizen Kane*, 13.
5. Cobos and Rubio, "Welles and Falstaff," 162. Barbara Leaming points out that Welles adopted this all-powerful director's stance during his black *Macbeth* (*Orson Welles: A Biography* [New York: Penguin, 1985], 122).
6. Cobos and Rubio, "Welles and Falstaff," 162.
7. Higham, *Orson Welles*, 11.
8. Cobos and Rubio, "Welles and Falstaff," 162.
9. Gyles Brandreth, *John Gielgud: A Celebration* (London: Pavilion Books, 1984), 152.
10. Higham, *Films of Orson Welles*, 169.
11. Robin Wood, *Personal Views: Explorations in Film* (London: Gordon Fraser Gallery, 1976), 138.
12. Truffaut, *"Citizen Kane,"* 130. Louis Giannetti calls Orson Welles "the most daring sound innovator since the early talkies of Lubitsch" ("Paradise Lost," 284–85).
13. Goldfarb's comment and the remarks that follow contradict the opinions of reviewers such as Pauline Kael, who regard Welles's later sound tracks as

distracting from rather than enhancing the films ("Orson Welles: There Ain't No Way," in *Kiss Kiss Bang Bang* [London: Calder and Boyars, 1970], 198–99).

14. Phyllis Goldfarb, "Orson Welles' Use of Sound," in Gottesman, *Focus on Orson Welles*, 85.

15. Andrew, *Film in the Aura of Art*, 165–66. Speaking of *Chimes at Midnight*, James Naremore says, "the battle is nearly as impressive if one simply listens to the sounds" (*The Magic World of Orson Welles* [New York: Oxford University Press, 1978], 274).

16. Wood, *Personal Views*, 138.

17. Leaming, *Orson Welles*, 43–44.

18. Robert Hapgood ("*Chimes at Midnight* from Stage to Screen," 39) gives this date as 1938, but according to Charles Higham, "On Monday, February 27, 1939, *Five Kings* opened in Boston without a proper dress rehearsal" (*Orson Welles*, 133).

19. Higham, *Orson Welles*, 342.

20. Hapgood, "*Chimes at Midnight* from Stage to Screen," 39–43.

21. Ibid., 43.

22. Higham, *Orson Welles*, 134.

23. Future parenthetical references to the shooting script of *Chimes at Midnight* will be abbreviated as "WSS" for Welles, Shooting Script. Parenthetical references to the dialogue release script of *Chimes* will be abbreviated as "WDRS" for Welles, Dialogue Release Script.

24. W. H. Auden, *The Dyer's Hand and Other Essays* (London: Faber, 1975), 186.

25. Gordon Gow, "Gordon Gow at Welles' Lament for the Passing of Merrie England . . .," *Films and Filming* 13, no. 8 (1967): 25.

26. Heston, *The Actor's Life*, 343.

27. Bevington, *Oxford Shakespeare: 1H4*, 85.

28. Brian Henderson, "The Long Take," *Film Comment* 7, no. 2 (1971): 11.

29. As I indicated in the introduction, only Robert Hapgood in his *Shakespeare Survey* article, "*Chimes at Midnight* from Stage to Screen," has previously examined the shooting script.

30. Sylvan Barnet's comments offer an extreme example. He says of *Chimes*, "Almost all Shakespeare specialists detest the film, understandably and rightly. . . . The film is a mess and is utterly unfaithful to Shakespeare" ("*Henry IV, Part I* on Stage and Screen," 282).

31. Joseph McBride, "*Chimes at Midnight*," in Gottesman, *Focus on Orson Welles*, 183.

32. As Anthony Davies says, "The speech is essentially presented as a soliloquy, but the words are said in Falstaff's hearing, so that he is visibly affected by them" ("Shakespeare and the Eloquence of Cinematic Space," 268). Bridget Gellert Lyons does not recognize this or record Falstaff's reactions to Hal's speech in her continuity script. She also misses Hal leaping in the air and clicking his heels at the end of the scene ("*Chimes at Midnight*," 51–52). Such omissions are, of course, usual in release and continuity scripts.

33. To avoid confusion, I have not cited either Shakespearean line numbers or page numbers from Welles's shooting script or dialogue release script when the words quoted are from the film itself.

34. Cobos and Rubio, "Welles and Falstaff," 159.

35. Henderson, "The Long Take," 11.

36. Cobos and Rubio, "Welles and Falstaff," 159.

37. Pierre Billard, "*Chimes at Midnight*," *Sight and Sound* 34 (1965): 64.

38. Jorgens, *Shakespeare on Film*, 111–12.

39. Higham, *Orson Welles*, 331.

40. Leaming, *Orson Welles*, see especially pp. 528–32.

41. Ibid., 39.

42. Ibid., 42.

43. Ibid., 43.

44. Ibid., 567.

45. Ibid., 568.

46. John Houseman, *Run-Through: A Memoir* (London: Allen Lane, Penguin Press, 1972), 167.

47. Higham, *Orson Welles*, 289.

48. Frank Brady, *Citizen Welles: A Biography of Orson Welles* (New York: Charles Scribner's Sons, 1989), 539.

49. Richard T. Jameson, "An Infinity of Mirrors," in Gottesman, *Focus on Orson Welles*, 66.

50. Higham, *Orson Welles*, 308.

51. Cobos, Rubio, and Pruneda, "A Trip to Don Quixoteland," 19.

52. A. C. Bradley, "The Rejection of Falstaff," in *Shakespeare "Henry IV, Parts I and II": A Casebook*, ed. G. K. Hunter (London: Macmillan, 1983), 62.

53. William Johnson, "Orson Welles: Of Time and Loss," *Film Quarterly* 21, no. 1 (1967): 18.

54. Bordwell, *"Citizen Kane,"* 47.

55. Ibid.

56. Lorne Michael Buchman, "From Globe to Screen," 107.

57. Ibid., 104.

58. Auden, *The Dyer's Hand*, 184.

59. Jorgens, *Shakespeare on Film*, 115.

60. Manvell, *Shakespeare and the Film*, 68.

61. Jorgens, *Shakespeare on Film*, 113.

62. Anthony Davies notes the pattern of visual separation between Hal and Hotspur ("Shakespeare and the Eloquence of Cinematic Space," 284).

63. Buchman, "From Globe to Screen," 108.

64. Cobos and Rubio, "Welles and Falstaff," 159.

65. Ibid., 160.

66. Ibid., 161.

67. Welles achieved a similar effect in the stage *Chimes* by putting Mistress Quickly's account of Falstaff's death at the beginning (Hapgood, *"Chimes at Midnight* from Stage to Screen," 43).

68. Louis Giannetti, *Understanding Movies* (Englewood Cliffs, N.J.: Prentice-Hall, 1987), 415.

69. William Johnson, "Orson Welles: Of Time and Loss," 15. Joseph McBride assembles the evidence (*"Chimes at Midnight,"* 113).

70. William Johnson, "Orson Welles: Of Time and Loss," 21.

71. Stephen Farber, *"The Magnificent Ambersons,"* in Gottesman, *Focus on Orson Welles*, 124.

72. Leaming, *Orson Welles*, 30.

73. Reginald Hill, *An April Shroud* (London: Grafton, 1975), 9.

74. William Johnson, "Orson Welles: Of Time and Loss," 16.

75. Higham, *The Films of Orson Welles*, 170.

76. Anthony Davies, "Shakespeare and the Eloquence of Cinematic Space," 270.

77. Bordwell, *"Citizen Kane,"* 47.

78. See Henderson, "The Long Take," 11.

79. Winny, *Player King*, 125.

80. Jorgens, *Shakespeare on Film*, 113. In his comments on the film, Jean-Louis Comolli says, "The parallel between court and hovel affects not only the settings and arrangement of the places; the King finds in Falstaff his double and his reversed image" ("Jack le Fataliste" *Cahiers du Cinema in English* 11 [September 1967]: 21).

81. Winny, *Player King*, 125.

82. Bevington, *Oxford Shakespeare: 1H4*, 26.

83. Speaight, *Shakespeare: Man and Achievement*, 169.

84. As James Naremore states, "it is Fall when Hal and Falstaff go off to war with the Percys, but the battle scenes are fought in a summer landscape" (*Magic World of Orson Welles*, 275).

85. Jorgens, *Shakespeare on Film*, 115.

86. Samuel Crowl sees Falstaff's disappearance through the trap door as foreshadowing "the eventual rejection scene, where King Hal sends Falstaff toward the grave" ("The Long Goodbye: Welles and Falstaff," *Shakespeare Quarterly* 31 (1980): 376–77.

87. Maynard Mack, *Killing the King: Three Studies in Shakespeare's Tragic Structure* (New Haven: Yale University Press, 1973), 26.

88. Nuttall, *A New Mimesis*, 161.

89. Charles Affron, *Cinema and Sentiment* (Chicago: Chicago University Press, 1982), 86.

90. McBride, *"Chimes at Midnight,"* 184.

91. Jorgens, *Shakespeare on Film*, 121.

92. McBride, *"Chimes at Midnight,"* 181.

93. Ibid., 184.

94. Saccio, *Shakespeare's English Kings*, 71–72.

95. James Hamilton Wylie, *The Reign of Henry the Fifth*, 3 vols. (Cambridge: Cambridge University Press, 1914–1929), 1 : 260.

96. Seward, *Henry V as Warlord*, 43–44. "London was in panic and the rumour ran that they were going to kill the king and proclaim Oldcastle regent" (Wylie, *Reign of Henry the Fifth* 1 : 264).

97. Wylie, *Reign of Henry the Fifth* 1 : 277.

98. A. R. Humphreys, ed., *The Arden Shakespeare: "The First Part of King Henry IV"* (London: Methuen, 1960), xli.

99. Seward, *Henry V as Warlord*, 171.

100. Gary Taylor, "The Fortunes of Oldcastle," *Shakespeare Survey* 38 (1985): 95–96.

101. Lorne Michael Buchman puts the matter of Falstaff, Orson Welles, and film critics in perspective: "If all sides of Falstaff had not been realized, the film would not be so interesting nor would it illuminate Shakespeare's world nearly so well" ("From Globe to Screen," 96–97).

102. McBride, *"Chimes at Midnight,"* 182.

103. Cowie, *Ribbon of Dreams*, 189.

104. See, for instance, Frankie Rubinstein, *A Dictionary of Shakespeare's Sexual Puns and Their Significance* (London: Macmillan, 1984), 65–66.

105. Robin Wood says, "It might be argued that a strong homosexual undercurrent runs through Welles's work, the more potent perhaps for never being exposed to the light" (*Personal Views*, 138). In terms of Welles's personal life and the mentor-protégé theme, it might also be argued that there was a homosexual undercurrent. Discussing Welles's relationship with Skipper Hill, Barbara Leam-

ing says, "the boy's designs on the older man were nothing less than romantic" (*Orson Welles*, 27).

106. McBride, *"Chimes at MIdnight,"* 185.

107. Juan Cobos and Miguel Rubio, "Welles on Falstaff," *Cahiers du Cinema in English* 11 (September 1967): 14. Daniel Seltzer says that in Welles's film, Falstaff "knows that Hal—far from being only superficially amused with him—loves him and understands him, even if that understanding clearly carries with it an element of contempt" ("Shakespeare's Texts and Modern Productions," in *Reinterpretations of Elizabethan Drama: Selected Papers from the English Institute*, ed. Norman Rabkin [New York: Columbia University Press, 1969], 105).

108. Bordwell, *"Citizen Kane,"* 47.

109. McBride, *"Chimes at Midnight,"* 185.

110. Jorgens, *Shakespeare on Film*, 118.

111. Bordwell, *"Citizen Kane,"* 47.

112. Joseph McBride (and Jack Jorgens quoting him) sees "Poins eating an apple (the end of innocence)" (*Shakespeare on Film*, 182). Poins is certainly eating something, and he holds it and bites it in such a way as to make an apple the best guess. He has, however, mysteriously managed to make it disappear by the time he reaches Falstaff's coffin, even though he is continuously onscreen.

113. William Johnson, "Orson Welles: Of Time and Loss," 16.

114. D. Curren Aquino, *"Chimes at Midnight:* Retrospectively Elegiac," *Shakespeare on Film Newsletter* 4, no. 1 (1979): 7.

115. William Johnson, "Orson Welles: Of Time and Loss," 19.

116. McBride, *"Chimes at Midnight,"* 12.

117. Cobos and Rubio, "Welles and Falstaff," 161.

## Chapter 8. Conclusion

1. David Norbrook, "No Holds Bard," review of *Reinventing Shakespeare: A Cultural History from the Restoration to the Present*, by Gary Taylor, *New Republic*, 16 October 1989, 50.

2. Brad Darrach, "Laurence Olivier Dies: 'The Rest Is Silence,'" *People*, 24 July 1989, 76.

3. Anthony Davies, *Filming Shakespeare's Plays*, 34–35.

4. Brady, *Citizen Welles*, 540.

5. Stanley S. Rubin, "Welles/Falstaff/Shakespeare/Wells: The Narrative Structure of 'Chimes at Midnight,'" *Film Criticism* 2, no. 2–3 (Winter-Spring 1978): 66.

6. Seltzer, "Shakespeare's Texts and Modern Productions," 109.

7. Zitner, "Wooden O's in Plastic Boxes," 2.

8. Roger Ebert, *A Kiss Is Still a Kiss* (New York: Andrews, McMeel and Parker, 1984), 1.

9. Ibid.

10. Kathy Chin Leong, "Hypertext: The Ever-Growing Interconnected Whole," *PC/Computing*, July 1989, 76.

11. Zitner, "Wooden O's in Plastic Boxes," 11.

12. Ebert is incorrect; in the United States, the number is 525.

13. Ebert, *A Kiss Is Still a Kiss*, 4.

14. Bob Brewin, "Smarter Than the Average TV," *Premiere*, November 1989, 119.

15. For a discussion of the problem of the television screen image and some

of its solutions, see Stewart Brand's *The Media Lab: Inventing the Future at MIT* (New York: Viking Penguin, 1977), 75–6.

16. Ibid., 81.

17. Jorgens, "BBC-TV Shakespeare," 415.

18. Michael Mullin, "Orson Welles' *Macbeth:* Script and Screen," in Gottesman, *Focus on Orson Welles,* 137.

19. Heston, *Actor's Life,* 338.

20. Ibid., 359.

21. Roman Polanski, *Roman* (London: Heinemann, 1984), 298. Some perspective on the smallness of these budgets in film terms (though inflation and currency fluctuations must be kept in mind) can be obtained by noting that the cost of *Who Framed Roger Rabbit* is "rumored to be somewhere between $40 million and $50 million" (Kim Masters, "What's Up, Doc?" *Premiere,* July 1988, 34). A "small" movie such as *Dirty Dancing* (1987), where, as producer, Linda Gottlieb says, "everybody flew economy class, and we took small fees . . . I made tuna sandwiches at home for the director," cost around $6 million (Michael Ryan, ". . . And Then She Was Fired," *Parade,* 11 September 1988, 12).

22. Olivier, *On Acting,* 310.

23. Brand, *Media Lab,* 29.

24. Lawrence O'Toole, "Lost and Found: Films That Failed in Theaters Thrive on Cassette," *American Film* 9, no. 2 (1983): 64.

25. Gregory P. Fagan, "IVE to Help Belushi Bio Pic," *Video Review,* September 1989, 18.

26. Richard Corliss, "Lord Larry's Crowning Triumph," *Time,* 16 May 1983, 77.

27. Ray Bennett, "The Bright and Shining Stars," *Satellite Orbit,* August 1989, 14.

28. Michael Billington, "A 'New Olivier' Is Taking On *Henry V* on the Screen," *The New York Times,* 8 January 1989, sec. 2, p. 21, col. 1. The projected budget for this *Henry V* was $10 million (ibid.); since the film's release the budget has been reported as $9 million (Jack Kroll, "A *Henry V* for Our Time," *Newsweek,* 20 November 1989, 78) and as $7.5 million (Richard Corliss, "King Ken Comes to Conquer," *Time,* 13 November 1989, 119). In any event, it is below the industry average. A typical film costs $18 million, though only about 10 per cent gross more than $10 million at the box office; the remainder of the revenue must be "generated by video and other non-theater sources" ("Top Grossing Films Released in the U.S., 1983–88," *Color Country Spectrum,* 23 July 1989, p. B6).

29. R. Alan Kimbrough, "Olivier's *Lear* and the Limits of Video," *Shakespeare on Film Newsletter* 11, no. 1 (December 1986), 6. Kimbrough also refers to "limited-budget studio productions," but the limits are relative. Writing in *Newsweek,* Jack Kroll and Rita Dallas indicate that Olivier's *Lear* is "said to be the most expensive production in British television history" ("Return of the Prodigal King," 8 November 1982), 105.

30. Kimbrough, "Olivier's *Lear,* 6.

31. Billington, "Olivier Taking on *Henry V,*" sec. 2, p. 21, col. 2.

32. Ibid., sec. 2, p. 18, col. 6.

# Works Cited

## Typescripts

Olivier, Laurence, and Alan Dent. "*William Shakespeare's 'Henry V.':* Revised Treatment for Technicolor Film." Shooting script. City of Birmingham Public Library.

Olivier, Laurence. *"Henry The Fifth" Shooting Script.* British Film Institute.

Rank Film Distributors. Letter to the author. 23 December 1987.

Welles, Orson. "Chimes at Midnight." Shooting script. Northwestern University Library, Special Collections Department.

———. "Falstaff (Chimes at Midnight): Un film d'ORSON WELLES, d'apres SHAKESPEARE, LISTE DE DIALOGUES ANGLAIS." Dialogue release script. The Shakespeare Institute, University of Birmingham.

## Books and Articles

Affron, Charles. *Cinema and Sentiment.* Chicago: University of Chicago Press, 1982.

Agee, James. "*Henry V.*" In *Focus on Shakespearean Films,* edited by Charles W. Eckert. Englewood Cliffs, N.J.: Prentice-Hall, 1972.

Altieri, Joanne. "Romance in *Henry V.*" *Studies in English Literature, 1500–1900* 32 (1981): 223–40.

Andrew, J. Dudley. *Concepts in Film Theory.* Oxford: Oxford University Press, 1984.

———. *Film in the Aura of Art.* Princeton: Princeton University Press, 1984.

———. *The Major Film Theories: An Introduction.* Oxford: Oxford University Press, 1976.

Aquino, D. Curren. "*Chimes at Midnight:* Retrospectively Elegiac." *Shakespeare on Film Newsletter* 4, no. 1 (1979): 1, 7–8.

Auden, W. H. *The Dyer's Hand and Other Essays.* London: Faber, 1975.

Banham, Martin. "BBC Television's Dull Shakespeares." In *Shakespeare's Wide and Universal Stage,* edited by C. B. Cox and D. J. Palmer. Manchester: Manchester University Press, 1984.

Barber, C. L. *Shakespeare's Festive Comedy: A Study of Dramatic Form and its Relation to Social Custom.* Princeton: Princeton University Press, 1972.

Barnet, Sylvan. "*Henry IV, Part I* on Stage and Screen." In *The History of "Henry IV" (Part One),* edited by Maynard Mack. New York: Signet, 1987.

Bathrick, Serafina Kent. "Independent Woman, Doomed Sister." In *The Modern*

*American Novel and the Movies,* edited by Gerald Peary and Roger Shatzkin. New York: Frederick Ungar, 1978.

Bazin, André. *What Is Cinema?* Translated by Hugh Gray. 2 vols. Berkeley: University of California Press, 1967.

Beauchamp, Gorman. "*Henry V:* Myth, Movie, Play." *College Literature* 5 (1978): 228–38.

Bennett, Ray. "The Bright and Shining Stars." *Satellite Orbit,* August 1989, 12–15.

Bergman, Ingrid, and Alan Burgess. *Ingrid Bergman: My Story.* London: Michael Joseph, 1980.

Berry, Ralph. *Changing Styles in Shakespeare.* London: George Allen and Unwin, 1981.

Bevington, David. *The Oxford Shakespeare: "Henry IV, Part I."* Oxford: Oxford University Press, 1987.

Billard, Pierre. "Chimes at Midnight." *Sight and Sound* 34 (1965): 64–65.

Billington, Michael. "A 'New Olivier' Is Taking On *Henry V* on the Screen." *New York Times,* 8 January 1989, sec. 2, p. 21, col. 1.

Bird, Ruth. *The Turbulent London of Richard II.* London: Longmans, Green and Co., 1949.

Bordwell, David. *"Citizen Kane." Film Comment* 7, no. 2 (1971): 39–47.

Bradley, A. C. "The Rejection of Falstaff." In *Shakespeare "Henry IV, Parts I and II": A Casebook,* edited by G. K. Hunter. London: Macmillan, 1983.

Brady, Frank. *Citizen Welles: A Biography of Orson Welles.* New York: Charles Scribner's Sons, 1989.

Brand, Stewart. *The Media Lab: Inventing the Future at MIT.* New York: Viking Penguin, 1987.

Brandreth, Gyles. *John Gielgud: A Celebration.* London: Pavilion Books, 1984.

Brewin, Bob. "Smarter Than the Average TV." *Premiere,* November 1989, 119.

Brown, John Russell. "Narrative and Focus: *Richard II.*" In *Shakespeare "Richard II": A Casebook,* edited by Nicholas Brooke. London: Macmillan, 1978.

Brownlow, F. W. *Two Shakespearean Sequences: "Henry VI" to "Richard II" and "Pericles" to "Timon of Athens."* London: Macmillan, 1977.

Bruce, Marie Louise. *The Usurper King: Henry of Bolingbroke, 1366–99.* London: Rubicon Press, 1986.

Bulman, James C. "The BBC Shakespeare and 'House Style.'" *Shakespeare Quarterly* 35 (1984): 571–81.

Calderwood, James L. *Metadrama in Shakespeare's Henriad: "Richard II" to "Henry V."* Berkeley: University of California Press, 1979.

Campbell, Joseph. *The Hero with a Thousand Faces.* Princeton: Princeton University Press, 1968.

Carr, Virginia M. Review of *Measure for Measure,* by William Shakespeare. BBC-TV/Time-Life Inc. Production. PBS Stations, 11 April 1979. "The Shakespeare Plays on TV: Season One." *Shakespeare on Film Newsletter* 4, no. 1 (1979): 4–5.

Charney, Maurice. "Shakespearean Anglophilia: The BBC-TV Series and American Audiences." *Shakespeare Quarterly* 31 (1980): 287–92.

Church, Michael. "*Henry IV* BBC 2." *The Times,* 17 December 1979, 7.

Clayton, Sylvia. "Caesar Dominates a Cautious Production." *Daily Telegraph,* 12 February 1979, 11.

———. "Shakespeare Played Safe Without Tears." *Daily Telegraph,* 4 December 1978, 15.

Cobos, Juan, Miguel Rubio, and J. A. Pruneda. "A Trip to Don Quixoteland: Conversations with Orson Welles." In *Focus on Citizen Kane,* edited by Ronald Gottesman. Englewood Cliffs, N.J.: Prentice-Hall, 1971.

Cobos, Juan, and Miguel Rubio. "Welles and Falstaff: An Interview." *Sight and Sound* 35 (1966): 158–63.

———. "Welles on Falstaff." *Cahiers du Cinema in English* 11 (September 1967): 5–15.

Comolli, Jean-Louis. "Jack le Fataliste." *Cahiers du Cinema in English* 11 (September 1967): 20–21.

Cook, Judith. *Shakespeare's Players: A Look at Some of the Major Roles in Shakespeare and Those who have Played Them.* London: Harrap, 1983.

Corliss, Richard. "King Ken Comes to Conquer." *Time,* 13 November 1989, 119–20.

———. "Lord Larry's Crowning Triumph." *Time,* 16 May 1983, 77.

Cotes, Peter. *George Robey: "The Darling of the Halls."* London: Cassell, 1972.

Cottrell, John. *Laurence Olivier.* London: Weidenfeld and Nicolson, 1975.

Cowie, Peter. *A Ribbon of Dreams: The Cinema of Orson Welles.* London: Tantivy Press, 1973.

Crowl, Samuel. "The Long Goodbye: Welles and Falstaff." *Shakespeare Quarterly* 31 (1980): 369–80.

———. Review of *Henry IV, Part 1,* by William Shakespeare. BBC-TV/Time-Life Inc. Production. PBS Stations, 26 March 1980. "The Shakespeare Plays on TV: Season Two." *Shakespeare on Film Newsletter* 5, no. 1 (1980): 3–4.

Cubeta, Paul M. Review of *Henry V,* by William Shakespeare. BBC-TV/Time-Life Inc. Production. PBS Stations, 23 April 1980. "The Shakespeare Plays on TV: Season Two." *Shakespeare on Film Newsletter* 5, no. 1 (1980): 4–5.

Darrach, Brad. "Laurence Olivier Dies: 'The Rest Is Silence.'" *People,* 24 July 1989, 70–77.

David, Richard. *Shakespeare in the Theatre.* Cambridge: Cambridge University Press, 1978.

Davies, Anthony. *Filming Shakespeare's Plays: The Adaptations of Laurence Olivier, Orson Welles, Peter Brook and Akira Kurosawa.* Cambridge: Cambridge University Press, 1988.

Davies, Russell. "The Nightmare Results of a Designer's Dream." *The Sunday Times,* 16 December 1979, 41.

———. "Shakespeare in Close-up." *The Sunday Times,* 23 December 1979, 43.

Davison, Peter. *"Hamlet": Text and Performance.* London: Macmillan, 1983.

Day-Lewis, Sean. "Giving Shakespeare the Works." *Daily Telegraph,* 11 December 1978, 10.

———. "Naturalism Overcomes the Bard." *Daily Telegraph,* 18 December 1978, 9.

———. "Years of the Bard." *Daily Telegraph,* 5 March 1979, 11.

Durgnat, Raymond. *A Mirror for England: British Movies from Austerity to Affluence.* London: Faber, 1970.

Ebert, Roger. *A Kiss Is Still a Kiss.* New York: Andrews, McMeel and Parker, 1984.

Eckert, Charles, W., ed. *Focus on Shakespearean Films.* Englewood Cliffs, N.J.: Prentice-Hall, 1972.

Eco, Umberto. "*Casablanca:* Cult Movies and Intertextual Collage." In *Travels in Hyperreality: Essays,* translated by William Weaver. London: Picador, 1987.

Egan, Robert. "A Muse of Fire: *Henry V* in the Light of *Tamburlaine.*" *Modern Language Quarterly* 29 (1968): 15–28.

Fagan, Gregory P. "IVE to Help Belushi Bio Pic." *Video Review,* September 1989, 18.

Farber, Stephen. *"The Magnificent Ambersons."* In *Focus on Orson Welles,* edited by Ronald Gottesman. Englewood Cliffs, N.J.: Prentice-Hall, 1976.

Fenwick, Henry. "The Production." In *The BBC TV Shakespeare: "Henry V."* London: British Broadcasting Corporation, 1979.

———. "The Production." In *The BBC TV Shakespeare: "Henry IV, Part I."* London: British Broadcasting Corporation, 1979.

———. "The Production." In *The BBC TV Shakespeare: "Henry IV, Part 2."* London: British Broadcasting Corporation, 1979.

———. "The Production." In *The BBC TV Shakespeare: "Julius Caesar."* London: British Broadcasting Corporation, 1979.

———. "The Production." In *The BBC TV Shakespeare: "Richard II."* London: British Broadcasting Corporation, 1978.

Frazer, J. G. *The Golden Bough: A Study in Magic and Religion.* London: Macmillan, 1983.

Frye, Roland Mushat. *The Renaissance "Hamlet:" Issues and Responses in 1600.* Princeton: Princeton University Press, 1984.

Garrett, George P., O. B. Hardison, Jr., and Jane R. Gelfman, eds. *Henry V.* In *Film Scripts One,* 37–136. New York: Appleton-Century-Crofts Educational Division, Meredith Corporation, 1971.

———. Introduction. In *Film Scripts One,* 1–35. New York: Appleton-Century-Crofts Educational Division Meredith Corporation, 1971.

Gaskell, Philip. *From Reader to Writer: Studies in Editorial Method.* Oxford: Clarendon Press, 1978.

Geduld, Harry M. *Filmguide to "Henry V."* Bloomington: Indiana University Press, 1973.

Giannetti, Louis. "Paradise Lost: The Cinema of Orson Welles." In *Masters of the American Cinema.* Englewood Cliffs, N.J.: Prentice-Hall, 1981.

———. *Understanding Movies.* Englewood Cliffs, N.J.: Prentice-Hall, 1987.

Gielgud, John. "King Richard the Second." In *Shakespeare "Richard II": A Casebook,* edited by Nicholas Brooke. London: Macmillan, 1978.

Goldfarb, Phyllis. "Orson Welles' Use of Sound." In *Focus on Orson Welles,* edited by Ronald Gottesman. Englewood Cliffs, N.J.: Prentice-Hall, 1976.

Gottesman, Ronald, ed. *Focus on Orson Welles.* Englewood Cliffs, N.J.: Prentice-Hall, 1976.

Gow, Gordon. "Gordon Gow at Welles' Lament for the Passing of Merrie England . . ." *Films and Filming* 13, no. 8 (1967): 25.

Gurr, Andrew, ed. *King Richard II.* Cambridge: Cambridge University Press, 1984.

Hall, Peter. Introduction. In *The Wars of the Roses: Adapted for the Royal Shakespeare Company from William Shakespeare's "Henry VI," Parts I, II, III and "Richard III."* By John Barton, in collaboration with Peter Hall. London: British Broadcasting Corporation, 1970.

Halliwell, Leslie. *Halliwell's Filmgoer's Companion.* London: Granada, 1984.

Hapgood, Robert. "*Chimes at Midnight* from Stage to Screen: The Art of Adaptation." *Shakespeare Survey* 39 (1986): 39–52.

———. "Shakespeare on Film and Television." In *The Cambridge Companion to Shakespeare Studies,* edited by Stanley Wells. Cambridge: Cambridge University Press, 1986.

Hazlitt, William. *Characters of Shakespeare's Plays.* Chelsea House Publishers, 1983.

Henderson, Brian. "The Long Take." *Film Comment* 7, no. 2 (1971): 6–11.

Heston, Charlton. *The Actor's Life: Journals, 1956–76.* Edited by Hollis Alpert. New York: Dutton, 1978.

Higham, Charles. *The Films of Orson Welles.* Berkeley: University of California Press, 1970.

———. *Orson Welles: The Rise and Fall of an American Genius.* London: New English Library, 1986.

Hill, Reginald. *An April Shroud.* London: Grafton, 1975.

Hirsch, Foster. *Laurence Olivier.* Boston: Twayne, 1979.

Hodgdon, Barbara. "Two *King Lears:* Discovering the Film Text." *Literature/Film Quarterly* 11 (1983): 143–51.

Holderness, Graham. "Radical Potentiality and Institutional Closure." In *Political Shakespeare: New Essays in Cultural Materialism,* edited by Jonathan Dollimore and Alan Sinfield. Manchester: Manchester University Press, 1985.

———. *Shakespeare's History.* New York: St. Martin's, 1985.

Homan, Sidney. "A Cinema for Shakespeare." *Literature/Film Quarterly* 4 (1976): 176–86.

"Homage to Olivier's *Henry V.*" *Shakespeare on Film Newsletter* 6, no. 1 (1982): 1 and 3.

Houseman, John. *Run-Through: A Memoir.* London: Allen Lane, Penguin Press, 1972.

Humphreys, A. R., ed. *The Arden Shakespeare: "The First Part of King Henry IV."* London: Methuen, 1960.

———. Introduction. In *Henry V,* by William Shakespeare. Harmondsworth: Penguin, 1968.

———. *Shakespeare: "Richard II."* London: Edward Arnold, 1967.

Hutton, C. Clayton. *The Making of "Henry V."* London: Ernest J. Day, 1944.

Huxley, Aldous. *The Devils of Loudun.* London: Chatto and Windus, 1952.

Jacobi, Derek. "*Hamlet.*" In *Shakespeare in Perspective,* edited by Roger Sales, vol. 1. London: British Broadcasting Corporation, 1982.

James, Clive. *The Crystal Bucket: Television Criticism from the "Observer," 1976–79.* London: Jonathan Cape, 1981.

Jameson, Richard T. "An Infinity of Mirrors." In *Focus on Orson Welles,* edited by Ronald Gottesman. Englewood Cliffs, N.J.: Prentice-Hall, 1976.

Jamieson, Michael. "Shakespeare in the Theatre." In *Shakespeare: Select Bibliographical Guides,* edited by Stanley Wells. Oxford: Oxford University Press, 1973.

Johnson, Ian. "Merely Players." In *Focus on Shakespearean Films,* edited by Charles W. Eckert. Englewood Cliffs, N.J.: Prentice-Hall, 1972.

Johnson, Paul. *"Richard II."* In *Shakespeare in Perspective,* edited by Roger Sales, vol. 1. London: British Broadcasting Corporation, 1982.

Johnson, William. "Orson Welles: Of Time and Loss." *Film Quarterly* 21, no. 1 (1967): 13–24.

Jones, Emrys. *Scenic Form in Shakespeare.* Oxford: Clarendon Press, 1985.

Jorgens, Jack J. "The BBC-TV Shakespeare Series." *Shakespeare Quarterly* 30 (1979): 411–15.

———. *Shakespeare on Film.* Bloomington: Indiana University Press, 1979.

Kael, Pauline. "Orson Welles: There Ain't No Way." In *Kiss Kiss Bang Bang.* London: Calder and Boyars, 1970.

Kernan, Alvin B. "The Henriad: Shakespeare's Major History Plays." In *Modern Shakespearean Criticism; Essays on Style, Dramaturgy, and the Major Plays,* edited by Alvin B. Kernan. New York: Harcourt, 1970.

Kimbrough, R. Alan. "Olivier's *Lear* and the Limits of Video." *Shakespeare on Film Newsletter* 11, no. 1 (December 1986): 6.

Kirby, J. L. *Henry IV of England.* London: Constable, 1970.

Kliman, Bernice W., and Kenneth S. Rothwell. "A Tenth Anniversary Editorial." *Shakespeare on Film Newsletter* 11, no. 1 (1986): 1, 6, 12.

Kott, Jan. *Shakespeare Our Contemporary.* New York: W. W. Norton, 1974.

Kroll, Jack. "A *Henry V* for Our Time." *Newsweek,* 20 November 1989, 78.

Kroll, Jack, and Rita Dallas. "Return of the Prodigal King." *Newsweek,* 8 November 1982, 105.

Last, Richard. "Masterly Falstaff from Quayle." *Daily Telegraph,* 10 December 1979, 15.

———. " 'Shakespeare' Creates Boxed-In Feeling." *Daily Telegraph,* 11 December 1978, 11.

Leamer, Laurence. *As Time Goes By: The Life of Ingrid Bergman.* New York: Harper, 1986.

Leaming, Barbara. *Orson Welles: A Biography.* New York: Penguin, 1985.

———. *Polanski: The Filmmaker as Voyeur.* New York: Simon and Schuster, 1981.

Leeming, David Adams. *Mythology: The Voyage of the Hero.* New York: Lippincott, 1973.

Leong, Kathy Chin. "Hypertext: The Ever-Growing Interconnected Whole." *PC Computing,* July 1989, 75–78.

Lyons, Bridget Gellert, ed. *"Chimes at Midnight"/Orson Welles, Director.* New Brunswick, N.J.: Rutgers University Press, 1988.

Mack, Maynard. Introduction. In *The History of "Henry IV" (Part One)*, by William Shakespeare. New York: Signet, 1987.

———. *Killing the King: Three Studies in Shakespeare's Tragic Structure*. New Haven: Yale University Press, 1973.

Manheim, Michael. "Olivier's *Henry V* and the Elizabethan World Picture." *Literature/Film Quarterly* 11 (1983): 179–84.

———. Review of *Richard II*, by William Shakespeare. BBC-TV/Time-Life Inc. Production. PBS Stations, 28 March 1979. "The Shakespeare Plays on TV: Season One." *Shakespeare on Film Newsletter* 4, no. 1 (1979): 5–6.

Manvell, Roger. *Shakespeare and the Film*. New York: A. S. Barnes, 1979.

Margolies, David. "Shakespeare, the Telly and the Miners." *Red Letters* 17 (March 1985): 38–48.

Masters, Kim. "What's Up, Doc?" *Premiere*, July 1988, 32–37.

McBride, Joseph. *"Chimes at Midnight."* In *Focus on Orson Welles*, edited by Ronald Gottesman. Englewood Cliffs, N.J.: Prentice-Hall, 1976.

McCreadie, Marsha. *"Henry V:* Onstage and On Film." *Literature/Film Quarterly* 5 (1977): 316–21.

McGilligan, Patrick. *Cagney: The Actor as Auteur*. New York: Da Capo Press, 1979.

McKenzie, D. F. *The Panizzi Lectures, 1985: Bibliography and the Sociology of Texts*. London: British Library, 1986.

McLean, Andrew M. "Orson Welles and Shakespeare: History and Consciousness in *Chimes at Midnight." Literature/Film Quarterly* 11 (1983): 197–202.

Messina, Cedric. "Interview: Cedric Messina Discusses *The Shakespeare Plays*," with John F. Andrews. *Shakespeare Quarterly* 30 (1979): 134–37.

———. Preface. In *The BBC TV Shakespeare: "Richard II."* London: British Broadcasting Corporation, 1978.

Miller, Jonathan. "Interview: Jonathan Miller on *The Shakespeare Plays*," with Tim Hallinan. *Shakespeare Quarterly* 32 (1981): 134–45.

Miller, Russell. "And Now, the BBC's Schoolgirl Juliet." *The Sunday Times*, 29 January 1978, 32.

Mullin, Michael. "Orson Welles' *Macbeth:* Script and Screen." In *Focus on Orson Welles*, edited by Ronald Gottesman. Englewood Cliffs, N.J.: Prentice-Hall, 1976.

———. "Shakespeare USA: The BBC Plays and American Education." *Shakespeare Quarterly* 35 (1984): 582–89.

Naremore, James. *The Magic World of Orson Welles*. New York: Oxford University Press, 1978.

Norbrook, David. "No Holds Bard." Review of *Reinventing Shakespeare: A Cultural History from the Restoration to the Present*, by Gary Taylor. *New Republic*, 16 October 1989, 49–52.

Norman, Barry. *Talking Pictures*. London: BBC Books and Hodder and Stoughton, 1987.

Nuttall, A. D. *A New Mimesis: Shakespeare and the Representation of Reality*. London: Methuen, 1983.

O'Brien, Mary Ellen. *Film Acting: The Techniques and History of Acting for the Camera*. New York: Arco, 1983.

Olivier, Laurence. *Confessions of an Actor*. London: Coronet Books, 1983.

———. "The Making of *Henry V.*" In *Classic Film Scripts: "Henry V,"* edited by Andrew Sinclair. London: Lorrimer, 1984.

———. *On Acting.* New York: Simon and Schuster, 1986.

O'Toole, Lawrence. "Lost and Found: Films That Failed in the Theaters Thrive on Cassette." *American Film* 9, no. 2 (1983): 64, 68–72.

Page, Malcolm. *"Richard II": Text and Performance.* London: Macmillan, 1987.

Palmer, D. J. "Casting off the Old Man: History and St. Paul in *Henry IV.*" *Critical Quarterly* 12 (1970): 265–83.

Polanski, Roman. *Roman.* London: Heinemann, 1984.

Purser, Philip. "Going Round Again." *Sunday Telegraph,* 18 February 1979, 13.

———. "In Tight Focus." *Sunday Telgraph,* 17 December 1978, 15.

Quinn, Michael. Introduction. In *Shakespeare "Henry V": A Casebook.* London: Macmillan, 1983.

Rabkin, Norman. *Shakespeare and the Problem of Meaning.* Chicago: University of Chicago Press, 1981.

Richardson, Ian. *"Richard II."* In *Shakespeare in Perspective,* edited by Roger Sales, vol. 1. London: British Broadcasting Corporation, 1982.

Rothwell, Kenneth S. "'The Shakespeare Plays': *Hamlet* and the Five Plays of Season Three." *Shakespeare Quarterly* 32 (1981): 395–401.

Rubin, Stanley S. "Welles/Falstaff/Shakespeare/Welles: The Narrative Structure of *Chimes at Midnight.*" *Film Criticism* 2, no. 2–3 (Winter-Spring 1978): 66–71.

Rubinstein, Frankie. *A Dictionary of Shakespeare's Sexual Puns and Their Significance.* London: Macmillan, 1984.

Ryan, Michael. ". . . And Then She Was Fired." *Parade,* 11 September 1988, 12.

Saccio, Peter. Review. *Henry the Fourth, Part 2,* by William Shakespeare. BBC-TV/ Time-Life Inc. Production. PBS Stations, 9 April 1980. "The Shakespeare Plays on TV: *Henry the Fourth, Part Two.*" *Shakespeare on Film Newsletter* 6, no. 1 (1982): 2.

———. *Shakespeare's English Kings: History, Chronicle, and Drama.* New York: Oxford University Press, 1977.

Seltzer, Daniel. "Shakespeare's Texts and Modern Productions." In *Reinterpretations of Elizabethan Drama: Selected Papers from the English Institute,* edited by Norman Rabkin. New York: Columbia University Press, 1969.

Seward, Desmond. *Henry V As Warlord.* London: Sidgwick and Jackson, 1987.

———. *Richard III: England's Black Legend.* London: Country Life Books, 1983.

"Shakespeare on Video: Good News for Teachers." *Shakespeare on Film Newsletter* 8, no. 2 (1984): 1, 8–10.

Shakespeare, William. *The BBC TV Shakespeare: "Henry V."* Peter Alexander Text, notes by Alan Shallcross. London: British Broadcasting Corporation, 1979.

———. *The BBC TV Shakespeare: "Henry IV, Part 1."* Peter Alexander Text, notes by Alan Shallcross. London: British Broadcasting Corporation, 1979.

———. *The BBC TV Shakespeare: "Henry IV, Part 2."* Peter Alexander Text, notes by Alan Shallcross. London: British Broadcasting Corporation, 1979.

———. *The BBC TV Shakespeare: "The Merry Wives of Windsor."* Peter Alexander Text, notes by Alan Shallcross. London: British Broadcasting Corporation, 1983.

———. *The BBC TV Shakespeare: "Richard II."* Peter Alexander Text, notes by Alan Shallcross. London: British Broadcasting Corporation, 1978.

———. *The Complete Signet Classic Shakespeare*, edited by Sylvan Barnet. New York: Harcourt, 1972.

Silviria, Dale. *Laurence Olivier and the Art of Film Making.* London: Associated University Presses, 1985.

Sontag, Susan. "Film and Theatre." In *Film Theory and Criticism: Introductory Readings*, edited by Gerald Mast and Marshall Cohen, 3d ed. Oxford: Oxford University Press, 1985.

Speaight, Robert. *Shakespeare: The Man and His Achievement.* London: J. M. Dent and Sons, 1977.

Stewart, Douglas J. "Falstaff the Centaur." *Shakespeare Quarterly* 28 (1977): 5–21.

Stewart, J. I. M. *Character and Motive in Shakespeare: Some Recent Appraisals Examined.* London: Longmans, Green and Co., 1965.

Stringer, Robin. "Miller's Spartan TV Bard." *Daily Telegraph*, 22 June 1979, 19.

Taylor, Gary. "The Fortunes of Oldcastle." *Shakespeare Survey* 38 (1985): 85–100.

———. *Moment by Moment by Shakespeare.* London: Macmillan, 1985.

———. *The Oxford Shakespeare: "Henry V."* Oxford: Oxford University Press, 1984.

Taylor, John Russell. *Hitch: The Life and Works of Alfred Hitchcock.* London: Sphere Books, 1981.

Tennenhouse, Leonard. *Power on Display: The Politics of Shakespeare's Genres.* London: Methuen, 1986.

Thomson, Peter. "Shakespeare Straight and Crooked: A Review of the 1973 Season at Stratford." *Shakespeare Survey* 27 (1974): 143–54.

Tillyard, E. M. W. *Shakespeare's History Plays.* London: Chatto and Windus, 1951.

"Top Grossing Films Released in the U.S., 1983–88." *Color Country Spectrum*, 23 July 1989, p. B6.

Treglown, Jeremy. Preface. In *"Richard III," by William Shakespeare*, edited by Julie Hankey. London: Junction, 1981.

Truffaut, Francois. *"Citizen Kane."* In *Focus on "Citizen Kane,"* edited by Ronald Gottesman. Englewood Cliffs, N.J.: Prentice-Hall, 1971.

———. *Hitchcock.* London: Secker and Warburg, 1967.

Walker, Alexander. *Vivien: The Life of Vivien Leigh.* New York: Weidenfeld and Nicholson, 1987.

Walter, J. H., ed. *The Arden Shakespeare: "King Henry V."* London: Methuen, 1985.

Weiss, Theodore. *The Breath of Clowns and Kings: Shakespeare's Early Comedies and Histories.* London: Chatto and Windus, 1971.

Wells, Stanley. *Royal Shakespeare: Four Major Productions at Stratford-upon-Avon.* Manchester: Manchester University Press, 1979.

———. "Television Shakespeare." *Shakespeare Quarterly* 33 (1982): 261–77.

Wharton, T. F. *"Henry the Fourth," Parts 1 & 2: Text and Performance.* London: Macmillan, 1983.

"Wilders Interview at MLA." *Shakespeare on Film Newsletter* 4, no. 1 (1979): 3, 9.

Wilders, John. "Introduction to *Henry IV, Part 2.*" In *The BBC TV Shakespeare: "Henry IV, Part 2."* London: British Broadcasting Corporation, 1979.

————. *The Lost Garden: A View of Shakespeare's English and Roman History Plays.* London: Macmillan, 1982.

————. Personal interview. 15 June 1987.

————. "Shakespeare and Television: A Marriage of True Minds?" De Quincy Society Lecture, Worcester College, Oxford. 3 November 1986.

————. "Shakespeare on the Small Screen." *Deutsche Shakespeare-Gesselschaft West Jahrbuch* 1982: 56–62.

Winny, James. *The Player King: A Theme of Shakespeare's Histories.* London: Chatto and Windus, 1968.

Wood, Robin. *Personal Views: Explorations in Film.* London: Gordon Fraser Gallery, 1976.

Wylie, James Hamilton. *The Reign of Henry the Fifth.* 3 vols. Cambridge: Cambridge University Press, 1914–1929.

Yeats, W. B. "At Stratford-on-Avon (1901)." In *Shakespeare "Richard II": A Casebook,* edited by Nicholas Brooke. London: Macmillan, 1978.

Zitner, Sheldon P. "Wooden O's in Plastic Boxes: Shakespeare and Television." *University of Toronto Quarterly* 51 (1981): 1–12.

## Unpublished Dissertations

Buchman, Lorne Michael. "From the Globe to the Screen: An Interpretive Study of Shakespeare Through Film (Welles, Kozintsev)." Ph.D. diss., Stanford University, 1984.

Davies, Anthony. "Shakespeare and the Eloquence of Cinematic Space: A Study of Spatial Strategy in Some Shakespearean Films." Ph.D. diss., University of Birmingham, 1983.

Jackson, Robert Darrell. "*Romeo and Juliet* on Film: A Comparative Analysis of Three Major Film Versions of Shakespeare's Play." Ph.D. diss., Wayne State University, 1978.

Singer, Sandra Sugarman. "Laurence Olivier Directs Shakespeare: A Study in Film Authorship." Ph.D. diss., Northwestern University, 1979.

Skoller, Donald S. "Problems of Transformation in the Adaptation of Shakespeare's Tragedies from Play-Script to Cinema." Ph.D. diss., New York University, 1968.

# Filmography

## *Chimes at Midnight/Falstaff* (1966)

| | |
|---|---|
| Production Company | Internacional Films Española (Madrid)/Alpine (Basle) |
| Executive Producer | Alessandro Tasca |
| Producers | Emiliano Piedra |
| | Angel Escolano |
| Production Manager | Gustavo Quintana |
| Director | Orson Welles |
| Second Unit Director | Jesús Franco |
| Assistant Directors | Tony Fuentes, Juan Cobos |
| Script | Orson Welles. Adapted from plays by William Shakespeare |
| Director of Photography | Edmond Richard |
| Camera Operator | Adolphe Charlet |
| Second Unit Photographer | Alejandro Ulloa |
| Editor | Fritz Mueller |
| Art Directors | José Antonio de la Guerra |
| | Mariano Erdorza |
| Music | Angelo Francesco Lavagnino |
| Musical Director | Carlo Franci |
| Costumes | Orson Welles |
| Sound Recordist | Peter Parasheles |
| Narrator | Ralph Richardson |

### CAST

| | |
|---|---|
| Sir John Falstaff | Orson Welles |
| Prince Hal/Henry V | Keith Baxter |
| King Henry IV | John Gielgud |
| Doll Tearsheet | Jeanne Moreau |
| Mistress Quickly | Margaret Rutherford |
| Henry Percy | Norman Rodway |
| Kate Percy | Marina Vlady |
| Justice Shallow | Alan Webb |
| Silence | Walter Chiari |
| Pistol | Michael Aldridge |
| Poins | Tony Beckley |
| Worcester | Fernando Rey |
| Westmoreland | Andrew Faulds |
| Northumberland | José Nieto |
| Prince John | Jeremy Rowe |

Falstaff's Page                     Beatrice Welles
Bardolph                            Paddy Bedford

## *Henry V* (1944)

Production Company                  Two Cities Films
Producer                            Laurence Olivier
Associate Producer                  Dallas Bower
Director                            Laurence Olivier
Assistant Director                  Vincent Permane
Screenplay                          Laurence Olivier and Reginald Beck
Text Editor                         Alan Dent
Film Editor                         Reginald Beck
Director of Photography             Robert Krasker
Costume Designer                    Roger Furse
Music                               William Walton

### CAST

King Henry V                        Laurence Olivier
Sir John Falstaff                   George Robey
King Charles VI of France           Harcourt Williams
Princess Katherine                  Renee Asherson
Lady Alice                          Ivy St. Helier
Queen Isabel                        Janet Burnell
The Dauphin                         Max Adrian
Duke of Burgundy                    Valentine Dyall
The Constable of France             Leo Genn
Duke of Orleans                     Francis Lister
Duke of Berri,
French Ambassador                   Ernest Thesiger
Montjoy                             Ralph Truman
Chorus                              Leslie Banks
Archbishop of Canterbury            Felix Aylmer
Bishop of Ely                       Robert Helpmann
Pistol                              Robert Newton
Mistress Quickly                    Freda Jackson
Corporal Nym                        Frederick Cooper
Lieutenant Bardolph                 Roy Emerton
Boy                                 George Cole
Fluellen                            Esmond Knight
Gower                               Michael Shepley
Jamy                                John Laurie
MacMorris                           Niall MacGinnis
Court                               Brian Nisson
John Bates                          Arthur Hambling
Michael Williams                    Jimmy Hanley
Sir Thomas Erpingham                Morland Graham
Earl of Westmoreland                Gerald Case
Duke of Gloucester                  Michael Warre
Exeter                              Nicholas Hannen

## *Henry V* (1979)

| | |
|---|---|
| Production Company | BBC/Time-Life TV |
| Producer | Cedric Messina |
| Director | David Giles |
| Script Editor | Alan Shallcross |
| Designer | Don Homfray |
| Costume Designer | Odette Barrow |
| Literary Consultant | John Wilders |

### CAST

| | |
|---|---|
| Chorus | Alec McCowen |
| King Henry V | David Gwillim |
| Duke of Gloucester | Martin Smith |
| Duke of Bedford | Rob Edwards |
| Duke of Clarence | Roger Davenport |
| Duke of Exeter | Clifford Parrish |
| Duke of York | Derek Hollis |
| Earl of Salisbury | Robert Ashby |
| Earl of Westmoreland | David Buck |
| Earl of Warwick | Rod Beacham |
| Archbishop of Canterbury | Trevor Baxter |
| Bishop of Ely | John Abineri |
| Earl of Cambridge | William Whymper |
| Lord Scroop | Ian Price |
| Sir Thomas Erpingham | George Howe |
| Sir Thomas Grey | David Rowlands |
| Gower | Brian Poyser |
| Fluellen | Tim Walton |
| MacMorris | Paddy Ward |
| Jamy | Michael McKevitt |
| Bates | Ronald Forfar |
| Court | Joe Ritchie |
| Williams | David Pinner |
| Nym | Jeffrey Holland |
| Bardolph | Gordon Gostelow |
| Pistol | Bryan Pringle |
| Boy | John Fowler |
| Herald | Simon Broad |
| King Charles VI | Thorley Walters |
| Lewis, the Dauphin | Keith Drinkel |
| Duke of Burgundy | Robert Harris |
| Duke of Orleans | John Saunders |
| Duke of Bourbon | John Bryans |
| The Constable of France | Julian Glover |
| Montjoy | Garrick Hagon |
| Queen Isabel | Pamela Ruddock |
| Katherine | Jocelyne Boisseau |
| Alice | Anna Quayle |
| Hostess | Brenda Bruce |

## *1 Henry IV* (1979)

| | |
|---|---|
| Production Company | BBC/Time-Life TV |
| Producer | Cedric Messina |
| Director | David Giles |
| Script Editor | Alan Shallcross |
| Designer | Don Homfray |
| Costume Designer | Odette Barrow |
| Literary Consultant | John Wilders |

### Cast

| | |
|---|---|
| King Henry IV | Jon Finch |
| Henry, Prince of Wales | David Gwillim |
| John of Lancaster | Rob Edwards |
| Earl of Westmoreland | David Buck |
| Sir Walter Blunt | Robert Brown |
| Thomas Percy, Earl of Worcester | Clive Swift |
| Henry Percy, Earl of Northumberland | Bruce Purchase |
| Henry Percy, Hotspur | Tim Pigott-Smith |
| Edmund Mortimer, Earl of March | Robert Morris |
| Earl of Douglas | John Cairney |
| Scroop, Archbishop of York | David Neal |
| Sir Michael | Norman Rutherford |
| Owen Glendower | Richard Owens |
| Sir Richard Vernon | Terence Wilton |
| Sir John Falstaff | Anthony Quayle |
| Poins | Jack Galloway |
| Bardolph | Gordon Gostelow |
| Peto | Steven Beard |
| Lady Percy | Michele Dotrice |
| Lady Mortimer | Sharon Morgan |
| Mistress Quickly | Brenda Bruce |

## *2 Henry IV* (1979)

| | |
|---|---|
| Production Company | BBC/Time-Life TV |
| Producer | Cedric Messina |
| Director | David Giles |
| Script Editor | Alan Shallcross |
| Designer | Don Homfray |
| Costume Designer | Odette Barrow |
| Literary Consultant | John Wilders |

### Cast

| | |
|---|---|
| King Henry IV | Jon Finch |
| Henry, Prince of Wales | David Gwillim |
| John of Lancaster | Rob Edwards |
| Humphrey of Gloucester | Martin Neil |

| | |
|---|---|
| Thomas, Duke of Clarence | Roger Davenport |
| Earl of Northumberland | Bruce Purchase |
| Scroop, Archbishop of York | David Neal |
| Lord Mowbray | Michael Miller |
| Lord Hastings | Richard Bebb |
| Lord Bardolph | John Humphry |
| Sir John Colville | Salvin Stewart |
| Morton | Carl Oatley |
| Earl of Warwick | Rod Beacham |
| Earl of Westmoreland | David Buck |
| Gower | Brian Poyser |
| Lord Chief Justice | Ralph Michael |
| Sir John Falstaff | Anthony Quayle |
| Poins | Jack Galloway |
| Bardolph | Gordon Gostelow |
| Pistol | Brian Pringle |
| Peto | Steven Beard |
| Page | John Fowler |
| Robert Shallow | Robert Eddison |
| Silence | Leslie French |
| Davy | Raymond Platt |
| Fang | Frederick Proud |
| Ralph Mouldy | Julian Battersby |
| Simon Shadow | Roy Herrick |
| Thomas Wart | Alan Collins |
| Francis Feeble | John Tordoff |
| Peter Bullcalf | Roger Elliot |
| Lady Northumberland | Jenny Laird |
| Lady Percy | Michele Dotrice |
| Mistress Quickly | Brenda Bruce |
| Doll Tearsheet | Frances Cuka |

## *Richard II* (1978)

| | |
|---|---|
| Production Company | BBC/Time-Life TV |
| Producer | Cedric Messina |
| Director | David Giles |
| Script Editor | Alan Shallcross |
| Designer | Tony Abbott |
| Costume Designer | Robin Fraser-Paye |
| Literary Consultant | John Wilders |

### CAST

| | |
|---|---|
| King Richard | Derek Jacobi |
| John of Gaunt | John Gielgud |
| Henry Bolingbroke | Jon Finch |
| Duchess of York | Wendy Hiller |
| Duke of York | Charles Gray |
| Duchess of Gloucester | Mary Morris |

| | |
|---|---|
| Duke of Northumberland | David Swift |
| Bishop of Carlisle | Clifford Rose |
| Duke of Aumerle | Charles Keating |
| Thomas Mowbray | Richard Owens |
| Queen | Janet Maw |
| Duke of Surrey | Jeffrey Holland |
| Henry Percy | Jeremy Bulloch |
| Bushy | Robin Sachs |
| Bagot | Damien Thomas |
| Green | Alan Dalton |
| Lord Ross | David Dodimead |
| Lord Willoughby | John Flint |
| Earl Berkeley | Carl Oatley |
| Sir Stephen Scroop | William Whymper |
| Earl of Salisbury | John Barcroft |
| Groom | Joe Ritchie |
| Abbot of Westminster | Bruno Barnabe |
| Gardener | Jonathan Adams |

# Index

205